une expérience de vie pour l'enfant

Le contenu de cette publication a été réalisé
par l'**Office des services de garde à l'enfance**
Direction **Recherche et information**

et

Raquel Betsalel-Presser, Ph. D. (Sciences de l'éducation, U. de Montréal)
Professeure agrégée
Faculté des sciences de l'éducation
Université de Montréal

Denise Garon, Ph. D. (Sciences de l'éducation, U. Laval)
Professeure en techniques de services
de garde d'enfants
Cégep Sainte-Foy

Photographies:
Ministère des Communications du Québec
Office des services de garde à l'enfance

Cette édition a été produite par
Les Publications du Québec
1279, boul. Charest Ouest
Québec (Québec)
G1N 4K7

Dépôt légal — 4ᵉ trimestre 1984
Bibliothèque nationale du Québec

ISBN 2-551-08973-5
ISBN 2-551-08971-9 (série)

La garderie

une expérience de vie pour l'enfant

Raquel Betsalel-Presser et Denise Garon

**Collection
Ressources
et petite enfance**

VOLET 2

L'âge
de la démarche
vers l'autonomie
de 2 à 3 ans

Avant-propos

L'Office des services de garde à l'enfance, organisme chargé par la loi sur les services de garde à l'enfance de veiller à ce que soient assurés des services de garde à l'enfance de qualité, se doit d'offrir un soutien technique et professionnel aux organismes et personnes oeuvrant dans ces services.

Dans cet esprit et devant la popularité de l'édition de rodage de «La garderie une expérience de vie pour l'enfant» publiée en 1976, l'Office proposait aux auteures de revoir le contenu et de l'actualiser en vue d'éditer à nouveau le document. Avec la collaboration de la Direction générale des publications gouvernementales (ministère des Communications du Québec), cette réédition était l'occasion de donner à ces ouvrages de référence un format plus pratique à consulter.

Maintenant en trois volets, « La garderie, une expérience de vie pour l'enfant » est publiée dans la collection «Ressources et petite enfance» à laquelle viendront s'ajouter d'autres ouvrages se voulant des outils et des instruments de travail à l'intention de toutes les personnes concernées par le développement des enfants de moins de six ans.

Nous tenons à remercier chaleureusement les auteures, Denise Garon et Raquel Betsalel-Presser, pour le sérieux et la compétence dont elles ont fait preuve dans la révision et l'actualisation de cette nouvelle édition. Denise Trudel, agente d'information à l'Office, les a accompagnées en leur apportant un soutien technique dans cette longue démarche qui nous conduit aujourd'hui à la publication de cet ouvrage.

Ces publications sont un témoignage concret de la collaboration entre les divers intervenants des milieux de l'éducation, de la recherche et l'Office des services de garde à l'enfance.

Nous osons croire que «La garderie une expérience de vie pour l'enfant» s'avérera un outil efficace pour tous ceux et celles qui, oeuvrant auprès des jeunes enfants, sont soucieux de leur offrir un cadre de vie pleinement adapté à leurs besoins.

Renée Spain, directrice
Recherche et information
Office des services de garde à l'enfance

Table des matières

Présentation générale des trois volets

Volet II

Âge de la démarche vers l'autonomie

Liste des tableaux

Volet II

Introduction

Depuis la première édition de rodage de *La garderie, une expérience de vie pour l'enfant* (1976)[1], des événements importants en matière de services de garde ont marqué l'évolution des ressources destinées à la petite enfance au Québec. Sans doute, le point tournant de l'histoire de ces services est lié au rapport du Comité interministériel sur les services d'accueil à la petite enfance (1978), suivi en 1979 de la loi 77, qui institue l'Office des services de garde à l'enfance. En 1980, cet organisme devient responsable d'appliquer la loi et de promouvoir cinq catégories de services de garde[2], c'est-à-dire le service de garde en garderie de jour, le service de garde en milieu familial, le service de garde en milieu scolaire, la halte-garderie et le jardin d'enfants. Une telle variété de services de garde possibles représente une richesse autour des ressources disponibles à long terme. Chacune d'elle ayant été conçue en vue de répondre aux demandes, aux priorités et aux besoins des familles à l'égard de leur enfant, cette variété témoigne d'un souci de pluralisme offrant un certain choix en fonction du type de support recherché par les parents. Ainsi, les familles qui réclament un service de garde pendant toute la journée peuvent faire appel à la garderie ou au service de garde en milieu familial en tenant compte, d'une part, des valeurs qu'elles privilégient et, d'autre part, de l'existence de ces services dans leurs quartiers ou dans leurs milieux de travail. De plus, le jardin d'enfants et la halte-garderie, suivant leur philosophie spécifique, offrent un programme plus court (généralement 2 à 3 heures par jour pour le premier, et à une fréquence et une durée intermittente pour le deuxième).

En conséquence, la présente version révisée et actualisée de *La garderie, une expérience de vie pour l'enfant* tient à maintenir son but premier, c'est-à-dire celui d'offrir un instrument de travail permettant de mieux adapter les interventions auprès des jeunes enfants. Dans le même sens, la nouvelle version se propose de rejoindre toutes les personnes concernées par la qualité du développement des moins de 6 ans, que ce soit dans une situation régulière ou occasionnelle de vie collective ou dans une relation individuelle avec un enfant de cet âge.

Cette série peut constituer, dans un sens large, une ressource pour des personnes impliquées dans des milieux hospitaliers, des cliniques, des classes maternelles, des terrains de jeu, des programmes récréatifs, et dans des programmes de formation et de perfectionnement du personnel destiné à la petite enfance. Somme toute, **c'est l'enfant d'âge préscolaire qui est le pivot de ce document, quelle que soit la nature du programme fréquenté**.

De plus, cette nouvelle version offre aux responsables de la formation et du perfectionnement des éducateurs[3] en service de garde l'occasion de mieux définir les multiples concepts issus des recherches portant sur le développement psycho-moteur et social de l'enfant et de les appliquer tout en tenant compte du contexte particulier dans lequel ils travaillent.

---

1. Nicole Ouimet-Malo, du ministère des Affaires sociales, a participé à la rédaction de cette édition.
2. En septembre 1983, les articles 5 et 6 de la Loi sur les services de garde à l'enfance portant sur les haltes-garderies et les jardins d'enfants ne sont pas encore en vigueur.
3. Afin de simplifier la lecture de ce texte, le terme éducateur sera utilisé, qu'il s'agisse d'une éducatrice ou d'un éducateur, et ce, quel que soit son statut professionnel.

Plusieurs réalisations québécoises et étrangères ont contribué, depuis 1976, à améliorer la qualité des services offerts à la petite enfance ; des publications concernant la situation des garderies au Québec, des guides portant sur des aspects de la santé et sur la vie de groupe en garderie ont aidé le personnel et les usagers des services de garde à être plus conscients des caractéristiques de ce milieu de vie. Il faut souligner également qu'une plus grande quantité de livres et de périodiques en langue française touchant ce domaine devient accessible au personnel et aux parents, et leur permet de mieux se renseigner. La démarche entreprise s'inscrit donc dans un courant de réflexion et d'application résolument actuel.

Objectifs généraux

Cette mise à jour de *La garderie, une expérience de vie pour l'enfant* veut rejoindre un grand public par le biais d'une documentation vaste et complexe concernant la petite enfance. Bien qu'il ne soit pas question de procéder à une analyse exhaustive des publications, les données issues des études les plus récentes seront synthétisées et intégrées suivant un esprit analogue à celui de la première version. En définitive, il s'agit de compléter les connaissances de l'univers de l'enfance et d'aborder des éléments de réflexion sur les changements vécus par les adultes, lorsqu'ils se trouvent dans un processus de développement professionnel.

En outre, cette nouvelle version se propose de favoriser l'auto-analyse, la réflexion, l'interaction et l'auto-évaluation du lecteur dans une perspective de croissance personnelle et professionnelle. En effet, les éducateurs en garderie ont maintenant suffisamment de recul et d'expérience pour mener une réflexion susceptible de les amener vers une analyse de leurs interventions pédagogiques. Dans le même sens, bien souvent des éducateurs recherchent un support auprès de leurs collègues, ou bien ils se tournent vers d'autres ressources dans le milieu. Cette série espère donc déclencher chez les éducateurs de la petite enfance une démarche de réflexion, à partir du contenu présenté et à l'aide de références incluses.

De plus, ce document peut être utilisé dans le but d'améliorer le niveau de communication entre les différents intervenants de la petite enfance ; grâce à une ressource commune, éducateurs et parents pourraient maintenir un esprit complémentaire à partir d'interactions quotidiennes avec le jeune enfant, de manière à favoriser le dialogue entre eux ainsi qu'une continuité entre les deux milieux de croissance.

En résumé, cet instrument de travail cherche à orienter les adultes engagés dans une situation éducative auprès de l'enfant d'âge préscolaire afin d'assumer les objectifs suivants :

● Assurer à l'enfant des expériences positives sur les plans physique, psychologique et social ; compte tenu de l'âge de l'enfant et du temps passé à la garderie, la qualité des services offerts est de première importance.

● Aider à situer l'enfant dans l'ensemble de son développement par rapport aux autres enfants.

- Aider à définir les éléments d'organisation d'une garderie par rapport aux besoins des enfants qui la fréquentent.

- Amener l'adulte à tirer profit des situations quotidiennes de façon à les rendre significatives pour tous les enfants et à développer leur autonomie et leur esprit créateur.

- Concilier les valeurs éducatives préconisées dans la famille et à la garderie.

- Établir une continuité dans la qualité des services entre la garderie et l'école.

Structure des trois volets

Selon les remarques présentées par certains lecteurs de l'édition du rodage, le format en deux tomes de l'édition originale s'avérait difficile à manipuler. Une nouvelle présentation a donc été conçue dans le but de favoriser la lecture selon les niveaux d'âge recherchés par le lecteur. C'est ainsi que l'idée d'une série de trois volets directement interreliés a été retenue. Chaque volet est regroupé à partir de caractéristiques propres à l'évolution de l'enfance :

- *l'âge de la recherche de l'identification* : **de un à vingt-quatre mois**, subdivisé en 4 sous-catégories : de un à six mois, de sept à douze mois, de treize à dix-huit mois, et de dix-neuf à vingt-quatre mois ;

- *l'âge de la démarche vers l'autonomie* : **de deux à quatre ans**, subdivisé en 3 sous-catégories : de deux à deux ans et demi, de deux ans et demi à trois ans, et de trois à quatre ans ;

- *l'âge de la conquête de l'initiative* : **de quatre à six ans**, subdivisé en 2 sous-catégories : de quatre à cinq ans et de cinq à six ans[4].

Ces catégories d'âge ne sont évidemment pas rigides. Elles regroupent les grands événements du développement de l'enfant et sont tributaires du processus de maturation qui s'opère de façon relativement universelle chez tous les enfants, mais à des rythmes différents. Elles doivent donc être considérées comme des points de repère. Pour chaque catégorie d'âge, les aspects suivants ont été retenus :

- le développement sensorimoteur ;
- le développement socio-affectif ;
- le développement du langage verbal ;
- les activités physiologiques.

Il devient donc essentiel de tenir compte, à la fois, de l'ensemble de la catégorie d'âge qui intéresse le lecteur et des sous-catégories de niveaux d'âge précédant ou suivant ledit niveau. Ces aspects du développement n'ont qu'une fonction d'organisation pour fins d'étude, mais ils sont toujours considérés comme intimement interreliés à l'ensemble du développement. À titre d'exemple, lorsque sur le plan

---

4. Il convient de souligner, cependant, qu'une attention particulière devrait être accordée dans un prochain document à la catégorie de cinq à six ans car il s'agit d'enfants qui sont souvent accueillis simultanément par une double organisation institutionnelle susceptible de rendre l'approche éducative relativement ambiguë et complexe, c'est-à-dire la maternelle et la garderie.

moteur l'enfant effectue un nouveau mouvement, c'est toute sa personne, et éventuellement son entourage, qui s'en ressentira ; l'enfant éprouvera le sentiment « d'avoir atteint un nouveau jalon dans la croissance » par les nouvelles possibilités d'autonomie que le mouvement en question met à sa portée et il peut utiliser cette nouvelle capacité d'entrer en relation avec les autres. Il est donc très important de préserver constamment cette interrelation entre chaque aspect du développement. C'est ainsi que chacun des volets présente systématiquement une démarche théorique et une démarche pratique, propre au niveau d'âge traité, même si celles-ci ne sont pas identifiées en tant que telles.

Dans un premier temps, **les aspects généraux du développement de l'enfant** familiarisent le lecteur avec les caractéristiques sensorimotrices, socio-affectives, langagières et les activités physiologiques qui marquent le développement de l'enfant de **un mois à six ans**.

Cette vue d'ensemble du développement de l'enfant d'âge préscolaire conduit, par la suite, au contenu de chaque volet selon la catégorie d'âge traitée. Ainsi, chacun des trois volets présente le portrait de l'enfant et la banque de ressources appropriées à l'âge.

Le portrait de l'enfant trace un profil sommaire du développement selon l'âge spécifique traité dans un volet en particulier (ex. : portrait de l'enfant de deux à quatre ans, l'âge de la démarche vers l'autonomie).

Suivant ce portrait, la **banque de ressources** développe en détail les sous-catégories d'âge en question.

En premier lieu, cette banque de ressources présente un tableau synthèse d'un aspect précis du développement selon la sous-catégorie d'âge respective (ex. : développement sensorimoteur de l'enfant de quatre à cinq ans).

Le tableau synthèse est composé d'énoncés théoriques qui ont été empruntés à diverses études scientifiques [4]. Ils précisent les principales caractéristiques identifiées dans chaque portrait de l'enfant. De plus, ces énoncés théoriques constituent la base de toutes les démarches pratiques qui les suivent. Toutefois, il est très important d'insister sur le fait que les synthèses et les énoncés théoriques doivent servir avant tout de points de repère destinés à mieux comprendre les comportements des enfants et à les situer dans leur processus individuel de maturation. **Il ne faudra donc jamais les utiliser comme grille d'évaluation**. Si des enfants présentent des difficultés particulières, il faut consulter des spécialistes qui les évalueront à l'aide d'instruments précis dont ils connaissent la valeur et la portée.

Par ailleurs, la démarche pratique, qui est présentée sous forme de **situations**, **attitudes** et **organisation matérielle**, constitue une sorte d'intégration des fondements inhérents d'un programme de garderie ; en d'autres termes, elles correspondent à l'ensemble indissociable des dimensions humaines, pédagogiques et environnementales proprement dites. Bref, la banque de ressources suivra toujours la séquence suivante :

---

4. Voir références et lectures recommandées à la fin du volet.

- tableau synthèse ;
- âge ;
- aspect du développement ;
- énoncé théorique ;
- situations ;
- attitudes ;
- organisation matérielle.

Afin d'établir clairement l'importance d'une interrelation entre les composantes théoriques et pratiques, la description suivante des trois axes de cette dernière dimension tentera de consolider l'orientation donnée à *La garderie, une expérience de vie pour l'enfant*.

La dimension humaine

L'enfant est l'élément central du service de garde. Il y arrive avec ses aptitudes, ses antécédents familiaux et ses besoins. Il est, par ailleurs, encore dépendant de l'adulte qui lui sert de point de référence et de modèle de comportement autant que de secours et de soutien. Il a des besoins qu'il ne peut satisfaire seul et qu'il peut parfois difficilement exprimer. Les activités doivent donc être organisées en fonction de lui.

Par ailleurs, la garderie se caractérise par le regroupement d'enfants et, en conséquence, la vie de groupe devient une réalité importante. L'enfant est en effet confronté à d'autres pairs qui, à cause de leur âge, ont des besoins et des appréhensions à la fois analogues et différents. Cela exige de chacun (enfants et adultes) un ajustement constant et un certain apprentissage de la tolérance et de la coopération. L'enfant d'âge préscolaire est au coeur du processus de socialisation qui lui crée souvent des difficultés d'adaptation (partager des jouets, attendre son tour, contrôler ses impulsions, etc.). Cependant, malgré le fait que le jeune enfant est incapable de partager toutes les activités collectives, le groupe est pour lui une source à la fois de contraintes et d'apprentissages très positifs. Il faut être aussi conscient que le groupe est une entité en soi qui conditionne le comportement des adultes et l'organisation de la garderie.

Les éducateurs sont les adultes qui influencent le plus le fonctionnement et le caractère propre de la garderie. En effet, à cause de l'importance de l'adulte pour l'enfant et du pouvoir de l'éducateur de choisir son mode d'intervention, il modèle directement le climat de la garderie et la qualité des relations. Son attitude et son comportement, le type d'activités qu'il suggère ou impose, les réponses de l'enfant qu'il suscite ou accepte, le degré et le type de communication qu'il privilégie sont autant de facteurs qui marquent le développement, et davantage le comportement des enfants.

Cette responsabilité doit être partagée par la personne responsable des programmes dont l'attitude et l'intervention en rapport avec les programmes, les horaires, l'organisation physique et matérielle déterminent le comportement du personnel. Son degré d'implication auprès des enfants peut également en faire une figure importante pour ces derniers.

Le personnel de la garderie a la responsabilité d'organiser les activités de la journée de façon à respecter autant que possible les besoins de chaque enfant.

Selon leur disponibilité, les parents peuvent aussi devenir une composante du monde de la garderie. On devrait encourager leur participation aux activités et tirer profit de leurs aptitudes ou talents particuliers.

La dimension pédagogique

L'importance accordée à la dimension humaine explique la place privilégiée réservée à l'enfant et à l'intervenant adulte dans les situations suggérées. Les éléments théoriques présentés dans la banque de ressources accordent une large place à l'interaction directe entre l'éducateur et l'enfant ; ces lignes directrices se prolongent en **situations** concrètes et en **attitudes** générales que l'intervenant adulte pourra adapter selon son style de personnalité et suivant son propre rythme. Les situations correspondent à une application concrète de la dimension pédagogique. Ce sont des jeux, des activités spontanées de l'enfant que l'éducateur utilise afin de favoriser le développement d'une habileté ou d'une capacité précise. Les situations peuvent aussi correspondre à des activités proposées et orientées par l'éducateur dans le but d'aider l'enfant à aborder ou à raffiner une acquisition spécifique lorsque le progrès de l'enfant réclame le support de l'adulte ; afin de conserver une certaine unité de présentation, les situations sont décrites en terme d'actions à faire, de gestes à poser, etc., mais une telle démarche n'est pas synonyme d'interventions rigoureuses ou rigides. En effet, l'éducateur reste le seul juge pour décider du moment qui convient, de la manière de présenter l'activité et de la pertinence de cette intervention. À titre d'exemple, s'il est proposé de prendre le bébé, de stimuler son regard par des jeux spécifiques, il va sans dire que c'est l'éducateur qui adapte une telle proposition comme et quand il convient.

Les situations et les activités proposées constituent des suggestions non exhausti-ves ; elles servent de point de départ à la réflexion et à la création d'autres situations susceptibles de stimuler le développement de l'enfant. Elles ne doivent donc pas être utilisées dans l'esprit de «trucs» ou de «**recettes pédagogiques**» et il s'avère important d'adapter les situations à chaque cas particulier.

De plus, il faut préciser que le concept de programme, utilisé parfois dans le présent ouvrage, doit être compris dans le sens large du terme. En effet, il fait référence à une conception globale (écologique) du milieu de la garderie, c'est-à-dire à l'ensemble des composantes humaines, matérielles et pédagogiques qui affectent la qualité de vie de l'enfant. En aucun cas, il ne faut interpréter la portée du concept de programme dans une perspective étroite, n'incluant que des activités dirigées. Tout élément du milieu peut devenir une composante des activités vécues en garderie (jeux spontanés, routines quotidiennes, etc.) et les buts poursuivis peuvent être multiples :

● Amener l'enfant à poser des actes de plus en plus autonomes et à développer le sens de la liberté et de la responsabilité.

● Amener progressivement l'enfant à penser et à exprimer sa pensée.

● Aider l'enfant à progresser dans la prise de conscience de lui-même comme personne humaine et morale, et dans sa compréhension de l'univers qui l'entoure.

● Permettre à l'enfant d'exprimer ses émotions et l'aider à les contrôler et à les orienter.

Somme toute, à l'intérieur d'un programme, les situations visent à favoriser la réflexion et l'analyse des formes d'interventions que chaque adulte adopte auprès de l'enfant. L'intervention est perçue à la fois en termes d'acte pédagogique auprès des jeunes et de support à la famille, qui peut adopter des attitudes analogues. Par ailleurs, les attitudes proposées dans les situations concrètes indiquent, dans le même sens, des pistes pédagogiques qui ne visent pas à modeler les comportements des adultes, mais plutôt à suggérer des approches respectueuses d'une philosophie d'intervention non directive. Une telle démarche permet à l'éducateur de mieux se situer en tenant compte des limites de sa propre personnalité ; l'auto-évaluation nécessaire à une telle approche rend possible une constante remise en question du rôle d'éducateur.

À la fin de chaque volet, des éléments de réflexion permettent de susciter chez l'éducateur une démarche d'évaluation personnelle, d'observation de l'enfant et d'interactions enfants-adultes-enfants.

Enfin, il faut souligner que toute activité d'un programme doit toujours découler de trois considérations fondamentales :

a) les besoins de l'enfant (âge et caractéristiques) ;

b) la nature du service de garde et les besoins des parents (garderie de jour, service de garde en milieu familial, jardin d'enfants, etc.);

c) le contexte général de la garderie comme milieu de vie : la situation géographique, le personnel, la place des parents, les locaux et les activités prévues.

La dimension environnementale

L'enfant se situe par rapport aux personnes, mais également par rapport au milieu physique (espace et objets surtout). Il y trouve des points de repère qui le sécurisent et aussi une source de découvertes qui stimulent son développement. L'aménagement du milieu physique est donc important. La garderie doit offrir aux enfants des espaces adaptés à leurs besoins, espaces qui tiennent compte de leur stade de développement et facilitent ainsi leur conquête de l'autonomie tant physique (capacité de déplacement), physiologique (alimentation, repos, propreté), que psychologique (capacité de choisir, etc.). L'organisation spatiale doit aussi être sécurisante (leur permettre la formation d'une image positive de soi, des autres, du milieu, etc.) et stimulante (encourager l'exploration, la découverte, favoriser les apprentissages).

L'aménagement doit également assurer la continuité : prévoir des espaces familiers établissant une continuité entre la famille et la garderie (espaces pour dormir, manger, jouer, etc.) ; planifier des espaces familiers correspondant aux normes du milieu, conformes au site de la garderie, pour éviter de créer des problèmes d'adaptation.

En plus des considérations sur l'espace intérieur et extérieur de la garderie, la dimension environnementale se réfère à l'utilisation du matériel comme source de stimulation pour l'enfant. Bien que la qualité du matériel soit un élément primordial pour favoriser une santé physique et mentale équilibrée, ce matériel perd sa valeur intrinsèque lorsque l'adulte néglige de le rendre accessible à l'enfant. C'est donc dans un esprit de ressource secondaire, associée à l'interaction éducateur-enfant, que l'utilisation du matériel est ici suggérée.

La pédagogie du quotidien.

Les services de garde doivent assurer la sécurité physique et émotive des enfants. Pour cela, il devient essentiel de prévoir des activités adaptées à leurs capacités et une certaine régularité afin de faciliter leur intégration. De plus, il est aussi important de planifier des activités de transition de façon à réduire les dangers de surexcitation et de désordre, surtout lors de périodes plus difficiles (avant le repas, période de rangement, etc.).

Les activités doivent également présenter suffisamment de souplesse pour permettre à l'enfant de se découvrir, de choisir ses jeux et ses amis et de faire varier ses intérêts au rythme de sa capacité de concentration et d'attention. S'adaptant à l'âge et au niveau de développement des enfants, ces activités doivent assurer un certain équilibre entre les périodes de détente et les périodes de jeux stimulantes, les situations individuelles et les situations collectives, les jeux dirigés et les jeux libres.

Les activités en garderie devraient permettre aux enfants d'apprendre au rythme des situations vécues naturellement. Dans cette perspective, il est important de prévoir une variété d'expériences qui favorisent la créativité et l'expression de l'enfant. Le jeu y tient une place de première importance puisqu'il est, pendant toute l'enfance, le pivot de l'apprentissage et qu'il favorise le développement de l'intelligence, de la motricité, du langage et de la socialisation.

La garderie prévoit aussi des occasions de stimuler le développement d'habiletés précises reliées aux soins personnels, c'est-à-dire d'amener l'enfant à une autonomie progressive sur le plan de l'alimentation, de l'hygiène et du repos.

La garderie doit reconnaître aux parents leur rôle et leurs responsabilités et respecter autant que possible les valeurs du milieu d'origine. Elle encourage donc les parents qui le peuvent à participer aux activités de la garderie ou à échanger avec les responsables pour assurer une certaine continuité des soins.

Aspects généraux du développement de l'enfant de un mois à six ans

Les caractéristiques de l'enfant d'âge préscolaire

Tel que précisé auparavant, quatre aspects du développement ont été retenus pour les fins de cette série : le développement sensorimoteur, le développement socio-affectif, le développement du langage verbal et les activités physiologiques. Cette division peut, sur bien des plans, être critiquée, et d'autres formules auraient pu tout aussi bien être choisies. Il est cependant apparu important de se limiter à des secteurs facilement observables et d'intégrer des concepts plutôt abstraits à des situations concrètes. Tel est le cas pour les concepts de la conscience de soi et le développement de l'intelligence en tant que tels. La découverte de soi se fait par l'intermédiaire du contact de l'enfant avec le milieu humain et physique. C'est à travers son développement sensorimoteur et physiologique (habitudes alimentaires, hygiéniques et de repos) que l'enfant découvre son corps avec ses possibilités et ses limites. C'est par son contact avec ses pairs et avec les adultes qu'il apprend à se définir comme individu et comme être social à la fois capable d'agir, de réagir et de communiquer. Tous les moments de sa vie contribuent à parfaire sa connaissance de soi. Rendre l'enfant plus conscient de lui-même et développer sa compétence à tous les niveaux devient ainsi l'objectif général à l'intérieur de toutes les activités d'une journée. On retrouvera donc dans les quatre aspects présentés des références à cet objectif fondamental.

Il en est de même pour le développement de l'intelligence. L'enfant d'âge préscolaire n'a pas atteint le niveau de la logique abstraite, il ne fonctionne qu'à partir de son contact avec le milieu humain et physique qui lui permet d'observer, de reconnaître, de se rappeler, d'associer ou de dissocier, de comparer, etc. Ces actions se retrouvent continuellement dans les activités des enfants et c'est pourquoi elles ont également été intégrées aux quatre aspects du développement.

Ce document veut mettre l'accent sur l'importance, pour un programme de garderie, de faire vivre des situations qui rejoignent le développement global, intégral des enfants et de *favoriser nettement le processus de développement plutôt que le produit résultant d'une action.* En d'autres termes, *l'habileté que l'enfant développe dans une activité doit avoir priorité sur la qualité physique ou plastique du produit qui en découle.*

On sait maintenant que tout apprentissage se fait par une expérience. L'enfant doit pouvoir s'essayer plusieurs fois, répéter, recommencer, se tromper pour parvenir à maîtriser une habileté quelconque ; il faut apprécier l'énergie déployée par l'enfant dans cette démarche de croissance physique et mentale. On reconnaît par là l'importance des premières années de la vie pour l'ensemble du développement et la nécessité de ne négliger aucun des éléments impliqués dans ce long processus.

Le développement sensorimoteur

L'organisation progressive des gestes, des déplacements, des actions d'un enfant au cours des premières années de sa vie est marquée par une double caractéristique : les habiletés sensorielles et motrices. Elles sont en effet, à cette étape, un instrument privilégié d'apprentissage. Grâce à la manipulation active, à l'acquisition de mouvements importants (la marche, le saut, la course, etc.), à la répétition d'expériences diverses pour le simple plaisir de l'action, l'enfant évolue à partir des réflexes des débuts de la vie jusqu'à une forme de pensée intériorisée, efficace et bien articulée. Lorsqu'il franchit le seuil de l'école, l'enfant de six ans a emmagasiné, par le biais de gestes, de mouvements et de perceptions sensorielles diverses, un bagage impressionnant de connaissances et d'informations.

Au cours des deux premières années, le nourrisson aborde et contrôle des acquis essentiels ; il reçoit en effet de multiples stimulations sensorielles concernant les objets et apprend à les associer de façon pertinente. Il s'exerce, répète les mêmes gestes et s'intéresse progressivement aux résultats qu'il produit ; ces gestes intentionnels illustrent bien l'intérêt de plus en plus marqué du bébé pour son environnement immédiat. Vers la fin des deux premières années de sa vie, l'enfant a généralement compris que les objets de son environnement sont des réalités permanentes dont l'existence ne dépend pas uniquement de ses propres perceptions qui lui permettent de voir, de toucher, de palper, etc. Le bébé a déjà suffisamment l'expérience de son petit univers pour savoir qu'un objet peut exister même s'il est absent. La compréhension d'une telle réalité (permanence de l'objet) est une compétence préalable à l'acquisition des notions spatiales et temporelles les plus simples. Si l'enfant ne parvient pas à comprendre que les objets autour de lui sont différents de lui-même et indépendants de ses propres perceptions, il ne pourra vraiment pas aborder la nature des choses telles qu'elles existent.

Les sons, les gestes, les mouvements, l'image du corps propre, l'organisation du temps et de l'espace autour de soi sont autant d'aspects qui font l'objet d'une démarche d'apprentissage intense au cours des six premières années de la vie.

Tous ces instruments de connaissance se polissent et se perfectionnent par la suite et contribuent, à l'âge adulte, à l'identification d'une personnalité bien organisée.

Le développement sensorimoteur de l'enfant de un mois à six ans
(Tableau I)

Le tableau I synthétise les composantes du développement sensorimoteur de l'enfant de un mois à six ans. Il passe en revue les différents sens (la vision, l'audition, le toucher, l'odorat, le goût) et les parties du corps qui rendent possible la préhension et la locomotion. Par ailleurs, l'accent mis sur l'une ou l'autre de ces composantes dépend de chaque groupe d'âge analysé.

Le concept **d'organisation perceptive** fait appel à la capacité de déceler, d'organiser et, éventuellement, d'interpréter une information fournie par l'environnement, à partir de différentes sources sensorielles. Par exemple, lorsqu'un enfant voit un écureuil se promener dans un arbre, il doit faire la démarche suivante avant d'être vraiment capable de décoder et de comprendre la situation qui est devant ses yeux :

— il voit (perception de l'objet) ;
— il fixe le regard (attention visuelle) ;
— il retient l'image (mémoire visuelle) ;
— il distingue l'image de façon sélective pour maintenir l'attention (discrimination visuelle).

Cette séquence dans la démarche d'apprentissage s'organise graduellement chez le jeune enfant et contribue directement au développement de l'intelligence.

Tableau I
Le développement sensorimoteur de l'enfant de un mois à six ans

Organisation perceptive*		Contrôle du geste	Contrôle du corps	Conscience du corps	Organisation de l'espace	Organisation du temps
Vision	**Audition**	**Préhension et manipulation**	**Locomotion**	**Schéma corporel**	**Relations spatiales**	**Relations temporelles**
• perception	• perception	• acquisition des mouvements de la main	• acquisition des mouvements	• image corporelle	• adaptation à l'espace	• adaptation au temps
• attention visuelle	• attention auditive	• coordination oeil-main		• concept du corps (connaissance)	• orientation dans l'espace	• orientation dans le temps
• mémoire visuelle	• mémoire auditive	• raffinement du mouvement (perception par le toucher)	• coordination	• schéma corporel (représentation)	• acquisition des notions	• acquisition des notions
• discrimination	• discrimination		• raffinement du mouvement	• latéralité	• structuration de l'espace	• structuration du temps
Ce qui est visible	**Les sons**	**Les gestes**	**Les mouvements**	**Le corps**	**L'espace**	**Le temps**
• objet • êtres vivants	• bruits • cris • voix	• tenir, lâcher, serrer, frapper, lancer, tracer	• s'asseoir, se tenir debout, ramper, grimper, marcher, courir, sauter, sautiller, galoper, tirer, pousser.	• et ses parties	• espace vide ou occupé • les objets dans l'espace	• les actions dans le temps
• dimension • couleur • forme • mouvement	• hauteur • intensité • durée • succession	• souplesse • précision • régularité • efficacité (textures, températures, résistance)	• souplesse • précision • rapidité • équilibre	• espace du corps • rythme du corps • possibilités • limites du corps	• **notions de relations :** hauteur, longueur, largeur, grosseur, distance • **notions de positions :** dessus, dessous, à côté, dedans	• durée • vitesse • succession • intervalle

* Ce tableau se limite à la vision et à l'audition. La perception par le toucher est incluse dans la section préhension et manipulation. La perception par le goût et l'odorat ne fera pas l'objet d'une présentation particulière.

Le tableau présente également le **contrôle du geste** et le **contrôle du corps** en suivant la même démarche progressive. Le tableau limite ici le geste à la préhension et à la manipulation, ces deux pôles étant considérés dans le présent contexte comme les plus significatifs.

Les trois dernières catégories du tableau, **conscience du corps, organisation de l'espace, organisation du temps**, font appel à la représentation mentale que l'enfant parvient à maîtriser et à l'exploration qu'il fait de lui-même et de son milieu.

Enfin, les deux paliers inférieurs du tableau d'ensemble présentent différents concepts et différentes habiletés qui font l'objet de chacun des aspects à développer. Ainsi, la vision met en cause ce qui est visible, objets ou êtres vivants, et débouche progressivement sur le contrôle des dimensions, des formes, des couleurs, etc. L'audition s'exerce à partir de sons, de bruits, de cris, etc., et permet de maîtriser avec le temps la hauteur, l'intensité, la durée des sons ; le contrôle du geste se développe par des comportements comme tenir, lâcher, serrer, etc., et s'associe à des qualités de souplesse, de précision, de régularité dans les mouvements et ainsi de suite pour chacun des thèmes présentés dans le tableau.

Ce tableau synthèse du développement sensorimoteur de l'enfant de un mois à six ans rassemble donc les principaux concepts qui seront présentés dans la banque de ressources. Il faut remarquer que certains aspects du développement sensorimoteur seront plus accentués que d'autres de manière à tenir compte des âges où ils se manifestent. Ainsi, l'organisation de l'espace et du temps est encore floue chez le nourrisson, mais ces concepts peuvent être davantage analysés à l'âge raffiné de la démarche vers l'autonomie, c'est-à-dire vers trois ans, et plus particulièrement à l'âge de la conquête de l'initiative (de quatre à six ans).

Finalement, le développement du nourrisson (volet I) présente des particularités plus marquées qui ne sont pas incluses dans le tableau[5]. À titre d'exemple, les fiches regroupent les aspects vision - préhension - succion - audition, à cause de la relation extrêmement étroite qui existe entre chacun de ces aspects du développement sensoriel. De plus, la locomotion présente l'évolution de la maîtrise de la tête, de la coordination des membres, de l'acquisition des positions assise et debout et de la marche.

Le développement socio-affectif

L'ensemble des sentiments, des émotions, des attachements et des rejets vécus par l'être humain tisse l'histoire affective personnelle et modifie jusqu'à un certain point la qualité de ses rapports sociaux.

La socialisation est un processus d'apprentissage infiniment complexe qui met en scène à la fois des comportements et des émotions; ainsi, le plaisir, la peur, l'anxiété, la joie ont des effets habituellement observables dans les interactions sociales (mimiques, gestes, sourires). Le jeune enfant doit donc apprendre à

---

5. Dans la banque de ressources, un tableau synthétique introduit chaque sous-catégorie d'âge en présentant les aspects qui lui sont particuliers.

communiquer ses propres émotions, à comprendre et à bien décoder celles des autres au contact des adultes qui l'entourent et, un peu plus tard, au contact des autres enfants ; il acquiert avec le temps des règles de vie, des habitudes sociales, des croyances spécifiques ; il endosse aussi progressivement des rôles sociaux conformes au milieu où il vit. Le jeu constitue, au cours des premières années de vie, le pivot même de ces échanges et de ces interactions et il permet à l'enfant d'expérimenter, à la mesure de son âge et de ses propres limites, les plaisirs et les contraintes de la vie collective.

Le développement socio-affectif de l'enfant de un mois à six ans
(Tableau II)

Le tableau II présente l'enfant en interaction avec les adultes et avec les autres enfants. L'expression des émotions, l'attachement ressenti pour les adultes significatifs de son entourage (figures parentales, adultes responsables à la garderie) et l'imitation de ces figures adultes sont autant de formes d'interactions adoptées par les enfants dans leurs rapports avec les adultes.

Dans leurs échanges avec les autres enfants, la maîtrise des impulsions, l'agressivité, le besoin de possession, les modes de participation sociale dans le jeu, l'acceptation des règles de groupe, les réactions positives ou négatives face aux autres camarades sont des aspects essentiels de la démarche sociale des enfants en garderie, car ils côtoient plus tôt que les autres les réalités sociales d'un groupe.

Le développement du langage verbal

Le langage verbal est l'instrument privilégié de la communication humaine. Il tient une place primordiale dans les échanges sociaux, et l'apprentissage des formes essentielles des structures linguistiques se fait généralement au cours de la petite enfance.

Certains aspects du développement déjà présentés dans les tableaux précédents sont en rapport étroit avec l'expression verbale ; ainsi, l'audition joue un rôle significatif dans la communication verbale et, par le fait même, dans les interactions sociales et affectives. Toutefois, pour unifier les caractéristiques du développement et pour faciliter l'utilisation de l'information spécifique concernant chaque groupe d'âge analysé, les compétences verbales comme telles seront présentées dans un tableau d'ensemble.

Si le langage verbal est l'objet d'une attention particulière, cela n'exclut pas l'importance à accorder aux diverses manifestations du langage corporel car ces signaux, mimiques, intonations, sourires, gestes, mouvements, etc., accompagnent et soutiennent le langage verbal.

Tableau II
Le développement socio-affectif de l'enfant de un mois à six ans

Interaction enfants - adultes			Interaction enfants - enfants		
Manifestations des émotions	Imitation de l'adulte	Apprentissage des rôles sociaux	Manifestations des émotions	Communication par le jeu	Participation à la vie de groupe
• Expression des émotions	• Compréhension et acceptation des règles des adultes	• Compréhension de la hiérarchie familiale et sociale	• Expression des émotions	• Type de jeu privilégié	• Respect des règles du groupe
• Attachement	• Attrait pour les jeux d'imitation	• Association et compréhension des comportements adultes	• Sentiment de propriété, de possession	• Type de participation aux jeux	• Connaissance et respect des membres du groupe
• Contact avec l'adulte	• Habileté à agir comme les adultes	• Compréhension des rôles sexuels	• Maîtrise des impulsions	• Contacts avec les pairs par le jeu	• Réactions face aux autres et au groupe
		• Connaissance de son identité sociale (nom, adresse, nom des parents, etc.)			• Relations avec les autres

Le langage corporel comporte en effet des centaines de signaux et de multiples combinaisons de mouvements significatifs qu'il est important de reconnaître et de ne pas négliger.

Les éducateurs responsables de groupes de très jeunes enfants devraient être très attentifs à ces modes de communication tels que hochements de tête, gestes d'appaisement, d'offrande ou de soumission. Ces messages corporels peuvent se glisser à tout moment dans les échanges sociaux des bébés et des jeunes enfants, quelles que soient les particularités de chaque étape de développement.

Le développement du langage verbal de l'enfant de deux à six ans
(Tableau III)

Le tableau III présente des éléments concrets d'observation retenus pour illustrer les principales composantes du langage verbal de l'enfant de deux à six ans (volets II et III). Deux pôles significatifs résument cette réalité ; d'une part, la compréhension des fondements linguistiques et, d'autre part, l'application et l'utilisation personnelle faite par les enfants dès la fin de la deuxième année de ces instruments de langage. La compréhension des mots, des phrases, des récits, la sensibilité à diverses formes d'intonation sont autant d'outils nécessaires à l'enfant pour maîtriser progressivement la communication verbale. Par ailleurs, l'imitation adéquate de sons nouveaux, l'utilisation du vocabulaire, l'application pertinente des mots, donnent à l'éducateur l'occasion d'identifier et d'améliorer les compétences ou les faiblesses du langage de l'enfant.

Les activités physiologiques

Le corps humain semble contrôlé par des horloges biologiques qui règlent en partie les cycles d'alimentation, de sommeil et d'élimination. Chez les bébés et les jeunes enfants, ces contrôles internes personnels déterminent les heures de sommeil et de veille, les besoins de nourriture solide et liquide, et l'évacuation des selles et des urines. Tout en suivant les mêmes cycles généraux, tous les enfants conservent pourtant leurs petites habitudes personnelles, leurs points forts et leurs limites particulières sur ce plan. Il est donc important à la fois de connaître les caractéristiques générales correspondant aux grandes étapes de développement communes à l'ensemble des enfants et d'observer avec attention les variantes individuelles.

Cette partie de la démarche d'observation des caractéristiques du développement rassemble les principales facettes des activités physiologiques des jeunes enfants, c'est-à-dire l'alimentation, le sommeil et l'élimination. De plus, à chacune de ces zones d'activités physiologiques correspondent des habitudes de propreté et des soins particuliers.

Tableau III
Le développement du langage verbal de l'enfant de deux à six ans

La compréhension	L'utilisation
— Compréhension des mots :	— Utilisation personnelle du langage et imitation des sons
— substantifs	
— adjectifs	
— verbes	— Utilisation des différentes formulations
— pronoms	
— Compréhension des phrases :	— Utilisation du vocabulaire
— interrogations	
— langage courant	— Définition des termes
— Compréhension des récits, des histoires	

* Bien que la compréhension du langage verbal débute durant la première année de vie, ce tableau vise à accentuer le processus de décodification mentale qui s'opère vers la fin de la deuxième année. Le développement du langage avant cette période a été intégré au portrait de développement intégral de l'enfant de un mois à vingt-quatre mois.

Les activités physiologiques de l'enfant de un mois à six ans
(Tableau IV)

Le tableau IV résume l'ensemble de ces particularités et les différents aspects dont il faut tenir compte.

La partie consacrée à l'alimentation met l'accent sur les capacités et les habitudes des enfants. Elle ne discute pas de la valeur alimentaire ni des quantités de nourriture à prévoir. Ces aspects sont présentés dans d'autres documents publiés par l'Office des services de garde à l'enfance et préparés par des spécialistes en nutrition. Le moment des repas est une période éminemment propice aux expériences sensorimotrices et socio-affectives, en plus d'avoir une importance évidente pour la santé physique et la croissance de l'enfant. L'attention portée aux enfants pendant cette période est donc très importante.

L'apprentissage du contrôle de l'intestin et de la vessie tient une place non négligeable dans le programme d'une garderie, surtout pour les très jeunes. La garderie doit offrir un milieu sain aux enfants et les aider à développer de bonnes habitudes de propreté.

Le sommeil ou le repos constituent également une période nécessaire dans la journée de la garderie. Il est indispensable au bien-être des enfants. Dans le sommeil, chacun adopte son style propre selon son âge et son type moteur; il importe de le respecter le plus possible. Les périodes de sommeil diminuent avec l'âge et font place à des périodes de sieste ou de détente qui sont tout aussi essentielles. Dans la mesure où l'enfant sera détendu et reposé, il profitera davantage de ses périodes de veille.

Voilà donc qu'avec cet aperçu des aspects généraux du développement de l'enfant de un mois à six ans s'achève cette présentation des volets I, II et III respectivement intitulés :

- l'Âge de la recherche de l'identification (un à vingt-quatre mois) ;
- l'Âge de la démarche vers l'autonomie (deux à quatre ans) ;
- l'Âge de la conquête de l'initiative (quatre à six ans).

Tableau IV		
Les activités physiologiques de l'enfant de un mois à six ans		
Alimentation	**Hygiène et élimination**	**Repos-sommeil**
Contrôle du geste	**Contrôle de l'intestin**	**Repos-sieste**
• Niveau d'autonomie	**Contrôle de la vessie**	• Variations dans le rythme
		• Caractéristiques et rituels
Caractéristiques particulières	**Habitudes de propreté**	
		Sommeil
• Appétit	• Niveau d'autonomie	
• Habitudes alimentaires	• Entretien des mains, du visage, des dents	• Variations dans le rythme, la nature et l'intensité
• Besoins spécifiques		• Caractéristiques et rituels
Habitudes de propreté		**Habitudes de propreté**

Volet II

Âge de la démarche vers l'autonomie

de deux ans à quatre ans

Le portrait de l'enfant de deux à quatre ans

Au cours des deux premières années de vie du petit enfant, une confiance mutuelle s'est progressivement tissée entre lui et des figures parentales significatives.

Toutefois, pour qu'il puisse grandir, il lui faut maintenant vivre l'expérience graduelle et dirigée de son autonomie.

Le sentiment de confiance acquis à l'étape précédente permet à l'enfant de prendre conscience de sa propre volonté. Cette volonté naissante a besoin de s'exercer ; l'enfant commence à exprimer ses propres désirs, il manifeste clairement ses exigences personnelles, il veut tout faire tout seul, sans aide, sans conseil. Il veut tout expérimenter, mais ses limites réelles supposent que des adultes qui l'aiment le laissent vivre avec ces nouveaux besoins, tout en veillant sur lui. Si ces adultes exercent trop de contrôle, l'enfant ne pourra jamais vérifier lui-même ses limites ; par ailleurs, s'ils n'établissent jamais de frontières bien définies, l'enfant ne devra compter que sur lui-même. Il limitera son expérience par crainte de perdre sa propre maîtrise et il lui sera toujours très difficile d'atteindre cette autonomie fonctionnelle.

Entre deux et quatre ans, l'enfant s'affirme, il dit « non » ; sa maturation physique, intellectuelle et sociale lui permet d'ailleurs de réussir tout seul de plus en plus de choses. Il peut maintenant marcher, courir, se nourrir, s'habiller seul plus facilement et il sait contrôler davantage son hygiène personnelle ; son langage se développe, il peut exprimer plus clairement ses désirs et ses refus. Il commence à s'associer aux autres enfants dans ses jeux, il s'invente même en toute autonomie des compagnons imaginaires ; il élargit, en somme, son petit univers par ses propres moyens.

L'affirmation de soi permet à l'enfant d'apprendre progressivement à contrôler des situations quotidiennes, mais elle implique un grand besoin de sécurité émotive et de stabilité affective. Les rites du sommeil et des repas, la constance dans le climat de vie qui entoure l'enfant, de même qu'une certaine permissivité au sujet d'expériences nouvelles constituent, à cet âge, une bonne attitude pour amener l'enfant à vivre cette période de façon positive.

Quoi qu'il en soit, cette marche vers l'autonomie est une étape essentielle, et les éducateurs devraient être pleinement conscients de l'importance de ces années dans le développement ultérieur d'un enfant.

Tableau V

Synthèse du développement sensorimoteur de l'enfant de deux ans

	Vision	Audition	Préhension et manipulation	Locomotion	Schéma corporel	Relations spatiales	Relations temporelles
E N T R E 2	• Meut ses yeux plus librement.	• Augmente sa capacité d'attention et de discrimination auditive.	• Se sert alternativement des deux mains.	• Marche bien.	• Explore son corps par l'activité motrice.	• Monte, descend, explore avec son corps l'espace vertical et horizontal.	• Expérimente la notion de temps en acceptant d'attendre.
E T 3	• Est sensible au champ périphérique.	• Aime la répétition de sons et de bruits.	• Aligne les objets horizontalement.	• Court bien, mais tombe soudainement.	• Explore les objets par une activité globale.	• Est plus conscient des distances mais ne comprend pas la continuité.	• Possède la notion du « maintenant ».
A N S	• Observe avec intérêt les mouvements rotatifs.	• Répète un plus grand nombre de mots par imitation auditive.	• Construit une tour de 5 ou 6 cubes.	• Monte les escaliers et descend avec appui, sans alterner les pieds.	• Identifie certaines parties de son corps : ventre, bras, jambes, etc.	• Expérimente dans ses activités sa situation dans l'espace et la place des objets.	• Comprend une succession simple (sans référence au passé).
	• Localise avec les yeux les objets et vérifie avec la main sa réponse visuelle.	• Aime s'entendre parler en faisant une action.	• Aime visser et dévisser.	• Peut donner un coup de pied.	• Nomme les parties de son corps : ventre, jambes, mains, tête, etc.		
	• Aime les petits objets.	• Chante généralement faux.	• Peut ouvrir les portes.	• Peut plier la taille et les genoux pour ramasser des choses.			
	• Identifie trois à cinq images.	• Aime le matériel rythmique : balançoire, bascule, berceuse.	• Accroît son adresse pour emboîter, démonter, réajuster.				
		• Répond en rythme à la musique : se balance, hoche la tête, tape du pied, etc.	• Aime remplir, creuser, vider.				
			• Aime manipuler les objets qui bougent, qui tournent, les joues mécaniques.				
			• Peut attraper une balle qui roule au sol.				

Deux ans

Le développement sensorimoteur

Vision

À deux ans, l'enfant peut localiser avec les yeux les objets, mais il veut encore vérifier avec la main sa réponse visuelle. Il localise mieux les distances plus rapprochées que les distances lointaines ; il est sensible aux champs visuels périphériques.

Situations
- **les jeux de surprise**

- pour susciter d'abord l'attention visuelle avant la manipulation, cacher dans un grand sac divers objets attrayants. Les sortir un à un, lentement, avant de les remettre dans les mains des enfants ;

- ne pas hésiter à réunir dans ce sac plusieurs objets semblables, de manière à doubler l'attention au sujet des mêmes caractéristiques. Surélever légèrement la position de ces objets par rapport à l'oeil de l'enfant ;

Attitudes
- prévoir la réaction des enfants qui voudront aussitôt toucher l'objet qu'ils viennent de voir ;

- ne pas laisser à la portée des enfants des objets dangereux ou fragiles, car ceux-ci voudront invariablement vérifier ce qu'ils ont vu et on ne peut leur demander encore de regarder longtemps sans toucher ;

- éviter de trop éloigner des enfants les objets sur lesquels il y a lieu d'attirer l'attention ;

- organiser le milieu de vie de manière à mettre à la portée des enfants les objets qui les intéressent ;

- accentuer les dimensions des objets ou des éléments qui doivent servir de point de repère pour l'enfant, de manière à susciter son attention même s'il s'agit d'objets éloignés.

- susciter des jeux où l'enfant devra poursuivre, dans un champ périphérique assez restreint, une direction visuelle donnée ;

- **le voyage du petit train**

- déterminer deux points qui servent de gare à gauche et à droite. Jouer à deviner, sans détourner la tête, si le train est rendu ou non à la gare ;

● présenter des objets mécaniques qui tournent d'eux-mêmes.

Attitudes ● être extrêmement prudent dans le choix des éléments qui peuvent être mis en mouvement en présence des enfants pour éviter tout danger, car l'enfant de cet âge n'a pas encore établi le lien essentiel qui existe entre un interrupteur et le fonctionnement immédiat d'un appareil;

● utiliser les objets qui présentent certains risques avec un seul enfant ou un très petit groupe, surveiller les gestes impulsifs de la main, des doigts et les mouvements des jambes.

Organisation matérielle ● prévoir l'achat d'objets mécaniques ou de jouets aux mouvements de rotation à cette époque de la vie de l'enfant (batteurs à oeufs rotatifs, que l'enfant pourra lui-même actionner);

● se procurer des objets qui soient solides et résistants, car l'enfant voudra sûrement en faire l'essai à son tour.

L'enfant de deux ans s'intéresse à ses propres mouvements; lorsqu'il gribouille et observe visuellement l'effet que cela produit sur un espace restreint, il peut facilement s'emporter et dépasser le cadre étroit de la feuille.

Situations ● tirer profit de toutes les situations quotidiennes ou d'événements inhabituels pour amener l'enfant à exercer l'oeil et la main.

Attitudes ● éviter de laisser des crayons un peu partout dans la pièce sans limite d'utilisation, car l'enfant s'en servira sûrement pour gribouiller sur les murs et les planchers;

● laisser, à certaines périodes, les enfants libres de gribouiller sur de grosses boîtes de carton ou de larges feuilles de papier, sans tenir compte des résultats du dessin; l'enfant de cet âge s'exerce encore pour le seul plaisir de s'exercer et de produire des résultats immédiats qui n'ont pas, pour lui, la même signification que pour l'adulte.

Organisation matérielle ● pour éviter des ennuis d'ordre pratique, donner à l'enfant des crayons avec des feuilles de papier de petites et de plus grandes dimensions, en plaçant en dessous, avec une couleur contrastante, une feuille de dimension encore plus importante;

● prévoir des espaces assez vastes pour que l'enfant puisse découvrir ses mouvements au delà des dimensions habituelles d'une feuille de papier. Exemple: mettre sur un mur des feuilles de papier journal fixées les unes aux autres, sur lesquelles l'enfant pourra tantôt gribouiller de petites surfaces ou suivre tout le mur avec son crayon, comme s'il marchait en se traçant un chemin. Maintenir un certain droit de contrôle en déterminant des espaces précis que l'enfant pourra utiliser.

- **les ballons en voyage**

- lancer deux ballons en même temps dans deux directions différentes. Faire rouler les ballons très lentement. Retenir l'enfant assis. Celui-ci suivra des yeux ;

- déplacer des objets lentement dans l'entourage de l'enfant et observer ses réactions ;

- observer l'attitude de l'enfant : celui-ci tentera invariablement de tourner la tête. Ne pas forcer l'attention au delà d'une certaine limite et utiliser des couleurs vives pour l'un et l'autre des objets.

L'attention visuelle se raffine : les objets retiennent son attention plus longuement. L'enfant de cet âge commence à montrer beaucoup d'intérêt pour les petits objets.

Situations
- placer en vrac une bonne quantité d'objets de grosseurs variables sans craindre d'y ajouter des objets de dimensions réduites, à condition qu'ils ne soient pas dangereux ;

- réunir des animaux miniatures de dimensions variables et assortir chaque espèce (tous les animaux, tous les chats) ; varier le plus possible les dimensions. Ex. : un gros, un moyen, un petit cheval... un gros, un moyen, un petit chat, etc. ;

- cacher devant l'enfant plusieurs petits objets à des endroits divers, le laisser les retrouver.

Attitudes
- être vigilant : surveiller avec beaucoup d'attention les enfants de cet âge ; ne pas tomber dans l'excès en donnant à l'enfant, malgré son intérêt, des objets trop petits et dangereux qu'il pourrait avaler.

Organisation matérielle
- utiliser des situations quotidiennes où l'enfant peut sans danger exercer et coordonner les mouvements de l'oeil et de la main, lui donner par exemple de petits raisins à saisir (manipulation) et à repérer visuellement dans un grand plat.

L'enfant de deux ans s'intéresse au mouvement produit par un objet ou un appareil : il observe avec un très grand intérêt les mouvements rotatifs.

Situations
- présenter à l'enfant une variété d'objets, d'appareils, de machines qui ont comme propriété de pouvoir effectuer des mouvements circulaires et rotatifs ;

- faire tourner devant lui des cerceaux, des toupies, des ballons qui pivotent sur eux-mêmes ;

- faire fonctionner des batteurs à oeufs manuels (pour éviter les blessures) ;

- utiliser les objets courants qui peuvent tourner, paniers, boîtes de conserve, etc. ;

Deux ans

Le développement sensorimoteur

Audition

L'enfant répond en rythme à la musique : il se balance, hoche la tête, tape du pied ; il aime donc beaucoup le matériel rythmique qui correspond à ce besoin : balançoires, bascules, berceuses.

Situations
- disposer plusieurs caisses de bois à la suite les unes des autres. Y faire asseoir les enfants comme dans un train, faire entendre de la musique douce et laisser les enfants s'exprimer à leur façon ;

- donner un bon coussin aux enfants. Les laisser s'installer dessus, à plat ventre, sur le dos ou comme ils voudront, et faire entendre de la musique ou chanter avec eux une chanson connue ;

- donner aux enfants des objets familiers, coussins, petites boîtes à tabac, boîtes de carton, tabourets, etc., sur lesquels ils pourront frapper en rythme.

Attitudes
- éviter d'intervenir lorsqu'un enfant, tout en exprimant le rythme, ne respecte pas le bon temps du rythme ;

- laisser cet enfant exprimer ce qu'il ressent sans évaluer la qualité de son expression rythmique, car il ne peut pas encore contrôler parfaitement tous ses mouvements ;

- ne pas craindre de laisser vivre au groupe un certain « désordre » sonore pendant quelques minutes ; c'est une bonne façon d'exprimer un trop plein d'énergie. Il faut toutefois éviter de prolonger trop longuement ces situations, car elles peuvent déboucher sur une surexcitation collective.

Organisation matérielle
- prévoir, dès cet âge (entre deux et trois ans), l'achat de matériel rythmique qui corresponde aux besoins des enfants : quelques chaises berceuses bien étudiées pour éviter les dangers (sans berceaux pointus mais plutôt de bois plein), des balançoires à bascules tubulaires où plusieurs enfants peuvent s'installer, des balançoires très basses, à l'intérieur comme à l'extérieur, non suspendues.

L'enfant accentue sa capacité d'attention et de reconnaissance auditive ; il identifie un plus grand nombre de bruits.

Situations	● remonter la sonnerie du réveille-matin et le cacher dans un circuit limité, facilement accessible. Faire retrouver le réveille-matin et faire contrôler le bouton d'arrêt (manipulation) par l'enfant lui-même ; l'enfant jouera sans se lasser pour le seul plaisir de pouvoir arrêter le réveil ;
	● dissimuler un ou deux réveille-matin, les régler à quelques secondes ou quelques minutes d'intervalles, et à des endroits différents. Ce jeu permet d'intéresser plusieurs enfants à la fois ;
	● imiter des cris d'animaux connus et faire associer à des cris des images très simples représentant l'animal qui vient d'être imité.
Attitudes	● rechercher toutes les occasions de susciter l'attention auditive de l'enfant, dans la mesure où il est possible d'isoler suffisamment le son ou le bruit à faire remarquer.
Organisation matérielle	● utiliser certains jeux d'attention auditive pour en faire une transition entre deux activités et pour faire retrouver le calme auprès du groupe en suscitant leur attention et en réalisant un meilleur contrôle du bruit environnant.

L'enfant aime entendre chanter : il aime la répétition de sons et de bruits familiers. Il chante encore généralement faux.

Situations	● faire régulièrement entendre à l'enfant les chansons qu'il aime en les chantant au cours de la journée. Pour varier, utiliser une grosse marionnette ou une toupie qui « chantera les airs que l'enfant lui demande ».
Attitudes	● éviter de reprendre l'enfant qui ne respecte pas l'air d'une chanson, continuer plutôt à chanter avec lui en insistant sur l'ensemble de la chanson plutôt que sur les détails. L'enfant raffine progressivement son oreille et finira par répéter avec plus de justesse.
Organisation matérielle	● aménager un petit coin spécial avec des coussins et du tapis, un peu en retrait des activités du groupe. Mettre à la disposition des enfants de petits livres en carton solide ou en tissus représentant surtout des animaux ou des objets familiers ; ces livres serviront de départ à de nombreuses activités mettant en cause l'audition et l'attention auditive de l'enfant.

L'enfant aime s'entendre parler en faisant une action et il répète un plus grand nombre de bruits et de mots par imitation auditive.

Situations	● favoriser le développement de la mémoire auditive de l'enfant de cet âge en faisant imiter après audition. Faire répéter le bruit caractéristique d'animaux ou d'objets familiers en regardant des images très simples ;

- utiliser des images, de petits animaux jouets ou des marionnettes, reproduire ces bruits connus des enfants. Raconter des histoires très simples, uniquement en faisant des bruits. Insister surtout sur les bruits produits par les éléments représentés en image.

Attitudes

- répéter correctement après l'enfant le ou les mots qu'il dit en jouant. Développer son attention auditive en ayant plutôt l'air de l'interroger que de le corriger et ajouter progressivement un mot nouveau. Vérifier si l'enfant ajoute ces mots à son vocabulaire croissant.

Organisation matérielle

- rester à portée de voix de l'enfant à l'occasion de telles expériences pour éviter d'avoir à parler trop fort et de l'ennuyer.

Deux ans

Le développement sensorimoteur

Manipulation

Perception par le toucher : L'enfant aime remplir, vider, creuser, transvaser de l'eau, du sable ou tout autre élément qui se prête à de telles manipulations ; il se lave fréquemment les mains, lave les pinceaux avec plaisir, joue à la lessive, etc.

Situations

- mettre à la disposition des enfants un carré de sable très fin à l'extérieur et un contenant de sable à l'intérieur, ajouter des accessoires comme des tamis ou des passoires à grains larges, des entonnoirs. Organiser des jeux d'eau où l'enfant pourra manipuler sans danger des contenants de toutes sortes ;

- laisser explorer librement les mouvements des objets qui flottent, qui s'enfoncent, qui se dissolvent, etc., dans des jeux d'eau et vérifier les sensations de chaleur, de froid, d'humidité, etc., avec le sable. Permettre aux enfants de transvaser du riz dans divers contenants, en incluant des contenants dans un plateau à large rebord, et comparer le sable et d'autres textures apparentées ;

- faire des jeux de rythme où l'enfant pourra taper sur deux ou trois matériaux différents : coussin, table, drap ou tissu tendu par deux adultes ; donner à toucher de la peinture aux doigts. Donner l'occasion aux enfants d'expérimenter les notions de dur, de mou, de rugueux, de liquide, de solide, sans nécessairement mentionner aucun des termes.

Attitudes

- accorder une attention particulière aux découvertes textiles faites par le biais des deux éléments favoris à cet âge. Le sable et l'eau sont des matériaux naturels et universels ;

- considérer les jeux d'eau et de sable comme des activités essentielles et les rendre accessibles aux enfants, malgré les contraintes que ces activités peuvent présenter à certains moments ;

- accorder beaucoup d'importance à la bonne organisation matérielle de ces jeux, car un manque de planification entraîne toujours un grand nombre d'interdits que l'enfant de cet âge ne peut pas respecter.

Organisation matérielle

- prévoir une organisation simple qui puisse donner l'occasion aux enfants de jouer à tour de rôle dans l'eau et le sable, même à l'intérieur au cours de l'hiver. Prévoir une double piscine sur un tapis au sol pour éviter les dégâts ou un espace autour du lavabo réservé aux enfants;

- utiliser plusieurs contenants pour éviter les disputes et laisser jouer un petit nombre d'enfants à la fois, à moins de disposer d'un très grand espace ;

- demander l'aide des enfants pour le rangement et le ramassage des accessoires de jeux.

L'enfant contrôle suffisamment bien ses mouvements de l'oeil et de la main pour attraper un ballon qui roule au sol.

Situations
- faire asseoir les enfants en cercle en écartant les jambes légèrement, faire rouler un ballon de bonne dimension en direction de chaque enfant à tour de rôle, en annonçant le prénom de l'enfant avant de faire rouler le ballon ;

- faire rouler un ballon en direction de l'enfant debout qui doit se déplacer pour attraper le ballon qui roule ;

- asseoir les enfants sur de petits bancs très bas ; faire rouler le ballon en direction d'un enfant, à tour de rôle, et faire pousser le ballon avec la main ou le pied sans se lever ;

Attitudes
- s'asseoir avec l'enfant pour encourager ses efforts et ne pas s'imaginer que celui-ci pourra jouer très longtemps seul avec un ballon ou sans directive et sans aucun encouragement.

L'enfant se sert alternativement de ses deux mains. Il aime manipuler les objets qui bougent, qui tournent, les jouets à clés ; il aime visser et dévisser. Il peut ouvrir les portes.

Situations
- réunir des bocaux et des couvercles de différentes grandeurs. Laisser tous les éléments en vrac dans une boîte. Observer la démarche des enfants et leur capacité de manipuler, de reconnaître et d'associer les bons éléments ;

- mettre à la disposition des enfants des séries de vieilles clés réunies par une ficelle et les laisser explorer les diverses serrures à l'intérieur de la garderie ;

- laisser les enfants faire tourner le banc du piano ou un tabouret pour explorer le phénomène à grande échelle.

Attitudes
- laisser l'enfant explorer lui-même et ne pas intervenir trop souvent, car c'est plus le plaisir de manipuler et d'explorer qui compte que le plaisir de réussir.

Organisation matérielle
- acheter avec beaucoup de précautions les divers jouets à visser et à dévisser pour les enfants de cet âge, car les objets doivent être souples et faciles à visser pour résister aux efforts des enfants qui explorent encore avec beaucoup de maladresse et de brusquerie tout jouet qui leur résiste ;

- prévoir des loquets de sécurité à hauteurs variables en tenant compte des dangers particuliers à chaque garderie.

Deux ans

Le développement sensorimoteur

Locomotion

L'enfant contrôle généralement bien la marche : il court bien, mais tombe fréquemment et soudainement vers l'avant.

Situations
- organiser des promenades autour de la pièce pendant lesquelles l'enfant doit courir autour d'un tas de coussins ou de petits matelas de mousse. Montrer aux enfants à se protéger la tête en se retenant avec les mains lorsqu'ils se laissent tomber sur l'amas de coussins.

Attitudes
- surveiller la course de certains enfants qui risquent de se blesser constamment au front ou à la tête parce qu'ils contrôlent encore très mal leurs réflexes de protection lorsqu'ils tombent vers l'avant.

Organisation matérielle
- éliminer tous les angles dangereux aux meubles de la garderie. Éviter de trop encombrer la pièce de jeux ou de meubles trop gros ou pointus ; utiliser de préférence de petites étagères très basses, au mur, et des coussins ou des tapis, au sol.

L'enfant raffine davantage ses mouvements d'ensemble ; il peut maintenant plier la taille et les genoux pour ramasser des objets.

Situations
- organiser des promenades durant lesquelles les enfants doivent marcher en petit bonhomme, en grenouille, en lapin, en chaton ;

- jouer à celui qui ramasse le plus rapidement un jouet tombé ;

- attendre le ballon qui roule au sol en prenant une position légèrement accroupie ;

- recevoir deux ou trois ballons à la fois, roulant ensemble au sol, dans la même position ;

- demander aux enfants de l'aide à l'occasion des activités de rangement ; faire ramasser les jouets qui sont en désordre sur le plancher et les mettre sur des tablettes.

Attitudes
- encourager l'enfant à plier la taille et les genoux pour ramasser des objets et montrer aux enfants qui ne le font pas encore la bonne manière de s'y prendre.

Organisation matérielle

- tirer profit d'une organisation matérielle qui varie les niveaux de planchers et force les enfants à monter et à descendre, à se pencher également pour ramasser des objets au sol ;

- éviter toutefois d'abuser des dénivellations du sol, car elles risquent de fatiguer l'enfant et l'adulte si elles sont en trop grand nombre.

L'enfant monte les escaliers et descend avec appui, sans alterner les pieds ; il dépose, à chaque marche, les deux pieds avant de monter la marche suivante.

Situations

- encourager l'enfant à monter l'escalier avec l'appui d'une part et l'aide de la main adulte, d'autre part.
  Retirer progressivement, l'aide de la main en commençant par les marches du bas ;

- encourager l'enfant de la même façon à descendre l'escalier progressivement, en ne s'appuyant que sur la rampe ;

- habituer l'enfant à la notion de hauteur en le faisant grimper sur une table, sur une petite armoire, sous surveillance, pour éliminer les problèmes de vertige ;

- laisser l'enfant grimper et l'aider par la suite à descendre, après avoir évalué avec lui le vide pendant quelques instants.

Attitudes

- suggérer, par imitation, l'idée de monter l'escalier en déposant les deux mains, comme appui, sur les marches qui précèdent ;

- accorder beaucoup d'importance aux louanges et aux encouragements pour aider les enfants craintifs. Établir des règles de sécurité très strictes pour protéger les enfants qui ne craignent en aucune façon les hauteurs ;

- tenir compte de la caractéristique particulière des enfants de cet âge qui ne craignent pas les véritables dangers ;

- tenir compte du fait que l'enfant de cet âge ne peut réussir à maintenir son équilibre qu'au prix d'une forte concentration. Il ne peut faire plus d'une activité à la fois.

Organisation matérielle

- pourvoir les jeux à grimper de barres d'appui, de rebords qui assurent toute la sécurité nécessaire. Prévoir que les tubulures des structures à grimper soient lisses, pour éviter la douleur et les blessures aux organes sexuels durant les escalades.

L'enfant développe progressivement, entre deux et trois ans, la capacité de pousser le ballon du pied. Un peu plus tard, il pourra frapper directement sur le ballon en mouvement, avec un seul pied.

Situations
- faire asseoir les enfants en cercle sur des chaises et faire pousser le ballon avec le bout des pieds ; lorsque l'enfant a acquis une certaine habitude et un certain contrôle des réflexes, étendre ce jeu à la position debout. Laisser en permanence sur le plancher un ou deux ballons. Ajouter un but à atteindre en plaçant une chaise ou une large boîte, ou encore en plaçant deux chaises écartées l'une de l'autre ; faire pousser du pied en direction d'un but, afin de faire tomber un obstacle placé entre les deux chaises.

Attitudes
- encourager les enfants, même s'ils réussissent difficilement à pousser le ballon. Éviter d'axer une telle activité sur le principe de la compétition, principe qui ne convient pas à cet âge.

Organisation matérielle
- prévoir l'achat de ballons assez gros (au moins six pouces de diamètre) et assez légers ; acheter aussi des ballons de poids et de textures différentes (caoutchouc mousse, ballons gonflés d'air, ballons pleins, etc.).

Deux ans

Le développement sensorimoteur

Schéma corporel

L'enfant de deux ans explore son propre corps par l'activité motrice. Il identifie certaines parties de son corps : ventre, bras, jambe, etc.

Situations
- **activités au cours de l'habillage**
- au cours de l'habillage et du déshabillage, lorsque l'enfant a besoin d'aide, jouer à entrer un bras dans le tunnel (manche), à sortir la tête du grand trou (col), etc. En faisant collaborer l'enfant, le vestiaire et l'activité d'habillage deviennent des occasions de jeux.

Attitudes
- ne pas avoir « peur de perdre du temps » à l'occasion des activités de routines. Les adultes ont trop souvent l'habitude de presser les enfants à aller toujours plus vite. En plus de pousser inutilement l'enfant à suivre un rythme qui ne lui convient pas nécessairement, ils perdent des occasions précieuses de faire de l'activité quotidienne un jeu continuel au profit d'un horaire imposé de façon souvent difficile. L'enfant aura assez tôt l'obligation de s'intégrer dans une routine quotidienne.

Organisation matérielle
- **le lit de neige**
- à l'occasion des jeux à l'extérieur de la garderie, au cours de l'hiver, permettre aux enfants bien habillés de se coucher quelques instants dans la neige, de tout leur long. Les faire se relever et observer avec eux la forme laissée dans la neige ; comparer les grandeurs, leur faire essayer les lits des voisins ;
- éviter de comparer avec des mesures d'adultes, mais utiliser plutôt des comparaisons directes entre les enfants eux-mêmes ou en fonction de plusieurs autres éléments présents dans l'entourage immédiat, observer les traces laissées par les bras étendus, les jambes écartées, etc. ;
- envisager la possibilité de fixer, dans la neige, la forme laissée par l'enfant en préparant, par exemple, une petite quantité d'eau colorée de diverses teintes.

- **le grand épouvantail**
- prendre quelques vêtements simples, chapeau, soulier, veste, pantalon et s'habiller devant les enfants en mêlant volontairement l'ordre des vêtements ;
- observer les réactions des enfants et, selon leur degré de compréhension, compliquer progressivement ce jeu en bâtissant d'abord un modèle conforme à l'ordre habituel et en multipliant ensuite les erreurs. Le chapeau dans les pieds, les souliers sur la tête, etc. ;

Deux ans

Le développement sensorimoteur

Relations spatiales

L'enfant monte, descend, explore avec son corps l'espace vertical et horizontal.

Situations
- laisser l'enfant marcher sur des rampes inclinées, glisser et rouler sur des pentes ;

- laisser l'enfant ramper sous les tables, rouler à plat ventre sur des cylindres, d'avant en arrière, avec ou sans soutien ;

- prévoir des éléments à grimper, très bas et sans danger, où l'enfant peut s'accrocher, et de petits escaliers, des pentes.

Attitudes
- encourager l'enfant craintif à monter et descendre, à franchir les obstacles avec un appui ;

- planifier des espaces variés pour l'enfant explorateur ou casse-cou, en surveillant plus particulièrement tous les aspects qui vont assurer sa sécurité.

Organisation matérielle
- organiser l'espace de façon à stimuler l'exploration. Limiter au maximum les risques et les dangers inhérents à l'inconscience particulière des enfants de cet âge.

L'enfant expérimente, dans ses activités quotidiennes, sa situation dans l'espace et la place des objets.

Situations
- établir pour les activités routinières une sorte d'ordre bien établi qui permette à l'enfant de se situer dans le cours de sa journée en rapport avec les espaces qu'il aura à occuper (un endroit pour manger, un endroit pour dormir, etc.) et les objets ou les jouets qu'il pourra utiliser ;

- se faire aider des enfants pour ranger les jouets, pour transporter les petites chaises et les bancs, et les remettre à leur place ;

- faire des rondes où les enfants doivent tourner autour d'une chaise, autour d'un autre enfant. Faire de petits jeux de cache-cache où l'enfant ne dipose que d'un gros objet pour se cacher.

Attitudes

- utiliser très souvent une attitude de jeu pour faire comprendre à l'enfant la notion de lieu et d'espace ;

- adopter une attitude de recherche (sous forme de jeu) pour obliger l'enfant, qui est pourtant placé tout près, à se situer par rapport à l'éducateur ; « Jean est parti. (chercher) ; il n'est pas *sous* la table, il n'est pas à la toilette, où est-il? Ah! il est assis *sur* sa chaise! »

Organisation
matérielle

- laisser l'enfant se cacher, tout en le surveillant; lui aménager des lieux un peu en retrait où il peut à la fois se retirer, se cacher et bien se situer par rapport aux jouets qui s'y trouvent.

L'enfant est davantage conscient des distances entre les personnes et entre les objets, mais il ne comprend pas la continuité.

Situations

- disposer des miroirs très larges à proximité de la porte d'entrée ou de sortie, de manière à permettre la prise de conscience d'une différence entre l'image du miroir (reflet) et la continuité des espaces au delà de la porte ;

- organiser des jeux de chemins de fer où les enfants se tenant les uns aux autres font simplement le tour de toutes les pièces de la garderie, plusieurs fois de suite ;

- laisser l'enfant anxieux revenir de temps à autre au vestiaire pour retrouver et revoir la porte d'entrée et de sortie.

Attitudes

- apporter à l'enfant une présence rassurante qui pourra suppléer à l'absence de compréhension de la continuité des espaces ;

- démontrer une compréhension du principe ci-haut mentionné en évitant de porter des jugements de caprices à l'endroit de certains enfants qui s'accrochent à la porte d'entrée ; donner à l'enfant des points de repères constants, permanents, et commenter devant lui la place successive qu'occupent les objets dans la garderie ;

- utiliser une petite maison de poupée ou la maquette de la garderie pour aider l'enfant à exprimer ses craintes.

Organisation
matérielle

- tenir compte des limites spatiales des enfants dans l'aménagement de la garderie ;

- simplifier à l'extrême l'aménagement des espaces où l'enfant doit très souvent se déplacer. Éviter, autant que possible, les couloirs en enfilade, les espaces intermédiaires sans fonction de jeu et qui masquent la troisième salle où l'enfant joue habituellement ;

- utiliser des miroirs spéciaux qui ne risquent pas de casser ;

- aménager des espaces ouverts sur l'extérieur au moyen de fenêtres à la portée des enfants ; pratiquer des ouvertures vitrées à différentes hauteurs, entre deux salles de jeu.

Deux ans

Le développement sensorimoteur

Relations temporelles

L'enfant expérimente la notion de temps en acceptant d'attendre son tour. Il possède la notion vécue du « maintenant ». Il comprend une succession très simple dans le temps (une action par rapport à une autre), mais sans référence au passé.

Situations
- donner à l'enfant une raison d'attendre son tour en l'aidant à se situer dans le temps. Distribuer les verres de jus ou la collation en commençant à un bout ou à un autre de la table, mais en suivant désormais l'ordre des places et en annonçant le prénom à venir (« Après Nicolas, c'est le tour de François. », etc.) ;

- aux changements d'activités, annoncer à l'avance à l'enfant que le jeu se termine et le lui laisser terminer avant de ranger le matériel. Reprendre le même principe lorsqu'il s'agit de l'action de l'adulte. Annoncer à l'enfant qu'il aura son tour dans un moment, lorsque le travail sera fini ;

- remercier l'enfant qui a attendu ou le féliciter de sa patience.

Attitudes
- tenir les promesses faites à l'enfant lorsqu'on le fait patienter avant de répondre à son désir et lui faire remarquer ensuite qu'on a répondu à sa demande, même s'il a dû attendre quelques instants ;

- essayer de ne pas s'impatienter lorsque l'enfant tarde lui-même à répondre aux demandes des adultes, mais le lui faire remarquer.

Organisation
matérielle
- alterner l'ordre de distribution du matériel de jeu et de la nourriture, en commençant chaque fois par un autre enfant. Faire remarquer à l'enfant impatient qu'il a eu son tour le premier au repas ou qu'il sera le premier à la salle de toilette, etc.

Tableau VI

Synthèse du développement sensorimoteur de l'enfant de deux ans et demi

2	Vision	Audition	Préhension et manipulation	Locomotion	Schéma corporel	Relations spatiales	Relations temporelles
A N S E T	• Est capable d'une attention visuelle plus soutenue.	• Est sensible aux rythmes marqués.	• Tend à serrer trop fort, à relâcher trop brusquement.	• Saute à pieds joints.	• Reconnaît le front, le dos, le côté, la tête, les pieds.	• Explore les contours, la profondeur des objets par le biais du modelage.	• Acquiert la conscience d'un passé immédiat.
D E M I	• Retient brièvement son attention sur des objets éloignés.	• Chante spontanément en tierce mineure.	• Peut bouger les doigts séparément.	• Se tient sur un pied pendant deux secondes.	• Situe les objets par rapport à son corps.	• Comprend la notion de haut et de bas.	
	• Commence à distinguer les lignes verticales et des lignes horizontales.	• Peut répéter des passages de chansons s'il n'est pas inhibé par la présence des autres.	• Construit une tour de 6 ou 7 cubes.	• Fait quelques pas sur le bout des orteils.	• S'appelle par son prénom.	• Acquiert la notion de « dehors » et « dedans ».	
	• Repère visuellement un objet à distance et vérifie avec la main sa réponse visuelle.	• Ne se lasse pas de la répétition des mêmes airs.	• Commence à observer la symétrie.	• Saute d'un point légèrement élevé.			
	• Peut suivre des yeux un objet en mouvement.	• Peut préférer galoper, courir, sauter en musique plutôt que de marcher.	• Aime pousser les jouets.	• Se soulève à partir de la position à genoux.			
			• Aime presser, broyer, écraser, taper divers matériaux.	• Aime grimper, sauter, se cacher, glisser.			
			• Expérimente la peinture aux doigts en barbouillant la table, ses mains, son visage, celui des autres, etc.				

Deux ans et demi

Le développement sensorimoteur

Vision

L'enfant est maintenant capable d'attention visuelle plus soutenue et fait des observations à des distances éloignées ; il peut, par conséquent, repérer visuellement un objet à distance, mais il vérifie toujours avec la main sa réponse visuelle.

Situations

- à l'occasion de promenades extérieures, à l'occasion de jeux dans la cour de la garderie, faire observer aux enfants les objets, les oiseaux, les automobiles ou les camions qui se trouvent à une assez grande distance. Dans la salle de jeu, faire repérer les jouets les plus éloignés. Placer l'ensemble du groupe loin de la porte d'entrée. Faire entrer un seul camarade et le faire nommer par les autres enfants ;

- faire souffler, par l'éducateur, des bulles de savon que les enfants doivent repérer visuellement et faire éclater ;

- gonfler des ballons de baudruche et en disposer librement dans la pièce pour que les enfants puissent les repérer et taper dessus (vision, manipulation, locomotion).

Attitudes

- considérer comme tout à fait normal le fait que l'enfant de cet âge désire toujours toucher à tout ce qu'il voit ;

- mettre à sa disposition des objets peu fragiles, nombreux et très colorés, pour que sa démarche visuelle soit facilement suivie d'une manipulation.

Organisation matérielle

- prendre du savon spécialement conçu pour fabriquer des bulles de savon, afin d'éviter l'irritation des yeux des petits ;

- ne pas laisser souffler les bulles aux enfants, car le degré de réussite très incertain risque de gâcher leur joie. Prévoir un assez grand nombre de ballons de baudruche ; éviter de trop les gonfler, car les bruits d'éclatement font peur ou énervent les enfants.

L'enfant peut suivre des yeux un objet en mouvement. Sa capacité d'attention visuelle est suffisamment importante pour qu'il fixe un ensemble d'objets et qu'il commence à distinguer les lignes verticales des lignes horizontales.

Situations
- fabriquer de petits objets de papier : avions, fusées, etc., et les lancer doucement à portée visuelle de quelques enfants ;

- tenter diverses expériences dans ce sens, avec des jouets mobiles, des ballons, des jouets mécaniques, sans autres buts que celui de prendre conscience visuellement du mouvement comme tel ;

- aligner divers objets (coussins, blocs, assiettes, etc.) devant l'enfant et le laisser reproduire les mêmes séries dans le sens horizontal, ou empiler les mêmes objets.

Attitudes
- susciter diverses activités autour de ces thèmes, sans verbaliser outre mesure et sans insister au delà de l'étape d'observation. Ces expériences sont le fondement de toutes une série de recherches que l'enfant fera lui-même, avec le temps, avec un niveau de conscience de plus en plus important ;

- observer les réactions des enfants de manière à bien identifier chez certains l'existence possible de problèmes visuels.

Organisation matérielle
- réunir très souvent des objets identiques devant les enfants, les aligner ou les empiler selon le cas. La ressemblance des objets fait ressortir les caractéristiques d'horizontalité et de verticalité.

Deux ans et demi

Le développement sensorimoteur

Audition

L'enfant de cet âge est sensible aux rythmes précis ; dans ce sens, il peut préférer galoper, courir, sauter plutôt que de marcher lorsqu'il suit la musique.

Situations
- organiser des rondes simples : toute chanson plaisant aux enfants de cet âge peut devenir une ronde ; varier les rythmes, chanter en tournant, tourner en cercle en s'accompagnant de musique, d'instruments rythmiques, etc.

Attitudes
- accepter de bon coeur que la ronde se dénoue rapidement ;

- éviter de prolonger l'activité et ne pas s'attendre à ce que les enfants s'intègrent rigoureusement à un cercle parfait. Les enfants perdront rapidement le contrôle pour s'emporter et courir un peu partout.

Organisation matérielle
- disperser les meubles qui peuvent nuire au centre de la pièce avant de faire une ronde en prévision des jeux d'emportement qui ne manqueront pas de se produire à la fin de l'activité.

L'enfant peut répéter des passages de chansons s'il n'est pas inhibé par la présence des autres ; il chante spontanément en tierce mineure.

Situations
- utiliser l'intérêt spontané des enfants pour chanter en tierce mineure des bouts de phrases ou des mots du langage courant. Faire appel à cet élément pour terminer une querelle ou pour faire rire l'enfant ou opérer une diversion après une querelle ou une dispute entre enfants. Ex. : Pim-pom, les pompiers, Pim-pom, les garçons salut, salut, les amis, etc.

Attitudes
- éviter de trop insister sur l'aspect « spectaculaire » des périodes d'activités consacrées à la musique ; considérer simplement cette période comme une façon d'être bien ensemble, sans exiger des enfants des performances pour épater les autres ou les adultes.

Organisation matérielle
- organiser un coin particulier avec des coussins, un tourne-disque et quelques instruments faciles à contrôler ou à manipuler. Utiliser, de préférence, un endroit calme, en retrait, et même plus entouré qu'ailleurs de manière à assourdir les bruits.

L'enfant de cet âge aime le familier, le connu, la routine, les mêmes habitudes. Il ne se fatigue pas de la répétition des mêmes airs et il les redemande inlassablement.

Situations
- reprendre comme transition entre deux activités un air connu de l'enfant, en conservant très longtemps le même air de manière à conserver une certaine routine. Utiliser un air chanté ou un air joué sur un instrument très simple, flûte à bec ou harmonica, guitare, piano, etc.

Attitudes
- accepter de répéter les mêmes airs que les enfants redemandent très souvent, même si l'adulte en ressent un certain ennui ; c'est un trait caractéristique à cet âge et il convient de le respecter.

Organisation matérielle
- faire une place dans la routine quotidienne de la journée à une période de temps prévue pour chanter ou jouer d'un instrument de musique ;

- faire appel aux talents de certains parents ou de diverses personnes ressources capables de jouer d'un nouvel instrument de musique.

Deux ans et demi

Le développement sensorimoteur

Manipulation

L'enfant de cet âge commence à observer la symétrie dans ses constructions, les ressemblances et les similitudes dans ses manipulations, lorsqu'il fait du triage ou qu'il associe des paires.

Situations
- **jeux de construction**

- prévoir plusieurs éléments simples mais identiques en terme de formes et de couleurs, de manière à favoriser l'observation de la symétrie dans les jeux de construction. L'enfant peut déjà construire une tour de six à sept cubes ;

- **discrimination — contrôle du geste**

- apporter de petites serviettes, des serviettes de bain, etc. Les mettre en vrac devant les enfants, les laisser étendre le linge dans le coin de poupée ou simplement replier le tout en ordre suivant les dimensions et la couleur. Apprendre à plier, à reconnaître, à discriminer les formes et les couleurs.

Attitudes
- accorder une certaine attention à la symétrie dans le rangement des objets familiers et demander aux enfants de participer à ces activités ;

- disposer souvent les enfants avec une certaine symétrie au cours de leurs activités ou leur faire poser des gestes ou faire des mouvements identiques de chaque côté des adultes ; faire observer le phénomène simplement, dans des mots accessibles aux enfants.

Organisation matérielle
- utiliser des chaises de chaque côté de la table. Disposer les enfants en cercle et alterner la place des éducateurs en fonction du nombre d'enfants assis en cercle, de manière à habituer l'oeil de l'enfant à une régularité qui aura à la longue un certain effet dans ses jeux de manipulation.

L'enfant aime à barbouiller tout ce qu'il voit et il s'intéresse plus particulièrement à la manipulation de la peinture aux doigts.

Situations
- mettre à la disposition des enfants une bonne quantité de peinture tactile, mais en utilisant une seule couleur à la fois ;

- s'adresser à un très petit nombre d'enfants à la fois ; laisser les enfants se faire des gants, barbouiller un petit coin de la table, un bon espace de feuille ;

- laisser les enfants se débarbouiller seuls au lavabo ; pendant quelques minutes, ils pourront voir l'eau changer de couleur et leurs mains redevenir blanches et propres.

Attitudes
- accorder une attention de tous les instants au petit groupe qui fait l'expérience de la peinture tactile, car les enfants pourraient perdre tout contrôle s'ils sont laissés à eux-mêmes et barbouiller de façon inconsidérée les murs ou le visage de leurs camarades, ou encore leur propre visage. La fantaisie peut être admise, mais à l'intérieur de certaines limites.

Organisation matérielle
- disposer d'un espace à proximité d'un point d'eau ; donner des tabliers de plastique aux enfants et ajouter un peu de savon en cristaux (savon à laver) à la peinture pour la diluer un peu et la rendre plus glissante.

L'enfant aime pousser les jouets. Il aime également presser, broyer, écraser, taper divers matériaux.

Situations
- investir dans les jouets à tirer et à pousser ; petits chariots, jouets musicaux montés sur tiges, caisses de bois montées sur roulettes. Laisser souvent un enfant pousser un autre enfant assis dans une caisse ou un chariot, en alternant les rôles de temps à autre ;

- prévoir des périodes de temps où les enfants pourront taper, broyer, etc., simultanément. Procurer aux enfants divers matériaux de modelage présentant des degrés de résistance variables ; pâte très dure qui demande beaucoup de force ; pâte plus molle qui force l'enfant à contrôler ses gestes et la force de ses mouvements, etc.

Attitudes
- observer les réactions des enfants en fonction de la résistance des matériaux mis à leur disposition ;

- apporter une aide et une attention supplémentaires aux enfants qui n'adaptent en aucune façon leurs mouvements et leurs efforts, ou qui semblent incapables d'établir des nuances dans leurs mouvements.

Organisation matérielle
- donner du matériel identique particulièrement à cet âge, à cause des querelles interminables et de l'incapacité pour l'enfant de résister au jeu différent que possède son voisin ; acheter une grande quantité d'objets et de matériaux de ce genre.

Développement sensorimoteur - Manipulation

L'enfant contrôle mal ses impulsions opposées à cause de ses mécanismes d'inhibition qui sont encore imparfaits. Certaines activités motrices sont donc mal freinées ; l'enfant tend à serrer trop fort et à relâcher brusquement.

Situations
- **contrôle du geste**

- présenter des situations où l'enfant qui tend trop à serrer ou à relâcher peut raffiner son sens de la précision et délier ses muscles fins ;

- remplir une grande quantité de petites bouteilles à mi-hauteur et colorer l'eau de diverses teintes. Prévoir une quantité égale de bouteilles vides. Donner des compte-gouttes aux enfants ou des poires à jus de manière à laisser l'enfant expérimenter les situations où il doit contrôler avec ses doigts, pincer et relâcher.

Attitudes
- observer la démarche de chaque enfant et voir jusqu'à quel point celui-ci contrôle ou non ses mécanismes d'inhibition, reprendre l'observation également au niveau de la locomotion.

Organisation matérielle
- mettre à la disposition des enfants un très grand nombre de compte-gouttes identiques, afin d'éviter les disputes entre enfants. Rattacher ces manipulations aux jeux d'eau.

Perception par le toucher : L'enfant de cet âge aime taper, presser, écraser et il accorde toujours beaucoup d'importance à l'eau ; il contrôle mieux ses gestes, peut tapoter et aplatir certains matériaux.

Situations
- organiser des jeux autour de la pâte à modeler. Donner deux ou trois boules de pâte à modeler de fabricants différents et faire évaluer la résistance de ces matériaux : dur, mou. Faire taper, écraser ou tapoter plus légèrement, etc. ;

- cacher sous un grand tapis mousse des objets de consistance différente, faire passer la main sur l'un et l'autre des objets, deviner. Choisir des objets mous et les faire palper aux enfants ;

- donner aux enfants des feuilles de papier à sabler de diverses textures, vérifier avec les doigts et ensuite sur du bois la sensation et l'effet obtenus.

Attitudes
- tirer profit de toutes les occasions pour faire expérimenter à l'enfant la résistance de divers matériaux, la texture, la température de divers objets, et donner le terme juste décrivant la sensation qui se dégage de cet objet.

Organisation matérielle
- prévoir de tels jeux pour de petits groupes, car les enfants se querelleront facilement à cet âge s'ils doivent attendre trop longtemps leur tour et ils voudront tous toucher au même moment.

L'équilibre de l'enfant se stabilise de plus en plus. Il arrive à se tenir sur un seul pied entre deux et cinq secondes et il peut faire quelques pas sur le bout des orteils, avec de l'aide et beaucoup de concentration.

Situations

- donner à l'enfant l'occasion de se tenir momentanément sur un pied en frappant du pied un ballon ;

- passer un pied dans un cerceau disposé sur le plancher en gardant l'autre pied en dehors et essayer de faire alterner ;

- placer l'enfant entre deux chaises, ou appuyé à un mur et à une chaise, et chanter ou compter pendant qu'il se tient en équilibre ;

- disposer sur le sol des pistes de pas dessinées sur du papier ou taillées dans la feutrine. Faire suivre le sentier ;

- reprendre les mêmes pistes et faire marcher l'enfant sur le bout des orteils, imiter les cailloux pour traverser la rivière ;

- disposer des objets dans un endroit surélevé. Laisser les enfants se mettre sur le bout des orteils pour les atteindre.

Attitudes

- encourager les enfants dans leurs tentatives et dans leurs efforts pour conserver un certain équilibre, leur apporter volontiers un appui momentané. Tirer profit de toutes les occasions quotidiennes, à l'intérieur comme à l'extérieur ;

- féliciter souvent les enfants qui font des réels efforts pour atteindre une certaine réussite.

L'enfant aime grimper, sauter, se cacher, glisser. Lorsqu'il se soulève, il peut maintenant le faire à partir de la position à genoux. Il a besoin d'espace pour courir à son aise sans avoir à toujours rencontrer des résistances.

Situations

- aménager, de temps à autre, toute la salle de jeu en course à obstacles. Utiliser tous les éléments qui se trouvent habituellement dans la salle et établir une direction, un ordre à suivre par le groupe d'enfants. Marcher sur les calorifères (avec l'appui de l'éducateur, le dos au mur, etc.). Glisser dans un cylindre de carton, marcher entre les barreaux d'une échelle, etc. Suivre une route dessinée en papier adhésif ;

- les petits lapins : tous les enfants sont à genoux et, au signal de la musique (tam-tam, flûte), les petits lapins se soulèvent et vont faire une promenade. À l'arrêt de la musique, ils se remettent à genoux ;

- ranger tous les meubles dans un coin de la salle de manière à libérer le centre (se faire aider des enfants) et laisser ceux-ci libres de courir avec des ballons au sol ou des cerceaux (faire rouler avec l'adulte, courir et rapporter à l'adulte).

Attitudes • établir des règles de sécurité très rigoureuses en planifiant bien l'organisation matérielle des salles de jeu et de la cour extérieure et laisser les enfants libres de jouer sans trop intervenir.

Organisation matérielle • apporter une surveillance d'ensemble à ce genre d'activités, mais éviter le plus possible d'avoir à intervenir. Il convient par ailleurs d'aménager les lieux et de dégager le plus possible l'espace central;

• accorder beaucoup d'importance au choix des éléments de jeux pour glisser, grimper, etc., (glissoires, portiques de jeux, cages à singes). Les choisir en tenant compte de leur solidité et de leur aspect sécuritaire;

• accorder régulièrement à l'enfant une bonne période de jeux, d'exercices de ce genre; si aucun espace n'est prévu en permanence dans la garderie, déplacer les principaux obstacles et laisser l'enfant libre de courir et de sauter.

Connaissance et identification des parties du corps : l'enfant reconnaît davantage de parties de son corps : le front, le dos, le côté, la tête, les pieds, et il localise les objets en rapport avec son propre corps comme point de repère.

Situations • **jeux de reconnaissance des parties du corps**

• **le jeu de la serviette**

• donner une serviette sèche et faire passer d'un enfant à l'autre. Les enfants nomment à tour de rôle, en frottant la partie désignée avec la serviette. Ex. : je me lave les yeux. Le suivant prend la serviette : je me lave le nez, etc. ;

• **identification et représentation de soi**

• dessiner sur le mur la forme debout d'un ou de plusieurs enfants, les uns à côté des autres. Faire essayer à tour de rôle, en face d'un grand miroir, la forme correspondant à chaque enfant, en leur faisant prendre exactement la même position.

• **situation des objets par rapport à soi**

• demander à l'enfant de dire, en s'habillant, où il met le chapeau (sur sa tête à lui), ses mitaines, ses bottes, et situer ces mêmes vêtements : chapeau, mitaines, bottes, mais sur l'éducateur, au cours de l'habillage ou en situation de jeu. Ces jeux font rire les enfants mais attirent leur attention sur les dimensions différentes des objets et sur les parties identifiées du schéma corporel.

Attitudes • respecter le rythme individuel d'apprentissage de chaque enfant sans trop insister sur la perfection de la phrase qu'il faut nommer, mais considérer plutôt l'importance d'un très grand nombre d'expériences où l'observation de l'enfant et son intérêt pour la reconnaissance des parties sont respectés;

- une observation assez précise permettrait de déceler à quel point les enfants se situent eux-mêmes en rapport avec leur propre perception.

Organisation matérielle

- prendre soin de fixer de grands papiers au mur dans les jeux de portraits de personnages, pour éviter de salir ou d'abîmer la peinture et pour conserver plusieurs « modèles » d'enfants. Il est alors possible d'établir des comparaisons plus frappantes en choisissant des modèles très contrastants, au plan des formes et des positions.

Situations

- **reconnaissance des parties du corps**

- faire toucher les parties du corps avec une autre partie : les genoux avec le nez, l'oreille avec l'épaule, le dos avec la main.

- **à l'heure de la sieste**

- après avoir fait l'obscurité dans la pièce, jouer, en changeant d'enfant chaque jour, à mettre la petite marionnette au lit : avec une lampe de poche, fixer une partie du corps et la rendre immobile, comme si elle dormait. Ex. : je fais dormir le bras de Julie ; je fais dormir la main de François, etc. ;

- il est possible de faire ce jeu pour un seul enfant chaque jour ou de le faire très rapidement pour chaque enfant. Varier en faisant dire tout bas à l'enfant quelle partie va s'endormir en premier lieu ;

- **conscience lointaine de la latéralité**

- faire enlever un soulier à chaque enfant (manipulation), les mettre en vrac ; demander à chacun de retrouver son propre soulier et de le remettre dans le bon pied — un seul pied est déchaussé, ce qui facilite la prise de conscience d'un pied d'un côté en particulier ; varier selon les jours le côté à retrouver. Mettre à la disposition des enfants une large quantité de vieux gants de différentes couleurs. Les laisser retrouver ceux qui conviennent à la bonne main et qui forment la paire, selon la couleur ;

- accepter de bon cœur le surplus de travail que de tels jeux peuvent apporter et laisser à l'enfant le temps de vraiment réussir dans sa recherche ;

- éviter toute tentative pour inculquer directement la notion de droite et de gauche ; il est toutefois possible de mentionner ces mots à l'occasion et selon le cas.

Organisation matérielle

- faire ce jeu, au début, avec un très petit nombre d'enfants et augmenter par la suite, progressivement, le nombre d'enfants participants.

Attitudes

- accorder beaucoup d'importance à l'attention apportée par l'enfant à l'occasion de ces jeux et insister pour fixer cette attention, ne serait-ce que quelques secondes.

L'enfant de cet âge explore le contour des objets, la profondeur et la forme de ce qu'il voit, de ce qu'il touche ; il y a un lien très étroit entre la manipulation d'objets et la compréhension ultérieure de certaines relations spatiales.

Situations
- favoriser très particulièrement l'utilisation de toutes les situations où l'enfant pourra toucher divers objets ayant des formes variées ; pour les mêmes raisons, donner le plus souvent des matériaux identiques.

Organisation matérielle
- prévoir suffisamment de matériaux pour éviter les disputes entre enfants, car ils ont l'âge où ils tentent de s'approprier ce qu'ils voient dans les mains de leurs compagnons.

Situations
- mettre à profit toutes les occasions de faire grimper l'enfant sur des structures de formes variées, de manière à lui permettre de ressentir avec tout son corps les différences entre une caisse de bois (concept du carré) et un énorme ballon (concept du cercle), etc. ;

- permettre à l'enfant de manipuler divers matériaux (pâte à modeler, terre glaise) pour construire lui-même diverses formes ;

- être attentif à toute situation pouvant aider l'enfant à prendre conscience de l'importance des différences dans l'espace environnant et tirer profit de façon spontanée de ces occasions en promenade, dans la cour de jeu, etc.

Deux ans et demi

Le développement sensorimoteur

Organisation spatiale

L'enfant s'intéresse à la position des objets par rapport à lui-même et aux autres objets.

Situations
- pour assurer une transition entre deux activités, disposer des bancs ou des tables basses en nombre suffisant. Alterner les consignes : assis sur le banc, sous le banc, sur la table, sous la table, etc. Ce jeu peut s'accompagner de musique ;

- apporter un élément d'imitation en imaginant que les enfants sont au bord de l'eau : à l'arrêt de la musique ou de la chanson, il y a une grosse vague qui s'en vient, les enfants montent sur le quai, se cachent sous le pont, dans la chaloupe.

Attitudes
- mettre à profit les situations quotidiennes pour familiariser l'enfant avec le concept et avec la terminologie la plus simple, mais également la plus juste pour décrire le concept ;

- être attentif aux déformations inévitables qui se glissent dans le vocabulaire du jeune enfant lorsqu'il s'agit de décrire ces différentes réalités ; il y a même lieu d'exagérer un peu la prononciation pour attirer l'attention de l'enfant.

Organisation matérielle
- établir clairement les limites lorsque les enfants montent sur la table. Il faut préciser les différentes utilités d'une table (jeu, repas, etc.) de manière à dissiper toute ambiguïté.

L'enfant de cet âge comprend la notion de « haut » et de « bas », et il acquiert progressivement la notion de « dehors » et de « dedans ».

Situations
- l'enfant comprend la notion de « haut » et de « bas » et il utilise cette notion dans les jeux de construction de tour aussi bien que dans la vie courante ;

- apporter des objets divers choisis par les enfants dans la garderie, blocs, jouets, petits bancs, caisses de carton ou de bois et tenter de construire en hauteur tout en respectant l'équilibre, etc. ;

- avec de petits blocs, construire des tours où chacun apporte son bloc, à tour de rôle, en alternant jusqu'à ce que la tour finisse par tomber.

Attitudes
- être très attentif à l'utilisation des mots à employer avec les enfants. Accentuer la prononciation dans les demandes faites aux enfants et insister pour utiliser le terme juste.

Deux ans et demi

Le développement sensorimoteur

Relations temporelles

L'enfant vit encore beaucoup dans le présent, mais il commence à acquérir la conscience d'un passé immédiat.

Situations
- situer le temps pour l'enfant en terme d'action. Donner à l'enfant des indices très simples pour lui donner des repères à courte échéance. Ex. : l'enfant mettra des pantoufles avant le dîner et des souliers après le dîner. L'éducateur portera un chandail jaune le matin, quand l'enfant a des pantoufles, et un chandail rouge l'après-midi, etc. ;

- rappeler très fréquemment à l'enfant le jeu qu'il vient de faire juste avant celui qu'il entreprend ; énumérer très souvent la succession de deux ou trois actions devant l'enfant : « Tu as mis la robe rouge et la robe jaune à la poupée : quelle robe vas-tu lui mettre maintenant? »

Attitudes
- parler beaucoup avec l'enfant des principales actions de sa journée, en établissant un rapport immédiat entre deux actions. Impliquer l'enfant dans des échanges en lui demandant de se situer lui-même dans ces actions ;

- permettre à l'enfant de saisir le sens du temps qui passe en lui faisant vivre des expériences du passé, mais d'un passé très proche.

Organisation matérielle
- utiliser une maison miniature pour aider l'enfant à s'exprimer autour de sa vie à la maison. Énumérer les actions quotidiennes faites à la maison et à la garderie, même si l'enfant ne semble pas toujours bien les situer, en prévoyant des personnages miniatures les plus proches de son univers personnel : père, mère, frère, etc.

Tableau VII

Synthèse du développement socio-affectif de l'enfant de deux à trois ans

	Interactions enfants-adultes			Interactions enfants-enfants		
	Manifestations des émotions	Imitation de l'adulte	Apprentissage des rôles sociaux	Manifestations des émotions	Communication par le jeu	Participation à la vie de groupe
ENTRE 2	• Peut souvent s'opposer aux adultes.	• Demande à aider l'adulte dans certaine tâches quotidiennes.	• Partage difficilement l'attention entre le père et la mère, peut s'entendre mieux avec l'un des deux.	• Peut s'opposer systématiquement aux autres enfants.	• Joue avec les autres, mais préfère encore le jeu parallèle au jeu de groupe.	• Observe d'abord ce que font les autres enfants.
ET 3	• Peut se montrer tantôt détaché de sa mère, tantôt extrêmement possessif et réclamer son attention exclusive.	• Imite les gestes de l'adulte avec beaucoup d'à-propos.	• Imite les gestes des adultes familiers et reproduit ces gestes en les associant au père ou à la mère, selon les milieux.	• Présente des variations brusques et imprévisibles dans ses attitudes.	• Représente dans ses jeux la réalité de façon symbolique.	• Laisse difficilement les autres jouer avec ce qui lui appartient.
ANS	• Peut manifester de l'autoritarisme dans sa famille.	• Peut perdre tout intérêt à aider et s'emporter si l'adulte ne lui accorde plus d'attention.	• Associe certains gestes au rôle précis d'un adulte familier.	• Passe brusquement du désir de possession à l'indifférence lorsqu'il possède un objet.	• Imite les choses, les personnes et les actions dans ses jeux de manière encore simplifiée.	• Différencie mieux les possessions.
	• Peut passer rapidement d'une grande soumission à une période de domination très accentuée.				• Joue parfois mieux avec les enfants plus âgés (5 ou 6 ans).	• Peut attendre son tour.
						• Considère les interventions des autres comme des menaces.
						• Peut s'opposer systématiquement aux autres enfants.

Deux à trois ans

Le développement socio-affectif

Interactions enfant-adulte

Manifestation des émotions : L'enfant peut passer rapidement de la soumission à la domination accentuée ; il peut se montrer très possessif et réclamer l'exclusivité ou se montrer très détaché ; il peut souvent s'opposer aux adultes.

Attitudes
- éviter de considérer ces brusques changements comme de simples caprices qu'il faut s'empresser de faire disparaître : ces diverses fluctuations résultent d'une certaine instabilité de son équilibre. À cause d'un manque de maturité, l'enfant qui apprend à choisir contrôle encore mal ses capacités d'inhibition ;

- adopter une attitude positive en utilisant des techniques simples qui changent momentanément le pôle d'intérêt en distrayant l'enfant et en le calmant.

Organisation matérielle
- aménager l'espace de manière à offrir à l'enfant des lieux stables, sécurisants, où il pourra se sentir à l'aise et calme ;

- adopter un rythme de vie assez routinier à cet âge. Éviter les changements trop fréquents et trop brusques.

Imitation de l'éducateur : L'enfant demande à aider l'éducateur dans certaines tâches quotidiennes et il imite ses gestes avec beaucoup d'à-propos, mais il peut perdre tout intérêt à aider et s'emporter si l'adulte n'accorde plus son attention.

Situations
- prévoir, dans l'organisation des tâches quotidiennes, certains travaux que les enfants peuvent faire : ranger les jouets sur les tablettes (donner aux enfants un petit chiffon humide pour épousseter les tablettes avant de les ranger), aider à replacer les coussins après la sieste, mettre en ordre les bottes, suspendre les mitaines et les gants à sécher, donner à manger et nettoyer les cages, etc. Empiler et rapporter les verres de carton, laver l'évier, transporter les jouets à l'extérieur, etc.

Organisation matérielle
- prévoir des plans d'eau et des plans de travail à la portée des enfants ;

- distribuer certains travaux de groupes autour d'une grande table ; il est alors plus facile de surveiller les enfants. Ex. : démêler des jouets comportant de petites pièces, etc. Les redistribuer dans plusieurs petites boîtes.

Attitudes
- accepter de « perdre un peu de temps » au profit des enfants pour répondre à leur besoin de se faire valoir auprès des adultes est une façon très positive de jouer un rôle significatif dans leur développement social ;

- suggérer aux enfants certains travaux à faire, mais sous forme de jeux, et confier des tâches à de petits groupes à la fois, pour éviter les querelles ;

- demander de l'aide avec gentillesse et sans jamais donner d'ordre ; remercier l'enfant et le complimenter après un effort. L'enfant retiendra ce principe à son tour lorsqu'il demandera quelque chose ; l'éducateur qui utilise lui-même la politesse est en droit d'exiger la même chose des enfants ;

- surveiller entièrement de telles activités et suivre l'enfant jusqu'à la fin de son travail ; procéder par petites périodes seulement.

Apprentissage des rôles sociaux : L'enfant associe certains gestes au rôle précis d'un adulte familier. Il imite les gestes des adultes familiers et reproduit ces gestes en les associant au père ou à la mère selon les milieux. Il partage difficilement l'attention et s'entend mieux avec l'un des deux parents à la fois.

Attitudes
- observer avec attention et discrétion les comportements des enfants à l'occasion des jeux symboliques ; c'est une très bonne façon de mieux connaître l'enfant ;

- discuter avec les parents des difficultés possibles pour l'enfant à l'heure du départ ou de l'arrivée ; observer l'attitude de l'enfant et des parents. Remarquer s'il y a continuité au niveau de ces problèmes, en rapport avec la présence de l'adulte (alternance de la présence du père ou de la mère à cette occasion ou irrégularité de la présence de l'un ou l'autre des parents ; cette étape est importante dans sa journée). Il peut en résulter une forme d'insécurité.

Organisation matérielle
- organiser un coin de jeux où l'enfant pourra librement imiter les gestes quotidiens de la maison en jouant à la poupée, à la dînette ;

- prévoir pour cet âge une petite automobile, jouet dans lequel les enfants peuvent s'asseoir et imiter des scènes qu'ils connaissent ;

- disposer d'un large choix de vieux vêtements d'adultes masculins ou féminins et laisser les enfants jouer librement avec ces divers accessoires, sans nécessairement établir d'horaire pour cette activité.

Deux à trois ans

Le développement socio-affectif

Interactions enfant-enfant

Manifestations des émotions : L'enfant peut présenter des variations brusques et imprévisibles au plan des attitudes à l'égard des autres enfants. Il peut passer du désir de possession à l'indifférence lorsqu'il possède un objet et il joue parfois mieux avec les enfants plus âgés.

Situations
- utiliser très souvent, en période de conflit ou de querelle, des techniques de substitution ou favoriser, pour ramener le calme, la tendance spontanée à cet âge vers le jeu parallèle, en distribuant un matériel identique : terre glaise, grosses perles à enfiler, etc.

Attitudes
- observer avec beaucoup d'attention le climat psychologique entre les petits groupes d'enfants et intervenir lorsque les attitudes deviennent trop négatives, en amenant une transition ou un changement d'activité ;

- traiter avec humour les caractéristiques les plus ennuyeuses de cet âge (hésitations, négativisme, etc.) en opérant une diversion ou en offrant des suggestions ou des solutions de rechange.

Organisation matérielle
- aménager l'espace de manière à pouvoir surveiller constamment les enfants sans avoir nécessairement à intervenir auprès d'eux ;

- prévoir des jouets suffisamment nombreux et très souvent identiques, de manière à prévenir un certain nombre de conflits et de querelles entre les enfants.

Communication par le jeu : L'enfant joue avec les autres, mais il préfère encore le jeu parallèle au jeu de groupe. Il imite les choses, les personnes et les actions de manière encore assez simplifiée, mais de façon symbolique, et il joue parfois mieux avec les enfants plus âgés.

Situations
- éviter de forcer l'enfant à perdre la face et à céder carrément dans une situation de conflit, car une telle situation débouche généralement sur de l'entêtement ;

- fournir à l'enfant des positions de repli, des solutions de rechange ;

- utiliser avec précaution, mais de façon plus systématique, les indications verbales pour calmer les querelles et pour convaincre l'enfant indécis ;

- recourir à l'interrogation lorsque c'est nécessaire pour créer une diversion ;

- intervenir le moins possible au départ, mais surveiller de très près les enfants qui se disputent, car ils risquent de se faire mal.

Organisation matérielle
- organiser l'espace de manière à pouvoir surveiller les enfants dans leurs jeux, mais aussi en fonction de regroupements en petit nombre pour diminuer les conflits ou les risques de conflit entre les enfants.

Participation à la vie de groupe : L'enfant observe souvent ce que font les autres enfants d'abord ; il laisse difficilement les autres jouer avec ce qui lui appartient car il différencie mieux les possessions. Il peut toutefois attendre son tour, mais considère souvent les interventions des autres comme des menaces.

Situations
- organiser des rondes très simples et accepter de bon coeur qu'il y ait autant d'enfants qui regardent que d'enfants qui participent ;

- initier l'enfant à l'obligation d'attendre son tour en utilisant des comptines et des formulettes enfantines à chaque fois qu'il est nécessaire de départager les tours. Les enfants acceptent généralement mieux la décision avec une telle formule, car c'est un peu le hasard qui décide, et ils en sont conscients.

Attitudes
- accorder une attention individuelle aux enfants qui veulent fièrement montrer leurs possessions ou leurs réussites, mais éviter de devenir injuste et de susciter des jalousies en complimentant toujours les mêmes enfants ;

- éviter de forcer un enfant à s'intégrer à un jeu de groupe s'il préfère observer le jeu ; cette période d'observation est aussi rentable sur le plan de la socialisation que le jeu lui-même ;

- respecter le besoin de possession qui s'accentue à cet âge et ne pas insister outre mesure pour faire partager ; prévoir une bonne quantité de jouets identiques (ce qui est à souhaiter).

Organisation matérielle
- prévoir un espace réservé à chaque enfant et situé à sa hauteur où il peut déposer les travaux qu'il fait ou encore ranger une culotte de rechange venant de la maison ou un tablier, une paire de mitaines, etc.

Tableau VIII	
Synthèse du développement du langage verbal de l'enfant de deux à trois ans	
L'utilisation	**La compréhension**

L'utilisation

— Dispose d'un vocabulaire de 100 à 200 mots.

— Associe au moins deux mots significatifs.

— Emploie de plus en plus le verbe.

— Parle de lui-même à la troisième personne.

— S'appelle par son prénom.

— Nomme ses jouets préférés, ses aliments préférés, quelques personnes familières, quelques parties de son corps ou celles d'une poupée (deux ou trois).

— Pose des questions.

— Utilise de façon soutenue les signes de dénégation.

— Emploie des substantifs avec article.

— Utilise des verbes sans conjugaison, utilise la phrase — action (au moins deux mots).

— Emploie des verbes à l'infinitif.

— Inverse l'organisation de la phrase, accumule les articles et les substantifs.

— Peut être sensible aux intonations (exclamations, surprises, chuchotements, etc.) et cherche à les utiliser par imitation.

La compréhension

— **Comprend les substantifs :**

   — Désignant une personne, des animaux (chat, chien, cheval), quelques parties du corps (tête, bras, pieds) et certains vêtements (culotte, bas, soulier, etc.), certains aliments connus, des jouets préférés.

— **Comprend des questions très simples :**

   — Signifiant le lieu (Où ?).

   — Signifiant la cause (Pourquoi ?).

— **Est capable de petites conversations suivies :**

   — Dialogues à partir de quelques mots simples.

   — Dialogues incluant des intonations variées.

— **A besoin d'être aidé sur le plan verbal à certains moments.**

Deux à trois ans

Le développement du langage verbal

Compréhension : L'enfant comprend les substantifs désignant une personne, des animaux, des parties du corps, des parties de vêtements, certains jouets et certains aliments connus. Il comprend des questions simples signifiant le lieu et la cause.

Situations
- nommer devant l'enfant le nom de certaines personnes familières, d'objets familiers ;

- lancer un ballon en direction de quelqu'un et dire à qui l'on s'adresse. Lancer en direction d'un objet et faire de même ;

- nommer des parties du corps et des pièces de vêtements à faire identifier, sans nécessairement les faire nommer par l'enfant.

Attitudes
- vérifier les capacités d'écoute et accentuer l'attention pour de courtes périodes ;

- éviter d'employer uniquement les mots que l'enfant peut dire lui-même, car la qualité et la clarté de l'écoute ont une heureuse influence sur son langage et il comprend souvent plus de mots qu'il n'en utilise vraiment.

Organisation matérielle
- ménager une période de temps pour écouter l'enfant attentivement, d'une part, et pour parler avec lui individuellement, d'autre part, de manière à apporter une aide individualisée au plan de la compréhension et de l'écoute.

Utilisation : L'enfant emploie les verbes à l'infinitif et il inverse souvent l'ordre des phrases en accumulant soit les substantifs, soit les verbes. Il commence à employer les articles avec les substantifs.

Situations
- utiliser les articles en marquant un point d'arrêt dans la phrase et en désignant l'objet au même moment ;

- poser des questions très lentement en soulignant chacun des mots. Reprendre lentement et correctement la réponse de l'enfant de manière à ce qu'il entende à nouveau la phrase corrigée, sans toutefois l'obliger à répéter ;

- poser des questions au sujet des événements qui viennent tout juste de se produire, de manière à encourager l'enfant à raconter l'événement.

Attitudes
- amener fréquemment l'enfant à parler en le laissant lui-même demander ce qu'il désire et en l'écoutant patiemment malgré ses difficultés et ses lenteurs. L'aider dans certains cas lorsque des étrangers, après quelques tentatives, n'arrivent pas

à le comprendre, pour éviter que l'enfant ne cesse de vouloir communiquer avec d'autres adultes et finisse pas craindre l'échec.

L'enfant nomme ses jouets et ses aliments préférés, quelques personnes familières, quelques parties de son corps ou celles d'une poupée (deux ou trois) et il pose des questions au sujet des choses qui l'entourent.

Situations
- faire des jeux rythmés où l'enfant doit répondre très rapidement et avec un certain rythme à une question simple : « Qu'est-ce que c'est que ça ? Montre-moi ton nez. » ;

- faire nommer, à l'occasion, l'objet que réclame l'enfant avant de le lui donner ; éviter toutefois d'être trop rigoureux sur ce plan ;

- mentionner clairement le nom de quelques objets non familiers pour stimuler la curiosité ;

- découper des photographies des objets familiers et poser fréquemment des questions autour de ces images ;

- reprendre ces mêmes questions dans les livres illustrés ;

- prendre la main de l'enfant pour indiquer, sous forme de jeu, une partie du corps tout en la nommant.

Attitudes
- poser des questions fréquentes au sujet des diverses parties du corps ;

- répondre toujours correctement à chaque question que l'enfant pose et éviter de négliger de répondre. Apporter une explication satisfaisante plutôt qu'un simple oui ou non.

Organisation matérielle
- utiliser des miroirs à plusieurs endroits et à portée de l'enfant pour que l'enfant identifie bien les parties de son corps et puisse mieux les nommer ;

- illustrer les objets familiers avec des photographies plutôt que par des dessins, pour conserver fidèlement la ressemblance.

L'enfant s'appelle par son prénom et il associe dans son langage au moins deux mots significatifs ; il emploie de plus en plus le verbe, mais il lui arrive encore de parler de lui à la troisième personne.

Situations
- poser des questions à tout le groupe de manière à ce que l'enfant qui désire quelque chose soit forcé de s'identifier ;

- reprendre après l'enfant son prénom et lui donner ce qu'il désire ;

- exprimer tout haut les actions faites par les enfants au moment où ils jouent. Reprendre après les enfants une phrase ne comportant pas l'action, en y ajoutant un verbe ; reposer ensuite la question : « Que fais-tu ? » Poser des questions au sujet des actions simples représentées dans les livres d'histoire ;

- utiliser des livres qui représentent des actions, mais avec des illustrations très simples et peu nombreuses, sur une seule image.

Attitudes
- commenter fréquemment à haute voix les actions faites par les enfants au cours de la journée ;

- encourager les progrès individuels après avoir accordé à chaque enfant quelques minutes d'écoute attentive, de manière à situer les faiblesses et les points particuliers à corriger.

Tableau IX
Synthèse des activités physiologiques de l'enfant de deux ans

Alimentation	Élimination	Repos-sommeil
Contrôle du geste	**Contrôle de l'intestin et de la vessie**	**Repos-sieste**
• Peut remplir la cuillère en poussant la pointe dans les aliments. Renverse encore beaucoup.	• Différencie mieux les fonctions de l'intestin et de la vessie — peut demander son pot, peut vouloir rester seul, peut vouloir s'installer seul, peut refuser le pot.	• Prolonge souvent le sommeil de la sieste, ce qui dérange le sommeil nocturne.
• Boit sans aide à la tasse et au verre (avec une ou deux mains).		• Peut refuser de dormir et jouer tranquillement dans son lit.
Caractéristiques		**Sommeil**
• Mastique avant d'avaler.		• Joue souvent dans son lit avant de s'endormir, rampe, gambade, se cache dans les couvertures.
• Commence à avoir des préférences selon la couleur et la consistance.		• Se réveille lentement et n'aime pas être bousculé par l'horaire.
• N'a pas besoin d'une grande variété d'aliments.		
Habitudes de propreté	**Habitudes de propreté**	**Habitudes de propreté**
• Veut décider de la façon dont il mange ; peut se salir beaucoup en mangeant, mais accepte de bien se laver la bouche et les mains à la fin du repas.	• S'amuse à laver et à sécher ses mains, s'intéresse davantage à sa toilette et peut préférer la débarbouillette à un jouet dans sa baignoire.	• N'aime pas dormir dans un lit mouillé et peut se réveiller en pleurant s'il a eu un accident.

ENTRE 2 ET 3 ANS

Deux ans

Les activités physiologiques

Alimentation

Caractéristiques, goûts, préférences : L'enfant mastique avant d'avaler. Il commence à avoir des préférences selon la couleur et la consistance des aliments. Il n'a pas besoin à cet âge d'une trop grande variété d'aliments et il n'aime pas beaucoup les mélanges.

Situations
- aider l'enfant à établir les différences entre les choses qui se mangent et celles qui ne se mangent pas, en faisant des jeux où il recherche cette distinction ; à partir des livres et des images, faire trouver ce qui se mange (imiter le geste) et ce qui ne se mange pas ;

- introduire très prudemment de nouveaux aliments à cet âge en utilisant des formules de présentation inhabituelles et amusantes. Cacher les aliments sous un couvercle, et les rechercher sous forme de jeu.

Attitudes
- demander la collaboration des parents pour dresser les menus et choisir les modes de préparation ;

- respecter le rythme particulier de chaque enfant et lui donner le temps de manger et de bien mastiquer, ce qu'il fera parfois trop consciencieusement ; éviter également de laisser trop longtemps un enfant à table.

Organisation matérielle
- simplifier le plus possible le menu en évitant les « camouflages » ;

- considérer l'âge des enfants pour déterminer les portions ;

- couper la viande en morceaux (fins) au lieu de la hacher ;

- *note :* Voir la série *Bien manger à la garderie* préparée par le M.A.S. en 1978.

Contrôle du geste : L'enfant peut remplir la cuillère en poussant la pointe dans les aliments ; il renverse encore beaucoup. Il peut boire sans aide à la tasse et au verre (avec une ou deux mains) sans trop renverser.

Situations
- assurer le confort physique de l'enfant à l'heure des repas afin de lui faciliter la tâche. Prévoir une chaise solide ou un banc, avec un appui pour les pieds ;

- donner des ustensiles plus petits pour faciliter la manipulation ; donner un verre ou une tasse incassable qui tienne bien dans la main. Ne servir que de petites quantités à la fois durant le repas ;

- faciliter la maîtrise de l'ustensile en donnant de vieilles tasses et cuillères semblables à celles utilisées aux repas et laisser les enfants les manipuler dans le sable et dans l'eau.

Attitudes
- établir un climat de calme, s'asseoir à côté des enfants et leur tenir compagnie ; tenir compte de leurs limites et les encourager à prendre le temps de bien manger tout en respectant leurs petites méthodes personnelles.

Organisation matérielle
- donner un peu de gaieté à la table, choisir des assiettes invitantes, laisser suffisamment d'espace entre les enfants pour éviter qu'ils ne se poussent les uns les autres à table ;

- prévoir une période de nettoyage à l'eau courante à la fin du repas. Éviter d'utiliser la même serviette pour plusieurs enfants ou le même plat d'eau ; les enfants de cet âge sont très sensibles à la contagion. Être très minutieux pour éviter de transmettre des problèmes d'un enfant à l'autre.

Deux ans

Les activités physiologiques

Élimination

L'enfant différencie mieux les fonctions de l'intestin et de la vessie. Il peut demander son pot, vouloir rester seul, vouloir s'installer seul ou refuser le pot.

Attitudes
- observer attentivement chaque enfant pour arriver à reconnaître les expressions individuelles qui annoncent leurs besoins d'éliminer ;

- rester à portée de voix de l'enfant qui réclame le départ de l'adulte, car il faudra sûrement l'aider lorsqu'il aura terminé ;

- féliciter l'enfant à chaque réussite et communiquer la bonne nouvelle aux parents ;

- apporter beaucoup d'attention à l'enfant qui pleure quand il a un accident, car, à cet âge, ces accidents prennent beaucoup d'importance ; consoler l'enfant et le changer immédiatement sans le gronder.

Organisation matérielle
- apporter beaucoup de soin à l'organisation du coin toilette pour les enfants de cet âge. Prévoir de petits pots, de petites toilettes très basses ou des sièges spéciaux fixés sur la toilette, car chaque enfant a un entraînement qui varie à la maison ;

- demander la collaboration des parents ;

- organiser un système pour tenir compte des particularités de chacun.

Habitudes de propreté : L'enfant s'amuse à laver et à sécher ses mains ; il s'intéresse davantage à sa toilette et peut préférer la débarbouillette ou un gant de toilette à un jouet dans sa baignoire.

Situations
- faciliter la décision de quitter le coin d'eau en le faisant collaborer au vidage de l'évier et en le laissant contrôler le bouchon de fermeture.

Deux ans

Les activités physiologiques

Repos-sommeil

L'enfant prolonge souvent le sommeil de la sieste et dérange ainsi son sommeil nocturne. Il peut refuser de dormir et vouloir jouer tranquillement dans son lit. Il joue souvent dans son lit avant de s'endormir, rampe, gambade, se cache dans les couvertures. Il se réveille lentement et n'aime pas être bousculé par l'horaire.

Situations
- jouer au train ou faire une marche chantée pour passer d'un lieu à un autre, ou encore envoyer un à un les enfants retrouver l'éducateur responsable de la surveillance du groupe au repos ; cela entraînera une première période de calme avant le repos.

Attitudes
- établir une entente avec les parents au sujet de la durée de la période de sieste ;

- permettre à l'enfant d'autorégulariser son repos en aménageant des lieux où il pourra se retirer quelques minutes sans nécessairement dormir ;

- accorder également une attention spéciale aux besoins des enfants qui demandent vraiment à dormir ;

- se montrer tolérant vis-à-vis des jeux et des bousculades qui précèdent toujours la période de repos, mais ramener le calme avant d'amorcer la période de repos proprement dite.

Organisation matérielle
- aménager de petites niches en retrait où l'enfant peut regarder un livre ou disposer simplement de petites nattes de caoutchouc mousse directement au sol ;

- établir un lieu fixe où l'enfant retrouvera sa place, son lit ou tout au moins son jouet préféré.

Tableau X
Synthèse des activités physiologiques de l'enfant de deux ans et demi

Alimentation	Élimination	Repos-sommeil
Contrôle du geste	**Contrôle de l'intestin et de la vessie**	**Repos-sieste**
• Saisit mieux la cuillère entre le pouce et l'index.	• Demande généralement lui-même pour éliminer.	• Peut ne pas protester mais désire apporter avec lui des jouets, peut vouloir sortir souvent de son lit.
• Tient sa tasse et son verre d'une main les levant et les reposant adroitement sur la table.	• A besoin d'aide pour s'installer, mais peut parfois réclamer de rester seul.	• Peut refuser de faire la sieste dans son lit et préférer d'autres formules : le plancher, le tapis, sous le lit, etc.
	• Annonce qu'il a fini ; a besoin d'aide pour s'essuyer et se rhabiller.	• Accepte le même lit, mais transformé en objet imaginaire (train, autobus, etc.).
Caractéristiques		**Sommeil**
• Exige souvent la répétition des aliments, des couverts, de l'arrangement des plats et même du moment où un aliment peut être offert.		• Peut tarder à s'endormir et prolonger ensuite son sommeil.
• A un appétit fluctuant ; préfère la viande, les fruits, le beurre ; peut refuser les légumes verts.		• Peut émerger du sommeil en pleurant et ne pas accepter d'être réveillé ; accepte mieux parfois d'être éveillé par un bruit doux ou une musique plutôt que par la voix humaine.
Habitudes de propreté	**Habitudes de propreté**	**Habitudes de propreté**
• Peut réclamer souvent de se laver les mains ou la bouche au cours du repas.	• Participe à sa toilette en s'intéressant davantage au rituel qui l'entoure qu'au simple nettoyage : aime tourner le robinet, tirer le bouchon, etc.	• Peut porter encore fréquemment les objets familiers à la bouche pour se réconforter lorsqu'il va s'endormir ; a besoin d'un minimum de surveillance pour ne pas mâchonner des objets sales à cette occasion.
• Aime laver la table pour le plaisir de frotter et de jouer dans l'eau.	• Peut se laver correctement les mains s'il décide de le faire.	

Deux ans et demi

Les activités physiologiques

Alimentation

L'enfant tient sa tasse et son verre d'une main, les levant et les reposant adroitement. Il saisit la cuillère entre le pouce et l'index. Il exige souvent la répétition des aliments, des couverts, de l'arrangement des plats et même du moment où un aliment est offert. Il a un appétit fluctuant. Il préfère la viande et le beurre, et peut refuser certains légumes.

Attitudes

- tenir compte des goûts particuliers des enfants en demandant l'avis des parents. Ceux-ci pourront déterminer ce qui peut être un caprice passager ou une préférence habituelle ;

- considérer le besoin de répétition et de routine comme une caractéristique particulière à cet âge et commune à presque tous les enfants ;

- établir une succession dans l'ordre de présentation des aliments et la respecter autant que possible ;

- éviter de forcer l'appétit de l'enfant et accepter généralement qu'il s'arrête de manger lorsqu'il en a assez ; éviter donc de servir de trop grandes portions.

Organisation matérielle

- aménager un espace pour les repas un peu en retrait et insister pour que l'enfant reste assis autant que possible, afin d'obtenir son attention et le contrôle de ses mouvements ;

- laisser l'enfant se verser l'eau au robinet (facile d'accès) en plaçant des verres de carton à la portée des enfants. Lui permettre de se laver les mains et le visage lorsqu'il le demande ;

- donner à l'enfant une certaine autonomie en déposant les aliments devant lui et en le laissant libre de se servir seul, même s'il en renverse encore de temps en temps.

Deux ans et demi

Les activités physiologiques

Élimination

L'enfant demande généralement lui-même pour éliminer ; il a besoin d'aide pour s'installer, mais réclame parfois de rester seul ; il annonce qu'il a fini et a besoin d'aide. Il participe à sa toilette et s'intéresse davantage au rituel qu'au simple nettoyage ; il aime tourner le robinet, tirer le bouchon, et il peut se laver correctement les mains s'il décide de le faire.

Situations
- amener l'enfant à mieux maîtriser ses mouvements d'habillage et de déshabillage en lui montrant à d'autres moments, ou simplement après coup, à ne pas enlever tous ses vêtements, mais seulement quelques parties des vêtements ;

- organiser des jeux où l'enfant pourra s'exercer à une meilleure maîtrise de l'habillage ou du déshabillage, afin qu'il devienne plus rapidement autonome.

Attitudes
- aider l'enfant à s'installer, prévoir et éliminer toute source possible d'accident, et laisser seul quelques instants l'enfant qui le réclame ;

- surveiller les attitudes particulières à certains enfants qui se retiennent trop, absorbés par un jeu ou un jouet, et les encourager à se rendre sans tarder à la salle de toilette.

Organisation matérielle
- aménager la salle de toilette dans un axe central qui permette à tous les enfants d'y avoir accès rapidement et aménager les petits cabinets à la hauteur des enfants, de sorte qu'ils soient facilement accessibles.

Deux ans et demi

Les activités physiologiques

Repos-sommeil

L'enfant désire apporter avec lui des jouets et il peut vouloir sortir de son lit ; il peut même refuser de faire la sieste dans son lit et préférer une autre formule. Il peut tarder à s'endormir et prolonger ensuite son sommeil. Il émerge souvent du sommeil en pleurant et n'accepte pas facilement d'être réveillé.

Situations
- éviter de réveiller l'enfant avec des bruits ou des sons de voix trop forts. Réveiller plutôt l'enfant par un chuchottement ou par une musique.

Attitudes
- donner à l'enfant l'occasion de se réveiller lui-même ou, s'il le faut, procéder avec beaucoup de calme et de discrétion. Éviter de trop parler. Baisser toujours la voix.

Organisation matérielle
- apporter à l'enfant diverses solutions pour sa sieste et le laisser choisir, en lui permettant toutefois d'apporter avec lui son ou ses jouets favoris. Aménager des espaces calmes, mais ne pas craindre de dépasser les aménagements traditionnels.

Tableau XI

Synthèse du développement sensorimoteur de l'enfant de trois à quatre ans

	Vision	Audition	Préhension et manipulation	Locomotion	Schéma corporel	Relations spatiales	Relations temporelles
ENTRE 3 ET 4 ANS	• Apprécie mieux les longues distances.	• Accorde beaucoup d'intérêt aux activités et aux expériences auditives.	• Contrôle davantage ses mouvements.	• Court plus rapidement, peut s'adapter à des courbes durant la course.	• Peut situer les objets par rapport à son corps.	• Situe les objets et la place des objets en relation avec lui-même.	• Peut attendre plus longtemps certains objets ou événements.
	• Effectue plus rapidement les changements d'orientation visuelle du loin au proche.	• Exprime sa compréhension et sa perception des sons par tout le corps : hoche la tête, chante en se berçant, etc.	• Construit une tour de 8 à 10 cubes.	• Monte les escaliers en alternant les pieds.	• Raffine ses perceptions du corps, perçoit mieux toutes les parties du visage.	• Est conscient de l'ordre des objets familiers.	• Ajoute de nouveaux mots pour décrire le temps : hier, demain, aujourd'hui.
	• Discrimine mieux et s'intéresse visuellement au relief et au contour des objets.	• Reconnaît une mélodie.	• Peut imiter un modèle simple (un pont).	• Saute d'environ 30 cm.	• Reconnaît et nomme davantage de parties ; le front, les coudes, le dos, le côté, les pieds, etc.	• Peut se repérer et s'orienter dans les itinéraires simples.	• Étend son vocabulaire à une dizaine de mots pour désigner le temps.
	• Utilise moins la main dans ses explorations visuelles.	• Chante les phrases d'une chanson.	• Aime verser, peut déboutonner.	• Se tient en équilibre sur un pied en se balançant.		• Peut se représenter l'espace vers lequel se dirige son action.	
	• Identifie les formes géométriques en les personnifiant : un ballon, une tente, une fenêtre, etc.	• Peut reproduire toute une chanson.	• Peut tracer deux lignes croisées.	• Peut conduire le tricycle avec les pédales.		• Acquiert la notion de lieu d'habitation.	
		• Conserve mieux le rythme.	• Peut encercler un espace.	• Peut marcher avec rythme.			
		• Aime les activités musicales de groupe.	• Commence à tracer des formes géométriques simples.	• Peut marcher sur une ligne droite.			

Trois à quatre ans

Le développement sensorimoteur

Vision

À trois ans, l'enfant apprécie mieux les longues distances.

Situations
- disposer des objets à des distances variables. Faire tourner le dos à un ou deux enfants. Changer les distances. Demander aux enfants de dire lesquels sont les plus près et les plus éloignés ;

- disposer à bonne distance des enfants trois ou quatre gros objets bien connus. Cacher avec un écran et faire disparaître l'un de ces objets. Demander quel objet est disparu. Faire participer les enfants au choix de l'objet disparu ;

- commencer à faire travailler l'enfant à la peinture avec la formule des palettes de couleurs placées à distance du tableau à peindre ;

- faire commenter à distance certains détails de diapositives, de films ou de photographies géantes

Attitudes
- organiser des activités qui tiennent compte de cette nouvelle possibilité d'attention et de fixation visuelle chez l'enfant, mais éviter de prolonger trop longtemps cette activité, car la capacité d'attention est encore réduite à quelques minutes à cet âge.

Organisation matérielle
- envisager la possibilité d'utiliser une seule image lorsqu'il s'agit de raconter une histoire ou de faire observer une illustration à un petit groupe d'enfants si les détails sont assez précis, car les enfants devront alors de temps en temps faire un effort d'accommodation visuelle et d'attention pour bien voir cette image.

L'enfant est capable d'observation visuelle plus systématique et il exploite moins la main dans ses explorations visuelles.

Situations
- commencer à observer avec l'enfant les diverses caractéristiques des nouveaux objets qu'il examine ; l'enfant pourra ainsi observer certains volets fragiles et délicats sans nécessairement toucher à l'objet ; apporter des outils plus complexes et en faire observer le fonctionnement à l'enfant, qui devra respecter la consigne de ne pas toucher ;

- l'attrait du neuf et de la surprise le motivera également à suivre le mot d'ordre pour avoir accès à de nouvelles surprises.

Attitudes
- ménager des éléments nouveaux et variés à faire voir à l'enfant. Celui-ci s'habituera à regarder avec les yeux plutôt qu'uniquement avec les mains ;

- apprendre progressivement à manipuler avec précautions des objets fragiles ;

- rester très prudent et ne rien apporter de vraiment dangereux, à cause du grand nombre d'enfants dont il faut tenir compte et des vieilles habitudes toujours présentes.

Organisation matérielle
- organiser l'espace en variant l'éclairage et la couleur, de manière à retenir l'attention des enfants et à soutenir leur intérêt pour les choses « vues » ;

- disposer avec soin les dessins et les travaux de chacun et apprendre à tous à respecter les travaux de leurs compagnons.

L'enfant discrimine mieux visuellement et s'intéresse au relief, au contour et à la forme des objets. Il identifie les formes géométriques en les personnifiant.

Situations
- **La boîte à secrets**

- pratiquer dans une boîte à chaussures ou une boîte plus grande une ouverture circulaire. Fixer le poignet d'une vieille mitaine et d'un vieux bas. Cacher dans la boîte deux ou trois objets aux contours précis et connus ; faire introduire la main à l'intérieur (manipulation) et faire identifier l'objet avant de le sortir de la boîte. Vérifier visuellement la réponse donnée par la seule perception tactile ;

- faire observer, en les nommant par leur vrai nom, diverses formes géométriques pures que l'on retrouve dans l'environnement de l'enfant : panneaux de circulation, maisons circulaires, etc. Laisser l'enfant identifier les formes des jeux à encastrer en les personnifiant : le triangle (une tente), le cercle (un ballon), et ne pas le reprendre constamment sur ce dernier point.

Attitudes
- ne pas laisser les enfants à eux-mêmes au cours de cette activité, car, à cet âge, ils risquent de ne pouvoir vraiment suivre les directives du jeu ; cela peut susciter des querelles inutiles entre ceux qui devinent et ceux qui cachent les objets.

Trois à quatre ans

Le développement sensorimoteur

Audition

L'enfant accorde à cet âge beaucoup d'intérêt aux activités et aux expériences auditives. Il est davantage capable de concentration, de contrôle musculaire et d'attention. Il peut accorder environ cinq minutes d'attention soutenue.

Situation
- **jeu pour retrouver le calme**

- **le roi du silence**

- réunir les enfants en cercle et jouer au roi du silence. Chaque enfant s'efforce d'être immobile et d'écouter un bruit le plus loin possible. Après une minute de silence, on proclame un roi du silence pour la journée ; il peut porter la couronne ou le chapeau cette journée-là.

- **jeux pour varier les expériences auditives**

- **les bruits mystérieux**

- apporter divers objets : bouteilles à col étroit pour souffler, papier cellophane à froisser, roues mal huilées, soufflet pour le feu, batteur rotatif manuel, etc. Faire deviner le bruit que chacun des objets peut ou va produire. Faire entendre par la suite les bruits que ces objets font effectivement. Faire imiter ces bruits à nouveau après la première audition.

- **les sons en bouteille (méthode Montessori)**

- apporter quelques bouteilles identiques et se faire aider des enfants pour fabriquer le contenu ; les remplir de haricots secs, de riz, de sucre, de petits clous, etc., et organiser un petit orchestre rythmique à partir de ces instruments ou faire des jeux de devinettes autour du contenu.

Attitudes
- respecter le rythme de chaque enfant, autant que possible en amenant, un peu à l'avance, un climat de calme lorsqu'il s'agit d'activités de groupe de ce genre ; les enfants agités prendront sûrement un peu plus de temps à retrouver leur calme que ceux qui sont plus pondérés de nature.

Organisation matérielle
- organiser les jeux de groupe de manière à toujours pouvoir être entendu par les enfants avant d'entreprendre toute autre forme de jeu. Le calme et le contrôle des enfants sont essentiels pour mener à bien toute expérience auditive.

L'enfant aime les activités musicales de groupe. De plus, il exprime sa compré-hension et la perception des sons par tout le corps : il hoche la tête, chante en se berçant, tape des mains en rythme.

Situations
- tirer profit des goûts et intérêts de cet âge en organisant des rondes simples, des jeux mimés, des danses, etc. ;

- établir des codes où l'enfant manifeste sa compréhension par des gestes et des mouvements : la sonnerie du réveil signifie se lever ; l'air de la flûte veut dire de se coucher au sol ; la clochette ou le grelot veut dire de s'asseoir, etc. Ceux qui commettent des erreurs se retirent du jeu ou doivent adopter une certaine position sans en changer (ils se reposent et restent couchés ou commencent un nouveau jeu) ;

- il est possible de varier en accentuant la distance entre la source sonore et les enfants.

Attitudes
- émettre des règles très simples, des codes faciles à comprendre ;

- reprendre très souvent les jeux qui ont semblé plaire à l'enfant, même si ce n'est pas tout à fait la perception de l'adulte. L'enfant de cet âge aime retrouver très souvent la même activité connue.

Organisation matérielle
- il est important de créer un climat de calme et d'attention avant d'aborder toute expérience sur le plan de l'audition, en prenant le temps de s'arrêter et de se détendre en aménageant l'espace de façon à favoriser ce climat détendu.

Attention et mémoire auditive : *L'enfant conserve mieux le rythme et reconnaît une mélodie. Il peut chanter une ou plusieurs phrases d'une chanson et il peut même souvent reproduire toute une chanson. Certains enfants le font beaucoup plus tôt, mais, vers trois ans, l'ensemble des enfants sont capables de réussir.*

Situations
- développer l'attention et la mémoire auditive selon l'intérêt de cet âge : demander aux enfants de répéter, chacun à leur tour, le nom de trois animaux, de trois personnes, de trois chiffres, de trois fleurs, etc. ; faire reconnaître des sons différents en fermant volontairement les yeux ; changer un air facile et très connu en sautant un mot ou une phrase et faire découvrir ce qui manque ; faire apprendre de petits airs très simples sous forme de comptines ou de formulettes ; varier les mots des comptines très connues ; utiliser des disques à l'occasion.

Attitudes
- susciter l'attention de l'enfant en variant le ton de la voix : en parlant parfois très bas et parfois un peu plus fort ;

- vérifier très souvent le niveau de compréhension et d'attention, de manière à bien évaluer la capacité d'attention selon les enfants et selon les groupes d'enfants.

Organisation matérielle
- éviter de prolonger toute activité auditive au delà de la période d'intérêt manifestée par l'enfant, car il y a un risque de voir monter la tension au lieu de la contrôler.

Trois à quatre ans

Le développement sensorimoteur

Manipulation

L'enfant peut réussir davantage des activités où la discrimination des formes et des dimensions lui permet de mieux regrouper les objets, mais généralement à partir d'un seul critère à la fois.

Situations
- **le jeu des boutons**

- demander aux enfants d'apporter dans une boîte une grande quantité de boutons de toutes les formes et de toutes les dimensions (vision et manipulation). Faire démêler les boutons et les placer soit dans des verres transparents selon les couleurs, soit dans de petits casiers selon leur forme, soit selon leur grandeur, en laissant choisir le critère de sélection par l'enfant ;

- réunir une grande quantité de livres de toutes les formes. Faire retrouver le ou les livres qui ont la même forme et les empiler ;

- refaire les mêmes jeux de triage et d'appariement en utilisant toutes sortes d'objets pouvant se regrouper sous diverses catégories.

Attitudes
- observer la démarche individuelle de l'enfant, ses choix et ses critères d'évaluation, de manière à situer son niveau de comportement tant sur le plan mental que sur le simple plan de la manipulation. Il est important toutefois de ne pas intervenir, car l'enfant choisit des critères de regroupement encore assez fantaisistes. Il faut le laisser faire, car il apprend de cette manière la nécessité de regrouper ;

- éviter d'organiser un tel jeu lorsqu'il y a de trop jeunes enfants autour, car il serait dangereux qu'un tout petit porte les boutons à sa bouche.

L'enfant peut imiter un modèle simple et il commence à reproduire des formes géométriques : il peut encercler un espace et peut tracer des lignes croisées.

Situations
- tenter de raffiner l'éducation du bras, de la main et des doigts en utilisant des jeux de doigts dans une petite boîte à sable (y déposer seulement une mince couche de sable) ;

● faire remarquer aux enfants comment tenir correctement les objets dans les mains : les objets lourds, fermement ; les objets légers, délicatement ; apprendre à tenir adéquatement de gros crayons ;

● laisser les enfants manipuler leurs vêtements lorsqu'il s'agit de boutonner et de déboutonner, etc., de manière à raffiner le geste de la main et des doigts ;

● laisser les enfants ramasser eux-mêmes les perles ou de petits objets lorsqu'ils tombent sur le plancher.

Attitudes   ● utiliser spontanément toute occasion donnant à l'enfant l'occasion de raffiner les gestes de la main et des doigts dans les activités de la vie quotidienne.

Perception par le toucher : L'enfant de cet âge aime manipuler avec une certaine précision, faire des trous dans la glaise ; il expérimente les objets avec des mouvements de doigts de même qu'avec toute la main.

Situations   ● donner à l'enfant de la terre glaise qui lui permette d'agir assez facilement sur le matériau ; presser avec le doigt, rouler avec les doigts étendus ;

● faire des jeux de devinettes en cachant dans une boîte, hors de la vue, un objet froid, un objet doux, un objet mou, un objet dur et faire deviner non pas le nom de l'objet, mais sa propriété tactile.

Attitudes   ● ajouter aux expériences tactiles les explications qui confirment les sensations vécues par les enfants, les causes et les effets ;

● susciter la curiosité de l'enfant dans le sens de la propriété des objets. Utiliser fréquemment des termes descriptifs en plus de mentionner le nom de l'objet. Ex. : cette terre glaise est rouge et elle est très dure parce qu'il y a longtemps qu'elle n'a pas été réchauffée par la chaleur de nos mains. La poignée de la porte est froide parce qu'elle est en métal.

L'enfant contrôle mieux ses mouvements. La coordination oeil-main est mieux réussie et lui permet d'ordonner.

Situations   ● **le jeu de la pêche aux poissons**

● dessiner des formes simples. Faire insérer au bout de chaque poisson un trombone métallique (demander aux enfants de participer à ce travail) ; au bout d'un petit bâton ou d'une baguette munie d'un bout protecteur, fixer une corde et un aimant. Déposer les poissons sur le plancher, assez éloignés les uns des autres. Laisser les enfants diriger l'aimant et la corde vers les poissons pour les saisir au passage ;

- confectionner aussi des poissons en relief à partir de bandes repliées de papier ou de carton.

Attitudes
- observer attentivement les comportements des enfants durant ce jeu, de manière à bien situer le niveau de difficulté que peut représenter cette activité pour chacun d'eux.

Organisation matérielle
- inviter les enfants à bien choisir leurs poissons, à les colorier avant la pêche ou même après, selon le cas ;

- éviter les bousculades en décrivant un grand cercle sur le sol pour délimiter l'espace. Les enfants respecteront probablement ce cercle ;

- tailler une très grande quantité de poissons, de manière à éviter les disputes et les querelles.

Trois à quatre ans

Le développement sensorimoteur

Locomotion

L'enfant court plus rapidement et il peut s'adapter à des courbes durant la course ; il peut sauter d'environ un pied (considérer de multiples variations individuelles comme étant normales).

Situations
- laisser les enfants s'organiser des jeux très simples de poursuite, car ils peuvent varier la trajectoire de leur course ;

- permettre des courses à un ou deux obstacles que les enfants devraient contourner en cours de route ;

- laisser les enfants sauter à l'intérieur de parcours de jeux ; encourager les enfants plus craintifs ou moins habiles à franchir des obstacles à leur portée.

Attitudes
- éviter de faire des comparaisons même au profit d'un enfant ou d'un autre, car les variations individuelles sont très grandes à cet âge et cela risquerait de blesser ou d'infirmer des enfants qui ne pourraient pas atteindre les performances les plus rapides.

Organisation matérielle
- délimiter des périodes consacrées aux activités de courses et de sauts à l'intérieur, à moins d'avoir un endroit permanent prévu à cette fin pour éviter tout danger de blessures ;

- profiter des sorties pour laisser les enfants courir à leur gré dans la cour.

L'enfant monte les escaliers en alternant les pieds ; il est maintenant capable de conduire correctement un tricycle en poussant les pédales pour avancer.

Situations
- jouer à imiter les mouvements de pédalage au sol, en variant le rythme et la vitesse ;

- encourager l'enfant craintif à monter et à descendre les escaliers de la garderie en se tenant d'abord et en alternant les pieds. Construire avec l'enfant un petit escalier solide qui permettra à l'enfant de jouer à monter et à descendre ; utiliser des caisses de bois ou des cubes ;

- laisser des tricycles solides, plutôt bas, à la disposition des enfants, à certaines heures de la journée.

Attitudes
- établir une surveillance étroite, partagée entre deux ou trois éducateurs, lorsque la période de jeux se prête à des activités de cet ordre ;

- éviter de réunir, à cette occasion, des enfants très jeunes et des enfants plus âgés, à cause des dangers pour les plus petits.

Organisation matérielle
- vérifier la solidité des petits escaliers mis à la disposition des enfants ;

- prévoir une intégration architecturale de petits escaliers, avec appui protecteur ; ces escaliers pourraient donner accès à des endroits bien délimités, à des espaces surélevés pour jouer ou regarder des livres ;

- prévoir l'utilisation des tricycles lorsqu'il n'y a pas trop d'enfants. Surveiller la vitesse des déplacements pour éviter les dangers.

L'enfant peut marcher en rythme et suivre une ligne droite. Il peut aussi se tenir en équilibre sur un pied en se balançant.

Situations
- laisser les enfants organiser des marches et des parades où un enfant doit suivre et précéder un camarade, en suivant un itinéraire simple ;

- imiter, en rythme, la démarche de certains animaux ; la parade des petits ours, le bain des canards, etc. Dessiner avec les enfants des lignes droites ou brisées, tracées en papier collant, sur le sol : le chemin de fer et le train, les voitures sur la route ;

- imiter les avions et les brouettes en se balançant sur un pied ; varier la vitesse dans le rythme de la marche, ralentir, accélérer.

Attitudes
- faire remarquer à l'enfant qui a toujours tendance à courir l'intérêt de la marche ; lui donner un but, un objectif, de manière à lui permettre de maîtriser ses mouvements pour en arriver à maîtriser également sa direction.

Organisation matérielle
- coller sur le plancher des bandes de papier adhésif de deux couleurs et dessiner une route qui se croise en formant une intersection, de manière à varier les diverses possibilités de marches sur des lignes droites. Relier divers espaces de la garderie par des chemins tracés au sol avec des couleurs et des textures différentes.

Trois à quatre ans

Le développement sensorimoteur

Schéma corporel

Identification des parties du corps : L'enfant identifie de mieux en mieux les parties de son corps et il en identifie un plus grand nombre. Il imite plus spontanément un modèle vivant en reprenant, sur demande, la position choisie par un compagnon ou un adulte au cours d'un jeu.

Situations
- **le bonhomme de neige**

- former un cercle ; y laisser un seul enfant, au centre, qui devient le bonhomme de neige. Les enfants chantent : lorsque la musique ou la chanson cesse, le bonhomme prend une position de gel ; tous ceux qui le veulent peuvent l'imiter. Celui qui reste le plus longtemps sans bouger devient à son tour le bonhomme de neige. Les enfants peuvent tenter d'imiter, les yeux fermés, un geste ou une position très simple : ouvrir la bouche, pencher la tête, taper du pied ;

- dessiner pour jouer un grand bonhomme incomplet et demander aux enfants de le compléter.

Attitudes
- insister davantage sur la clarté de l'identification verbale. L'enfant doit tout au moins commencer à nommer clairement un plus grand nombre de parties : le front, les coudes, le dos, le côté, etc.

L'enfant reconnaît et nomme davantage de parties de son corps : les parties du visage, les coudes, le dos, le côté, les pieds, etc.

Situations
- faire des rondes, des jeux chantés où l'enfant peut à tour de rôle répondre par des parties de son corps, soit pour s'habiller, comme dans le jeu très connu de « Promenons-nous dans le bois » ou dans des jeux où l'enfant doit nommer une partie de son corps ; ex. : les enfants sont en cercle. L'un d'eux dit : « Êtes-vous contents ? Mais oui ! (tous). Montrez-le avec le nez ». Et, à tour de rôle, chaque enfant nomme une partie différente en reprenant. Variante : « Savez-vous planter des choux ? »

Attitudes
- donner à chaque enfant l'occasion de nommer à son tour une partie qu'il connaît, même s'il répète celle que son voisin vient de nommer. La force de l'imitation finira par influencer l'enfant qui apprendra ainsi rapidement à reconnaître de plus en plus ces parties.

Représentation : L'enfant imite facilement divers modèles vivants prenant des positions différentes. De plus, il commence à bien localiser les objets ou les autres, en rapport avec son propre corps (principe de latéralité).

Situations
- **imitation de modèles**

- dessiner au sol la forme couchée de quelques enfants de grandeurs différentes avec les jambes et les bras écartés. Demander à un ami d'aider un autre à s'installer dans la même position que celle du dessin. Pour aider un enfant à prendre conscience de soi et de l'espace environnant, jouer de temps à autre, quelques secondes : à toucher le mur avec les mains, à mettre la tête sur la table, à mettre le dos au mur, à mettre le nez sur la vitre, à mettre le ventre sur le plancher ;

- utiliser très fréquemment les adverbes servant à localiser les objets et les positions des objets, de même que la position des enfants eux-mêmes. Animer des jeux qui permettent de localiser la position du corps par rapport aux objets : monter sur les chaises, tourner autour de la table, ramper sous la table, sauter dans la boîte, en dehors de la boîte.

Situations
- **prise de conscience et exploration des principes de latéralité**

- inversion — changement de position : le petit navire : assis au sol face à face, les enfants joignent leurs pieds écartés. Enlever à chacun un soulier, chanter le petit navire en balançant le corps et les pieds. Observer les changements de position ;

- faire déchausser un seul pied. En face d'un grand miroir, déplacer le mouvement des pieds. Combiner un seul gant, une seule chaussure du même côté. Alterner selon les jours ;

- prise de conscience de soi et exploration des principes de latéralité : inversion — changement de position — observation du phénomène : distribuer de vieux gants de diverses couleurs aux enfants, mais ne donner qu'un seul gant à chaque enfant. Placés devant un large miroir, les enfants jouent aux marionnettes de la main, de multiples façons. Variantes : faire jouer à la main chaude (les mouvements les plus simples), donnant à chaque enfant un seul gant ou deux gants de couleurs différentes.

Attitudes
- faire observer aux enfants la permanence du pied déchaussé malgré les mouvements. Ne pas insister au delà d'une simple remarque au point de départ ; progresser très lentement pour laisser aux enfants le temps de s'habituer ;

- s'assurer que chaque enfant a eu l'occasion de vérifier lui-même, face au miroir, le phénomène de constance du même gant dans la même main, tout au cours du jeu.

Organisation matérielle
- placer les enfants de manière à suggérer l'idée de bercement du navire.

Trois à quatre ans

Le développement sensorimoteur

Relations spatiales

L'enfant situe les objets et la place des objets en relation avec lui-même. Il commence à être conscient de l'ordre des objets familiers.

Situations
- favoriser, dans toutes les activités quotidiennes, la prise de conscience de son corps comme point de repère : situer les parties du corps qui sont en avant, sur le côté, en arrière ; situer les objets en avant de lui ou en arrière de lui ; situer les objets en mouvements par rapport à soi ; situer la position des camarades par rapport à soi ;

- aider l'enfant, en causant avec lui, à situer les objets familiers à leur place respective (mémorisation) ;

- reconstituer en miniature la place des meubles dans la maison en terme de rapport (maison de poupée).

Attitudes
- rechercher davantage l'idée de relation entre la position du corps et celle des objets, plutôt qu'une situation rigoureusement exacte ;

- donner à l'enfant l'occasion de retrouver un ordre familier et de parler, au cours de la journée, de sa maison et de sa famille ;

- éviter de rechercher un ordre exact. Situer plutôt les éléments dans l'ensemble. Ex. : la table dans la cuisine.

Organisation matérielle
- faire l'acquisition de maisons miniatures qui sont mises à la dispositon des enfants dans certaines circonstances où l'adulte peut parler avec l'enfant.

L'enfant commence à bien se représenter l'espace vers lequel se dirige son action. Il acquiert la notion de lieu d'habitation et il peut se référer et s'orienter dans les itinéraires simples.

Situations
- faire décrire à l'enfant, à l'occasion de sorties ou de promenades, les lieux où le groupe se propose de se rendre, lorsque ces lieux sont connus. Discuter avec l'enfant du chemin qu'il doit parcourir pour se rendre à la garderie et pour retourner à la maison le soir. Confier à des enfants le soin de conduire le groupe

durant une promenade dans les environs et suivre leurs indications, au retour, même si les enfants se trompent ;

- inventer des labyrinthes dans lesquels les enfants doivent se retrouver et atteindre un objectif ;

- proposer aux parents de jouer au pilote et au copilote lorsqu'ils viennent à la garderie reconduire leur enfant en voiture. Suivre très exactement le chemin décrit par l'enfant lorsqu'ils ont un peu de temps libre, quitte à se tromper ;

- enregistrer, à l'occasion, les indications que l'enfant donne pour se rendre à des endroits bien connus, et suivre les indications à mesure qu'elles sont données sur le magnétophone ;

- reprendre le même jeu avec les indications de l'adulte, comparer les résultats et recommencer ;

- étendre de grands papiers au sol et semer des repères de deux sortes que l'enfant doit suivre pour retrouver son chemin.

Attitudes
- suggérer à une réunion de parents de laisser l'enfant de temps à autre indiquer la route à suivre pour se rendre à des endroits qui lui sont familiers ; faire comprendre aux parents qu'il est important qu'ils « perdent parfois un peu de temps » dans ce sens.

Trois à quatre ans

Le développement sensorimoteur

Relations temporelles

L'enfant peut attendre davantage certains objets ou certains événements. Il ajoute de nouveaux mots pour décrire le temps : hier, demain, aujourd'hui. Il étend son vocabulaire à une dizaine de mots pour désigner le temps (différences individuelles).

Situations
- souligner, à l'occasion, des événements attendus dans un avenir très proche : demain et après-demain. Évaluer le temps en terme d'action : deux dodos, trois matins à déjeuner. Deux repas à la garderie, etc. ;

- situer les termes habituels : hier, demain, aujourd'hui, en rapport avec l'événement présent et au niveau d'une action finie (très spécifique) ou d'une action à venir. À court terme : la soupe avant le dessert, le jeu de ballon avant le dîner, etc. À plus long terme : aujourd'hui tu portes les bas jaunes, demain, tu porteras les bas rouges, etc. ;

- rester fidèle aux codes établis de manière à familiariser l'enfant assez rapidement.

Attitudes
- éviter d'utiliser un code, une entente, une journée et de changer de repère le lendemain, ou tout simplement de ne pas donner suite à la promesse faite la veille en terme d'événements ou d'objets promis ;

- utiliser toujours le terme juste immédiatement accolé au terme subjectif choisi par l'enfant.

Organisation matérielle
- diviser une feuille en deux ou trois casiers, selon le cas, et dessiner à chaque jour qui passe un signe caractéristique convenant à l'événement ou à l'objet qui s'annonce.

Tableau XII

Synthèse du développement socio-affectif de l'enfant de trois à quatre ans

ENTRE 3 ET 4 ANS

Interactions enfant-adulte			Interactions enfant-enfant		
Manifestations des émotions	Imitation de l'adulte	Apprentissage des rôles sociaux	Manifestations des émotions	Communication par le jeu	Participation à la vie de groupe
• Supporte plus mal l'isolement et le rejet.	• Est sensible aux éloges et aime aider les adultes et se faire complimenter pour ses efforts.	• Manifeste un esprit de conformisme, cherche à plaire, accepte mieux les conseils.	• Provoque souvent querelles et disputes pour la possession de matériel ou de jeux passagers.	• Imite dans ses jeux des personnages, transpose des scènes de la vie réelle.	• Préfère maintenant la société des autres enfants (deux ou trois).
• Manifeste un sens du comique et de l'humour.	• Aime répondre au téléphone comme l'adulte, mais sans efficacité véritable.	• Commence à obéir à un ordre en présence de l'adulte.	• Devient plus conscient des autres et développe jalousie et rivalité.	• Invente des personnages fictifs (compagnons imaginaires).	• Doit être surveillé lorsque les compagnons sont du même âge.
• Marque beaucoup d'affection pour la mère.	• Démontre une certaine initiative dans ses imitations.	• Commence à définir son appartenance à un sexe plutôt qu'à un autre.	• Commence à se vanter en présence des autres enfants.	• Accorde beaucoup d'importance à l'imaginaire et fait des transferts d'identité (s'imagine être un animal).	• Commence à partager ses jouets, à coopérer.
• Est capable de sympathie.	• Peut ranger en imitant l'ordre décrété par l'adulte.		• Est souvent très exigeant ou plein de sollicitude pour le compagnon imaginaire.	• Aime se déguiser pour les jeux et les danses.	• Aime apporter avec lui ses jouets pour les partager ensuite.
• Cherche à observer les expressions faciales pour découvrir ce qu'elles signifient.				• Peut s'amuser seul (sur simple suggestion).	• Acquiert un sens aigu de la propriété.
• Est plus conscient des besoins des autres et accepte d'y répondre.					

Trois à quatre ans

Le développement socio-affectif

Interactions enfant-adulte

Apprentissage des rôles sociaux : L'enfant manifeste un esprit de conformisme. Il cherche à plaire et accepte mieux les conseils. Il commence à obéir à un ordre en présence de l'adulte et commence à définir son appartenance à un sexe plutôt qu'à un autre de façon plus marquée.

Attitudes
- laisser les enfants traduire librement dans leurs jeux l'imitation de l'adulte, leur perception de ces rôles, et éviter de trop intervenir ;

- aider l'enfant à se définir comme un garçon ou comme une fille, mais éviter le piège de la discrimination ou des clichés traditionnels au plan des rôles : « un garçon ne joue pas à la poupée, une fille ne fait pas de construction, un garçon ne pleure pas, etc. ; »

- conserver une attitude positive et ne pas s'inquiéter devant des manifestations de curiosité sur le plan sexuel. Utiliser les termes justes pour décrire les parties génitales de l'enfant ; établir un climat de confiance avec la famille à ce sujet. Répondre aux questions de l'enfant simplement et avec franchise ;

- tirer profit de l'intérêt des enfants pour le monde des adultes en présentant, comme éducateur, un modèle facilement accessible à l'enfant : donner des conseils à l'enfant, mais avec des explications ; recommander la politesse et la courtoisie à l'enfant en le traitant lui-même avec politesse ;

- éviter de trop rationaliser en donnant toujours les raisons qui motivent les actions ; les enfants peuvent comprendre, mais pas encore autant que l'adulte.

Organisation matérielle
- aménager des espaces de jeux qui permettent aux garçons et aux filles une saine égalité dans les jeux. Éviter de surspécialiser les jeux d'imitation (jeux de poupée ou de construction) en leur donnant un caractère d'exclusivité. Donner accès à tous ces jeux, aux garçons comme aux filles.

Imitation de l'adulte: L'enfant est sensible aux éloges et aime aider les adultes et se faire complimenter. Il aime répondre au téléphone, mais sans efficacité véritable. Il peut ranger en imitant l'adulte. Il démontre une certaine initiative dans ses imitations.

Situations
- confier à l'enfant des tâches simples : passer le plateau à biscuits ; faire une commission à la cuisine. Demander son aide en lui expliquant pourquoi il faut ranger et comment il faut le faire ;

- organiser des jeux de téléphone avec des rouleaux de papier et de fils, prévoir un grand téléphone avec un cadran géant ;

- aider les enfants à amorcer des jeux d'imitation en suggérant des installations : aligner des caisses et des chaises pour un train, deux chaises avec des couvertures pour le toit, etc.

Attitudes
- complimenter mais ne pas tomber dans l'excès : éviter d'utiliser les éloges et les compliments à tout propos, au risque de diminuer la valeur d'une telle récompense ;

- ménager des réussites à l'enfant mais ne pas lui éviter tous les échecs, car il doit également expérimenter cette possibilité ; certains enfants supportent mal tout échec, à partir de cet âge, car ils deviennent sensibles aux réactions négatives de l'entourage s'ils n'ont pas l'occasion de vivre sainement de petits échecs dans leur quotidien ;

- aider à amorcer des jeux d'imitation en accord avec les intérêts des enfants, mais se retirer aussitôt que l'essentiel est mis en place.

Organisation matérielle
- aménager des espaces facilement accessibles pour ranger les jouets ; faire remarquer aux enfants les problèmes causés par le manque d'ordre : perte de jouets, incapacité de retrouver les pièces d'un jeu lorsque l'enfant désire s'en servir, etc.

Manifestation des émotions : L'enfant marque souvent beaucoup d'affection pour la mère et il supporte mal l'isolement et le rejet. Il est capable de sympathie et manifeste un sens du comique et de l'humour : il cherche à deviner le sens des expressions faciales, il commence à être conscient des besoins des autres et il accepte d'y répondre.

Situations
- écouter avec beaucoup d'attention et d'intérêt les « nouvelles » que l'enfant donne de sa famille et de ses parents au cours de la journée ;

- permettre à l'enfant d'organiser des jeux de mimes où il doit deviner le sens des gestes et des expressions imités par l'adulte ou par d'autres enfants ;

- inviter l'enfant à préparer des cadeaux ou des surprises pour sa maman ou son papa, sans toutefois exiger la perfection des objets fabriqués.

Attitudes
- utiliser les explications verbales pour obtenir la collaboration de l'enfant et faire appel, à l'occasion, à des mimiques particulières pour retenir son attention et créer une diversion ;

- éviter de faire appel à la pitié de l'enfant ou de jouer sur des notes dramatiques pour obtenir sa sympathie ou son obéissance (ex. : tu vas me faire mourir de fatigue, etc.) ;

- tirer profit de façon positive des expériences de l'enfant : du mal physique, de la fatigue, de la faim et du sommeil pour faire comprendre les besoins des autres ;

- conserver le sens de l'humour face aux querelles et aux disputes.

Organisation matérielle
- éviter de retirer complètement l'enfant trop indocile en l'isolant du reste du groupe : le mettre plutôt légèrement en retrait du groupe ;

- prévoir un espace particulier avec une ambiance chaleureuse et confortable : coussins, matelas, tapis feutres, où les enfants peuvent venir retrouver l'adulte à certaines heures pour parler et se reposer tout simplement de manière à retrouver un climat de sécurité affective.

Trois à quatre ans

Le développement socio-affectif

Interactions enfant-enfant

Participation à la vie de groupe : L'enfant préfère maintenant la société des autres enfants ; il commence à partager ses jouets et à coopérer ; il aime apporter ses jouets avec lui pour partager et il acquiert un sens aigu de la propriété.

Situations
- amener l'enfant à partager les jouets de la garderie. Accepter que l'enfant apporte à la garderie un jouet particulier ou un objet auquel il tient pour le montrer à tous les amis. Procéder officiellement, montrer l'objet à tout le groupe et par la suite, ranger l'objet hors de la portée des autres enfants pour éviter les pleurs, les pertes ou les bris.

Attitudes
- considérer avec beaucoup d'intérêt l'enfant qui exhibe ses nouveaux habits, ses nouveaux souliers ou son nouveau manteau, et éviter de prêter à un autre enfant le vêtement d'un compagnon, à moins d'y être vraiment obligé ;

- traiter avec beaucoup de respect et de sérieux les travaux des enfants et demander la participation des parents à ce sujet.

Organisation matérielle
- accorder un espace particulier à chaque enfant pour ranger bottes et vêtements et tirer profit de son intérêt quand une pièce de vêtement se perd ; l'enfant pourra généralement aider à le reconnaître ;

- ranger les travaux des enfants. Aider tous les enfants à respecter les travaux de leurs compagnons et à apprécier les travaux.

Communication par le jeu : L'enfant imite dans ses jeux des personnages fictifs, il accorde beaucoup d'importance à l'imaginaire et fait des transferts d'identité. Il aime se déguiser pour les jeux et les danses et il peut s'amuser seul sur simple suggestion.

Situations
- utiliser très souvent le goût particulier qu'ont les enfants de cet âge de se transformer en animaux et faire des jeux qui demandent une certaine imitation dans ce sens ;

- leur permettre de prolonger leur jeux d'imitation au delà des seules périodes consacrées à cette fin. Laisser un enfant qui désire faire un autre jeu conserver les accessoires qui l'identifiaient à son personnage, même s'il passe plusieurs heures dans la garderie avec son costume préféré.

Attitudes
- utiliser, sans trop encourager toutefois, les jeux imaginaires des enfants pour les aider à choisir entre diverses possibilités. Transformer les obligations les plus simples en jeux amusants par ces divers procédés ; se coucher pour la sieste dans son train ou dans son bateau ; venir dîner au restaurant de la garderie, laisser le jouet préféré (de la garderie) dormir dans un petit coin pour la nuit, etc. ;

- éviter d'exagérer les transferts d'identité au risque de faire perdre de vue le sens du réel et du quotidien.

Organisation matérielle
- prévoir divers accessoires pour supporter les jeux imaginaires de l'enfant : demander aux parents de réunir des vieux vêtements propres, des chapeaux, des gants, des souliers (éviter les talons hauts trop fins qui sont dangereux pour l'enfant).

Manifestation des émotions : L'enfant provoque souvent des querelles pour la possession de matériel ou de jeux ; il devient plus conscient des autres et développe de la jalousie et de la rivalité. Il commence à se vanter en présence des autres enfants et est souvent exigeant ou plein de sollicitude pour le compagnon imaginaire.

Attitudes
- tolérer avec un brin d'humour les interminables vantardises des enfants de cet âge et leur donner l'occasion d'exécuter des gestes simples qui leur redonneront le sens de la réalité et où ils pourront connaître également une part de succès et une part d'échecs ;

- considérer l'existence du compagnon imaginaire suffisamment sérieuse pour lui faire une place à l'occasion de diverses activités (certains enfants, toutefois, ne font jamais appel à des personnages imaginaires) ;

- éviter de susciter des rivalités et des jalousies en ayant recours à une justice rigoureuse dans la distribution du matériel, etc. ;

- accepter de «perdre du temps» pour donner à chaque enfant l'occasion d'exécuter la même tâche, de chanter la même chanson, de posséder le même élément de bricolage ;

- accepter la présence du compagnon imaginaire, mais éviter de trop encourager sa présence au détriment de la présence des autres enfants du groupe.

Organisation matérielle
- prévoir des jeux plus différenciés ; l'enfant est désormais capable d'attendre son tour et de contrôler ses jalousies (à petites doses) ;

- éviter de donner des jeux trop difficiles à réussir : les camions, tricycles, poupées, trousses de médecin et jeux d'imitation de rôle sont favoris à cet âge et aident les enfants à mieux s'accepter mutuellement.

Tableau XIII
Synthèse du développement du langage verbal de l'enfant de trois à quatre ans

La compréhension	L'utilisation
— Comprend les substantifs abstraits :	— Dispose d'un vocabulaire de 150 à 800 mots.
— La couleur.	— Peut donner son prénom et son nom.
— La différence, la similitude.	— Utilise des mots pour décrire l'action représentée sur une image.
— Comprend des adjectifs exprimant :	— Commence à employer le pluriel.
— Une dimension simple (petit, gros, grand).	— Peut nommer trois couleurs.
— Comprend les mots indiquant :	— Peut compter jusqu'à trois.
— Des notions spatiales (haut, bas) et	— Définit les objets par leur usage.
— temporelles (avant, après, aujourd'hui, demain).	— Explique les événements
— Comprend le sens de «comment»	— Utilise correctement les mots les plus connus de son vocabulaire.
	— Accumule successivement des pronoms et des substantifs sans nécessairement leur ajouter des verbes.
	— Évite encore très souvent d'employer les pronoms et utilise plus spontanément son prénom pour parler de lui-même.

Trois à quatre ans

Le développement du langage verbal

Compréhension

L'enfant comprend un plus grand nombre de substantifs abstraits impliquant la couleur, les dimensions, les différences et plusieurs mots indiquant des notions spatiales (haut, bas, etc.) et des notions temporelles (avant, après, etc.). Il peut comprendre le sens de «comment».

Situations
- demander très souvent aux enfants de reconnaître les objets par des caractéritiques telles que la couleur, la dimension (gros, petit) ;

- insister sur les différences entre la taille des enfants en utilisant des miroirs. Faire nommer ces différences ;

- donner des objets aux enfants ; les faire identifier en nommant celui qui a un gros cube, un cube rouge ;

- faire choisir aux enfants des objets semblables, mais de tailles différentes, dans le réel ou sur des images.

Attitudes
- prononcer toujours très clairement avec même une certaine exagération dans le débit ;

- poser des questions qui mèneront l'enfant à répondre au « comment » en définissant les objets ou les autres par une caractéristique principale : couleur, taille, forme, etc. ;

- amener les enfants à varier ces caractéristiques descriptives.

Organisation matérielle
- classifier très souvent les objets courants en nommant les principales caractéristiques ; utiliser plusieurs collections de petits objets variés et tirer profit des activités spontanées de triage que l'enfant peut faire pour préciser le niveau de compréhension des critères de triage utilisés par l'enfant.

Trois à quatre ans

Le développement du langage verbal

Utilisation

L'enfant peut utiliser correctement les mots les plus connus de son vocabulaire. Il accumule successivement des pronoms et des substantifs sans parfois ajouter de verbes. Il utilise encore spontanément son prénom au lieu d'un pronom.

Situations
- utiliser les objets courants, ceux qui entourent l'enfant, pour vérifier combien de mots sont prononcés correctement ;

- reprendre sans trop hésiter une phrase sans verbe ou mot d'action et y ajouter correctement le verbe le plus descriptif ;

- reprendre souvent des jeux où il faut désigner l'usage des objets, où il faut nommer et mémoriser quelques objets en petites séquences (à l'aide d'images ou sans support visuel, selon le cas.).

Attitudes
- être attentif aux erreurs les plus fréquentes chez certains enfants. Vérifier le niveau d'audition et la capacité d'écoute de l'enfant qui répète constamment la même erreur ;

- ne pas faire répéter l'enfant, mais reprendre soi-même lentement toute la structure de phrase correctement, afin que l'enfant entende bien la façon correcte de prononcer ;

- être très attentif à tout problème persistant et proposer aux parents une consultation avec l'audiologiste et l'orthophoniste dans le cas de surdité possible, de bégaiement, de zézaiement prononcé, etc.

Organisation matérielle
- voir à obtenir l'attention visuelle d'un enfant avant de répéter souvent un mot à son intention. La prononciation observée sur les lèvres de l'interlocuteur, peut aider à améliorer par la suite la clarté de la prononciation de l'enfant.

L'enfant peut donner son nom et son prénom. Il peut compter jusqu'à trois en comprenant bien le sens numérique et il peut également nommer trois couleurs.

Situations
- demander souvent à l'enfant son nom et son prénom. Lui suggérer, pour l'aider, les premières syllabes de son nom de famille ;

- mentionner, à l'heure des présences, les prénoms et les noms de famille ;

- compter avec lui les objets simples en frappant des mains ; laisser dire et répéter avec l'adulte le nom des chiffres en ordre ;

- mentionner souvent le nom des couleurs : la balle rouge, le crayon bleu, etc. Pointer les objets, faire préciser les couleurs qu'il connaît le mieux.

Attitudes
- encourager tout effort pour nommer un chiffre, un nom, une couleur ;

- parler avec lenteur et précision, sans exagérer au delà d'un certain naturel évidemment.

Organisation matérielle
- insister pour choisir des couleurs franches dans l'aménagement des locaux, de manière à pouvoir utiliser ces couleurs à tout instant, comme point de comparaison.

L'enfant explique les événements et définit les objets par leur usage. Il utilise les mots pour décrire l'action représentée sur une image et il commence à utiliser le pluriel.

Situations
- organiser par très courtes périodes des jeux où l'enfant doit s'exprimer ; l'adulte nomme un objet, l'enfant doit dire à quoi peut servir cet objet ;

- imiter une activité connue de l'enfant : se brosser les dents, se laver les mains, etc. Faire exprimer en termes clairs l'action représentée ;

- répéter les phrases où l'enfant pourrait employer le pluriel, mais sans trop insister.

Attitudes
- éviter de lasser l'enfant en insistant trop souvent sur les mêmes mots ;

- répéter simplement après lui les mots à corriger, sans trop exiger qu'il reprenne, et féliciter largement ceux qui répètent correctement le mot à apprendre ; prononcer clairement les mots désignant le pluriel ;

- utiliser toutes les occasions pour apprendre à l'enfant les termes désignant les objets qui l'entourent quotidiennement ; pour favoriser l'utilisation du pluriel, faire compter les objets, les doigts, les enfants, etc.

Tableau XIV
Synthèse des activités physiologiques de l'enfant de trois à quatre ans

	Alimentation	Élimination	Repos-sommeil
E **N** **T** **R** **E** **3** **,** **E** **T** **4** **A** **N** **S**	**Contrôle du geste** ● Peut se servir de la fourchette mais est encore peu conscient des autres autour de lui, ce qui présente un certain danger. ● Peut saisir la cuillère entre le pouce et l'index avec une rotation correcte du poignet. ● Se nourrit seul et sans trop renverser (cuillère et tasse). ● Prend la tasse par l'anse, rejette la tête en arrière pour boire les dernières gouttes. **Caractéristiques** ● Marque avec moins de force refus et préférence ; aime davantage les aliments à mâcher. ● Mange lentement et en lambinant ; aime aider à replacer tasses et verres. **Habitudes de propreté** ● Est capable de suivre certaines règles de propreté élémentaires (ne pas manger des aliments tombés sur le plancher, ne pas toucher aux aliments des autres, etc.) et des habitudes simples de politesse en groupe (attendre son tour, garder les aliments dans sa bouche, etc.).	**Contrôle de l'intestin et de la vessie** ● Peut aller seul à la toilette, sans prévenir ou en prévenant, et il a encore besoin d'aide quand il a fini pour attacher ou détacher les boutons. **Habitudes de propreté** ● Insiste moins sur les rites de lavage. ● Insiste davantage pour aider à se laver lui-même. ● Oublie fréquemment de refermer le robinet.	**Repos-sommeil** ● Peut ne plus dormir durant la sieste. ● Accepte de s'étendre pour « jouer » à la sieste qui peut durer jusqu'à une heure. **Sommeil** ● Se réveille lentement, mais de meilleure humeur s'il a réussi à dormir. ● Peut recommencer parfois à dormir à cet âge, même s'il ne dormais pas au cours des mois précédents. **Habitudes de propreté** ● Est capable de replier sa petite couverture sans la traîner au sol et peut éviter de marcher sur son matelas de repos.

Trois à quatre ans

Les activités physiologiques

Repos-sommeil

L'enfant peut ne plus dormir durant la sieste, mais il peut accepter de s'étendre pour jouer à la sieste avec un jouet ou un livre. L'enfant qui fait la sieste se réveille lentement, mais de meilleure humeur s'il a réussi à dormir ; il peut recommencer à dormir après un arrêt de quelques semaines.

Situations
- donner aux enfants qui ne dorment pas l'occasion d'organiser eux-mêmes leurs jeux sans trop d'interventions. Surveiller le calme avant tout, afin de ne pas déranger les autres enfants.

Attitudes
- éviter de retenir de force ou contre son besoin un enfant qui ne veut ou ne peut absolument pas dormir, car cela risque de perturber le sommeil de tous les autres et de le rendre lui-même agressif. Lui permettre à tout le moins de regarder un livre ou de jouer en silence.

Organisation matérielle
- aménager de façon attrayante et diversifiée la salle de repos pour inciter un nombre d'enfants à y venir ;

- aménager un coin de jeu pour ces enfants un peu en retrait du groupe et les laisser jouer à des jeux libres en petit groupe, sous la surveillance d'une étudiante, d'une grand-maman ou d'une aide venue à cette occasion ;

- demander la collaboration de l'enfant pour qu'il replie sa petite couverture sans la laisser traîner et lui demander de ne pas marcher sur son matelas avec ses souliers.

Trois à quatre ans

Les activités physiologiques

Alimentation

L'enfant peut se servir de la fourchette, mais il est encore inconscient du danger. Il peut saisir la cuillère entre le pouce et l'index ; il se nourrit correctement sans trop renverser et il prend sa tasse par l'anse. Il marque avec moins de force refus et préférences, il aime les aliments à mâcher, il mange lentement et en lambinant.

Situations
- donner aux enfants l'occasion de mimer des scènes de repas, de façon imaginaire, en aménageant un coin de poupée ; éviter d'établir une discrimination en qualifiant ces jeux de « petite fille » ;

- accepter, lorsqu'un enfant le réclame, de faire une place à table au compagnon imaginaire, sans toutefois encourager ces jeux à l'extrême ;

- participer en alternance aux repas des enfants de manière à ce qu'il y ait toujours un adulte avec eux.

Attitudes
- encourager l'enfant à manger correctement, sans trop renverser ;

- introduire progressivement des aliments nouveaux en félicitant les enfants qui acceptent tout au moins de goûter à ces aliments.

Organisation matérielle
- éviter de donner des fourchettes à l'enfant, même s'il peut s'en servir à la maison, parce que l'enfant, encore peu conscient de la présence des autres et des limites de l'espace immédiat, peut représenter un danger pour ceux qui l'entourent ;

- organiser l'espace de manière à ce que les enfants ne puissent pas trop renverser leurs aliments au sol ;

- participer au repas, comme adulte, en faisant remarquer aux enfants certaines habitudes de propreté ;

- regrouper les enfants lorsque c'est possible en cercle, à de petites tables, pour que les enfants puissent se voir et s'imiter de façon positive.

Trois à quatre ans

Les activités physiologiques

Élimination

L'enfant peut aller seul à la toilette sans prévenir ou en prévenant, lorsqu'il a fini. Il a encore besoin d'aide pour attacher et détacher les boutons. Il insiste moins sur les rites du lavage. Il insiste surtout pour se laver lui-même et il oublie fréquemment de refermer les robinets.

Situations

- établir certaines périodes qui se prêtent spontanément aux activités orientées vers l'hygiène personnelle de l'enfant ; après les repas, avant les promenades à l'extérieur, avant la sieste, etc. ;

- habituer l'enfant à une certaine régularité dans ce sens et lui donner par le fait même une occasion toute naturelle de se situer dans le temps.

Attitudes

- laisser à l'enfant une plus grande autonomie, mais ne pas le laisser complètement à lui-même, car même s'il maîtrise bien sa vessie et ses intestins, il peut encore survenir des accidents qui ne pourraient qu'être causés par des problèmes d'habillage ou de maîtrise des boutons (ces problèmes peuvent causer une anxiété inutile chez certains enfants).

Organisation matérielle

- aménager des espaces qui favorisent l'autonomie et qui centralisent à la fois le coin toilette et le coin lavabo ;

- rendre les espaces facilement accessibles.

Éléments de réflexion pour l'éducateur

Évaluation personnelle

L'éducateur s'interroge sur ses propres façons d'être sur le plan professionnel. C'est à lui d'apporter les réponses qui lui conviennent.

— Est-ce que mon action éducative tient compte des petits événements quotidiens tout autant que des ressources que j'ai en réserve dans mon savoir professionnel?

— Suis-je capable de remettre en question mes façons de vivre avec les enfants de deux ans à quatre ans?

— Quelle est la source principale de mon action quotidienne : moi et ma personnalité, moi et mon expérience, moi et mon interprétation des ressources théoriques?

— Quelle signification a pour moi ce document?

— Quelle est ma réaction devant un enfant qui, par fois, est en compétition avec moi?

— Quels comportements souhaiterais-je améliorer chez moi?

— Est-ce que le rythme collectif du groupe d'enfants de la garderie a plus d'importance à mes yeux que le rythme de chacun des enfants en particulier?

— Suis-je capable d'encourager la démarche vers l'autonomie chez les enfants de cet âge?

— Est-ce que la réussite d'une activité a plus d'importance pour moi que le plaisir que l'enfant a pu avoir dans cette activité?

Observation de l'enfant

L'éducateur utilise tous les événements du quotidien pour observer et pour mieux connaître les enfants de son groupe. C'est à lui de donner une valeur positive à ses observations.

— Comment ai-je l'habitude de réagir au moment de la période dite « négative » des enfants de cet âge?

— Comment ai-je l'habitude de régler les querelles des enfants à cet âge?

— Suis-je attentif aux manifestations de stéréotypes sexuels?

— Suis-je attentif aux enfants ayant des besoins spéciaux?

— Suis-je capable de reconnaître l'enfant leader dans mon groupe?

— Suis-je capable d'attendre un enfant qui veut terminer ce qu'il a commencé?

— Suis-je assez conscient des risques d'ordre physique que prennent certains enfants dans ce groupe d'âge précis?

— Comment se manifeste le quotidien des enfants de cet âge si je veux tenir compte de leur grand intérêt pour la fantaisie et l'imaginaire?

— Est-ce que je peux identifier rapidement les changements d'humeur qui surviennent chez un enfant au cours d'une journée de garderie?

— Suis-je assez attentif à ne pas exprimer mes remarques et commentaires concernant un enfant en sa présence ou devant les autres enfants du groupe?

Interaction professionnelle

L'éducateur tient compte des autres adultes qui interviennent également auprès de l'enfant. C'est à lui d'amorcer des échanges.

— Est-ce que les parents sont pour moi des informateurs privilégiés ou des personnes ressources significatives?

— Est-ce que les parents semblent se sentir à l'aise et suffisamment acceptés dans la garderie pour entrer et pour sortir librement et partager quelques minutes, à leur arrivée ou au départ, les jeux de leurs enfants?

— Est-ce que je cherche à échanger avec les autres éducateurs de la garderie sur des questions professionnelles, afin de prendre des décisions concertées sur l'approche pédagogique?

— Suis-je capable de remplacer, à la dernière minute, l'éducateur qui est responsable d'un autre groupe d'enfants à la garderie?

— Est-ce qu'il m'arrive de discuter du problème d'un enfant, en sa présence ou devant d'autres adultes moins concernés?

— Quel est mon rapport avec les différents intervenants adultes de la garderie?

— Quelles occasions est-ce que je me donne pour me ressourcer?

Résumé

Le désir d'autonomie de l'enfant de deux et de trois ans, sa volonté d'agir seul témoignent de sa capacité nouvelle de vouloir et de pouvoir maîtriser davantage sa propre vie et son environnement personnel.

Cette nouvelle attitude est à la fois une source de croissance et une contrainte pour les adultes qui sont concernés par sa sécurité et ses apprentissages. Le milieu de la garderie doit tenir compte de cette dynamique passionnante mais déroutante chez le tout-petit de cet âge, et il lui faut adapter l'environnement en fonction de ces priorités.

À ses besoins d'autonomie physique et d'expériences sensorimotrices variées, la garderie répondra par un aménagement matériel simple, susceptible de permettre à l'enfant de grimper, de courir, de sauter en toute sécurité, et elle mettra à sa disposition du matériel de jeu stimulant.

Sur le plan socio-affectif, la période d'opposition et les fréquents changements d'humeur, d'idées et de choix doivent être considérés comme une suite de comportements cohérents en terme d'étapes à franchir : s'armer de patience, cultiver le sens de l'humour et réduire au minimum les règles et les interdits sont des attitudes saines à adopter dans les circonstances. L'enfant qui se sent aimé sera généralement plus souple et plus facile à aborder.

La fantaisie, la fabulation et l'imaginaire dans les jeux spontanés et dans le langage même font également partie des caractéristiques particulières aux enfants de cet âge. Accepter le compagnon imaginaire sans toutefois remplacer les véritables relations sociales en sa faveur peut aider l'enfant à se situer dans son processus de socialisation.

L'agressivité, la colère, la frustration font partie en outre des manifestations possibles d'autonomie, au même titre que certaines formes de communication non verbale positive (sourire, hochements de tête, gestes d'apaisement, etc.). Mettre souvent l'accent sur ce qui est agréable ou préférable, tenter de traduire les interdits de façon positive, manifester la joie pour les efforts faits au lieu de s'attacher exclusivement aux déceptions de l'adulte devant les erreurs de l'enfant sont autant d'attitudes valables à développer comme éducateur.

L'autonomie physiologique accrue de l'enfant de cet âge libère progressivement les adultes de certaines contraintes. Il peut manger seul, il dort moins souvent, il peut se débrouiller de plus en plus facilement pour aller à la toilette ; tous ces progrès doivent être encouragés et soutenus par les éducateurs.

L'enfant de deux à trois ans, exprime plus clairement, à la fois sur le plan verbal et sur le plan émotif, ses désirs et ses refus. Il importe donc d'établir une certaine concertation entre les divers intervenants (parents, éducateurs en garderie, famille élargie, etc.), de manière à créer autour de l'enfant cohérence, stabilité et continuité. Pour atteindre un tel objectif, il est essentiel de pouvoir bien connaître cet enfant, de l'observer, de préciser périodiquement les étapes déjà franchies. Il est également nécessaire d'ajuster constamment les divers modes d'interventions éducatives. Pour y parvenir, il ne faut pas craindre de se remettre en question comme adulte et de remettre en question son propre savoir-faire.

S'il est reconnu que l'enfant de cet âge a un mode d'agir fluctuant et souvent imprévisible, il est par conséquent indispensable que les éducateurs, en contrepartie, puissent s'adapter en trouvant un point d'équilibre dans une attitude saine et positive puisée quelque part entre le laisser-faire insouciant et l'autoritarisme rigoureux.

Conclusion

Tout au long de ce document, le souci de traiter l'enfant d'âge préscolaire comme un tout harmonieux en constante évolution et interaction avec son environnement demeure très présent. Son environnement étant la famille, la garderie et le milieu où il habite, il serait juste de s'attarder aux éléments d'interaction de la famille avec la garderie ainsi qu'à l'importance pour l'enfant de vivre des expériences variées en dehors du foyer. Nous considérons cependant que ces sujets méritent une attention particulière qu'on ne pourrait minimiser en quelques paragraphes dans cette série. Par ailleurs, nous n'avons pas développé en détail des sujets tels que la participation des parents, les liens garderie-école, les besoins particuliers des enfants et du personnel allophones, ni des mesures particulières à prévoir pour les enfants souffrant d'un handicap sensoriel, physique ou mental. Cependant, le lecteur est encouragé à essayer de déceler, d'adapter et d'améliorer des situations susceptibles de l'aider pour des cas particuliers. Il est à souhaiter que d'autres documents s'ajoutent à cette série, pour permettre d'approfondir les thèmes qui sont moins développés dans le présent document.

Enfin, la présentation sommaire de la dimension des activités physiologiques est délibérée ; ce thème est traité dans le présent document dans une perspective plus globale que strictement descriptive, de manière à rappeler au lecteur l'importance également significative de cet aspect de la croissance. Le lecteur trouvera aussi, dans la liste de documents disponibles à l'Office des services de garde à l'enfance, une série d'ouvrages portant sur la nutrition et sur les habitudes alimentaires.

Bien que l'impact possible de la garderie sur le développement de l'enfant ne fasse pas encore l'unanimité, il est déjà reconnu que la qualité des soins reçus et la qualité du climat psychologique sont deux pôles essentiels qui déterminent le type d'expérience vécue à la garderie. En conséquence, miser sur la valeur positive des interventions éducatives et du caractère social de ce milieu de vie collectif constitue pour l'enfant une voie certaine vers des gains à long terme.

RÉFÉRENCES

AIMARD, Paule, *L'Enfant et le langage*, Villeurbanne, France, Éditions Simep, 1972.

BARCLAY MURPHY, Lois, « Children under Three Finding Ways to Stimulate Development, issues in research, dans *Children* 16, 46-52, 1969.

BERGES, J. et LEZINE, I., *Test d'imitation des gestes*, Paris, Masson & Cie, 1963.

BETSALEL-PRESSER, Raquel, *Centre de jour éducatif : implications psycho-pédagogiques d'un programme destiné aux enfants de moins de deux ans*, Thèse de doctorat présentée à la Faculté des études supérieures de l'Université de Montréal, 1974, (inédite).

BRIDGES, K.M.B., « Emotional Development in Early Infancy », dans *Child Development* 3, 1932, 324-341.

CALDWELL, Bettye M., « What Is the Optimal Learning Environment for the Young Child ? », dans *American Journal of Orthopsychiatry*, 37, 1967, pp. 8-21.

CENTRE NATIONAL D'INFORMATION SUR LA GARDE DE JOUR (Le), *La Garde de jour des enfants*, Ottawa, Direction du régime d'assistance publique du Canada, 1973.

CLOUTIER, R. et L. DIONNE, *L'Agressivité chez l'enfant*, Montmagny, Edisem, Le Centurion, 1981.

COMMISSION DES ÉCOLES CATHOLIQUES DE QUÉBEC, *Psychomotricité-maternelle 4 ans : Document de travail destiné aux jardinières des classes maternelles — 4 ans*, Québec, 1973.

CRATTY, J. Bryan, *Perceptual and Motor Development in Infants and Children*, Londres, MacMilan, 1970.

DOLL, E. *Vineland Social Maturity Scale Circle Pines*, Minnesota, American Educational Guidance Services, 1953.

ERIKSON, E.H., *Enfance et Société*, Neufchâtel, Delachaux et Niestlé, 1959.

EVANS, E.B., Beth. SHUB and Marlene WEINSTEIN, *Day Care*, New York, Beacon Press, 1971.

FEIN, Greta and Alison CLARKE-STEWART, *Day Care in Context*, New York, Wiley, 1973.

GAGNÉ, G. et M. PAGE, *Études sur la langue parlée des enfants québécois,* Montréal, Presses de l'Université de Montréal, 1981.

GARON-DUPONT, Denise, *Les étapes du développement de l'enfant de la naissance à six ans,* document inédit préparé pour le comité conjoint du ministère des Affaires sociales, du ministère de l'Éducation et du ministère de l'Immigration sur les services de garde, Gouvernement du Québec, 1975.

GESELL, A. et F.L. ILG, *L'enfant de 5 à 10 ans,* Paris, Presses universitaires de France, 5e édition, 1967.

GESELL, A., *Le Jeune Enfant dans la civilisation moderne,* Paris, P.U.F., 11e édition, 1980.

GETTY, L. et M. LEMAY, *Prévenir le bégaiement, c'est possible,* Longueuil, Prolingua, 1980.

GORDON, IL., *Baby Learning Through Baby Play,* New York, St. Martin's Press, 1970.

GOUIN-DÉCARIE, Thérèse, « Intelligence et affectivité chez le jeune enfant », dans *Actualités pédagogiques et psychologiques,* Neufchâtel, Delachaux et Niestlé, 1962.

GOUIN-DÉCARIE, Thérèse et Marcelle RICARD, « La Socialisation du nourrisson », dans *La Recherche,* 139, décembre 1982.

GRIFFITHS, R., *Record Form for Use with the Griffiths' Mental Development Scale for Testing Babies from Birth to Two Years,* Londres, Child Development Research Center, 6e édition révisée, 1965.

GRIFFITHS, Ruth, *The Abilities of Young Children,* Londres, Child Development Research Center, 1970.

HONING, Alice, S. and R.J. LALLY, *Infant Caregiving,* New York, Media Projects incorporated, 1972.

KEYSERLING, Mary D., *Windows on Day Care,* New York, National Council of Jewish Women, 1972.

KRITCHEVSKY, Sybil, Elisabeth PRESCOTT and Lee WALLING, *Planning Environments for Young Children - Physical Space,* Washington, National association for the education of young children, 1969.

LEACH, P., *Votre enfant de la naissance à l'école,* Paris, Albin Michel, 1979.

LEVY, Janine, *L'éveil du tout-petit,* Paris, Éditions du Seuil, 1972.

LEZINE, Irène, « Rôle des jeux et des jouets dans la vie de la crèche », dans *Les soins aux enfants dans les crèches* (pp. 99-107), Cahiers de santé publique n° 24, Genève, Organisation mondiale de la santé, 1965.

LEZINE, Irène, *Psychopédagogie du premier âge,* Presses universitaires de France, Paris, 2e édition révisée, 1969.

MINISTÈRE DE L'ÉDUCATION, *Guide pédagogique : Le langage au préscolaire,* Gouvernement du Québec, Direction générale des moyens d'enseignement, 1982.

PAINTER, Geneviève, *Teach Your Baby,* New York, Simon and Schuster, 1971.

PIAGET, J., *La Naissance de l'intelligence chez l'enfant,* Actualités pédagogiques et psychologiques, Neufchâtel, Delachaux et Niestlé, 6e édition 1968, 1936.

PIAGET, J., *La Construction du réel chez l'enfant,* Actualités pédagogiques et psychologiques, Neufchâtel, Delachaux, 4e édition 1967, 1937.

PIAGET, J., *La Formation du symbole chez l'enfant. Imitation, jeu et rêve. Imitation et représentation,* Actualités pédagogiques et psychologiques, Neufchâtel, Delachaux et Niestlé, 4e édition 1968, 1945.

PIAGET, J., *Six études en psychologie,* Genève, Éditions Gonthier, 1964.

PICKLER, E., *Le Développement moteur des enfants,* Paris, Presses universitaires de France, 1979.

PIERRE-JOLY, Régine, *Programme de développement psycholinguistique, Rapport de recherche,* Bureau de psychologie, C.E.C.M., 1978.

PRESCOTT, Elizabeth, Elizabeth JONES and Sybil KIRTCHEVSKY, *Day Care as a Child-Rearing Environment,* Vol. II, Washington, National association for the education of young children, 1972.

PROVOST, M., D. GARON et C. LARSEN, *Impact des garderies sur les jeunes enfants. Où va le Québec?* Avis sur les services de garde, Comité de la santé mentale du Québec, ministère des Affaires sociales du Québec, 1983.

REYMOND-RIVIER, Berthe, *Le Développement social de l'enfant et de l'adolescent,* Bruxelles, Mardaga, 1977.

RICIUTTI, M.N. and A. WILLIS, *A Good Beginning for Babies. Guidelines for Group Care,* National association for the education of young children, Washington, D.C., 1975.

ROBINSON, H.B., « From Infancy Through School », dans *Children,* n° 16, 62, 1969.

STEVENS, Karen, « Equipping and Arranging a Room for Kindergarten », dans Sylvia Sunderlin, Nan Gran (Eds.) : *Housing for Early Childhood Education* (pp. 53-57), Washington, Association for childhood education international, 1968.

VAYER, Pierre, *Le Dialogue corporel: l'action éducative chez l'enfant de 2 à 5 ans,* Paris, Éducation psychomotrice, 1971.

VINEL, Claude, *Les Jeux et l'enfant de 5 à 12 ans*, Paris, Amphora, 1980.

WHITE, B.L., *The First Three Years of Life*, New York, Avon, 1978.

WOLFF, P.H., « What We Must and Must not Teach our Young Children from What We Know About Early Cognitive Development », dans *Clinics in Developmental medicine*, 33, 1969, pp. 7-19.

YARROW, L.J., « Mesures et définitions des effets du milieu pendant la toute première enfance », dans *Les Soins aux enfants dans les crèches* (pp. 145-154), Cahiers de santé publique n° 24, Genève, Organisation mondiale de la santé, 1965.

ZAZZO, René *et al.*, *Manuel pour l'examen psychologique de l'enfant*, Tome I, Suisse, Delachaux et Niestlé, 1958.

Lectures recommandées

CLOUTIER, R. et R. TESSIER, *La Garderie québécoise*, Québec, Les Éditions Laliberté, 1981.

CLOUTIER, R. et L. DIONNE, *L'Agressivité chez l'enfant*, Montmagny, Édisem Le Centurion, 1981.

COHEN, D., *Faut-il brûler Piaget?*, Paris, Retz, 1981.

DENNER, A. et J. DANA, *L'Environnement de l'enfant*, Paris, Seuil, 1973.

DE SAUSSOIS, N., *Activités en ateliers à l'école maternelle organisées / animées*, Collection Pratique pédagogique, numéro 27, Paris, Armand Collin, 1980.

DE SAUSSOIS, N., DUTILLEUL, M.B. et GILABERT, H., *Les enfants de 2 à 4 ans à l'école maternelle*, Collection Pratique pédagogique, numéro 40, Paris, Armand Collin, 1983.

DE SAUSSOIS, N., *Le temps qu'il fait, le temps qui passe, Activités pour les ateliers à l'école maternelle*, Collection Pratique pédagogique, numéro 36, Paris, Armand Collin, 1983.

LEACH, P., *Votre Enfant de la naissance à l'école*, Paris, Albin Michel, 1979.

LEWIS, D., *Le Langage secret de votre enfant*, Paris, Belfond, 1980.

MONTAGNER, H., *L'enfant et la communication*, Paris, Permond-Stock, 1978.

PAINTER, G., *Guide des activités du tout-petit*, Paris, Calmam-Levy, 1973.

Liste des publications de l'Office des services de garde à l'enfance

Brochures d'information (Disponibles en version anglaise)
- Choisir un service de garde
- Offrir un service de garde
- Travailler en service de garde

Feuillets d'information (Disponibles en version anglaise)
- L'aide financière aux parents
- Les subventions aux services de garde
- La formation du personnel de garde des garderies

Répertoire des services de garde en garderie, en milieu familial reconnus par une agence et en milieu scolaire
- Où faire garder nos enfants? 1989-1990

Périodique bimestriel distribué sur demande d'abonnement
- Petit à Petit
- Index du Petit à Petit, octobre 1989

Collection «Études et recherches»
- À propos des garderies, Situation des garderies au Québec en 1985. DUMAIS, France, *avec la collaboration de* Suzanne BOUCHARD et Michèle DORBES, (1986, 193 p.), volume 5

Collection «Diffusion»
- Programme d'intégration éducative famille-garderie. FALARDEAU, Isabelle et Richard CLOUTIER, (1986, 172 p.), volume 2
- L'utilisation des services de garde au Québec. PAYETTE, Micheline et François VAILLANCOURT, (1984, 140 p.), volume 1
- La garderie en bas âge, perspectives bio-sociales sur les relations humaines pendant la jeune enfance. Ouvrage collectif sous la direction de F.F. STRAYER, (1986, 96 p.), volume 3

Résumés de politique
- La politique d'intégration des enfants handicapés dans les services de garde (1986, 28 p.)
- La politique de l'Office des services de garde à l'enfance au regard de la gestion des ressources humaines dans les services de garde (1987, 39 p.)

Divers
- Conseils pratiques à l'intention des haltes-garderies BOURGAULT, Louise, (1988, 6 feuillets)

Office des services de garde à l'enfance
100, rue Sherbrooke Est
Montréal (Québec)
H2X 1C3

Téléphone
Pour les appels provenant de la région de Montréal: (514) 873-2323
Pour les appels provenant de l'extérieur de la région de Montréal: 1-800-363-0310

Publications concernant la petite enfance et les services de garde vendues aux Publications du Québec

Collection «Ressources et petite enfance»

- Entrez dans la ronde... l'intégration des enfants handicapés dans les services de garde. BAILLARGEON, Madeleine, (1986, 139 p.)

- La garderie, une expérience de vie pour l'enfant. BETSALEL-PRESSER, Raquel et Denise GARON, (1984, 121 p., 126 p., 122 p.)

  Volet 1: «L'âge de la recherche et de l'identification de 1 mois à 24 mois»
  Volet 2: «L'âge de la démarche vers l'autonomie de 2 à 3 ans»
  Volet 3: «L'âge de la conquête de l'initiative de 4 à 6 ans»

- Des enfants gardés... en sécurité. GUENETTE, Rachel, (1988, 262 p.)

- Des enfants gardés... en santé. PROULX, Monique et Monique RICHARD, (1985, 157 p.)

Divers

- Créer un cadre de vie en garderie. Guide d'élaboration d'un programme d'activités. BROUILLET, Chantale, (1988)

- Faire garder ses enfants au Québec, toute une histoire. DESJARDINS, Ghislaine, (1984, 78 p.)

- L'aménagement d'une garderie. JOHNSON, Michel et Michel TURCOTTE, (édition revue et corrigée, 1989, 72 p.)

- La mise sur pied d'une garderie. LAPLANTE, Hélène, Monique DESLONG-CHAMPS et Gilles ÉMOND, (1987, 72 p.)

- Les infections en garderie. Guide de prévention à l'usage des professionnels et professionnelles de la santé. ALARY, Michel et al., (1988, 272 p.)

Ressources pour la petite enfance

Centre de la petite enfance/Hull
45, rue Ducharme
Hull (Québec)
J8Y 3P7
(819) 778-3527

Comité petite enfance
388, rue Lamarre
Longueuil (Québec)
J4J 1T2
(514) 463-2850
(CLSC Longueuil est)

Service de prêt de matériel pour nourrissons
2, 7e Rue, C.P. 790
Forestville (Québec)
G0T 1E0
(418) 587-2212
(CLSC de Forestville)

Association canadienne pour la santé mentale
550, rue Sherbrooke ouest
Suite 1080
Montréal (Québec)
H3A 1B9
(514) 849-3291

Programme éducatif Passe-Partout
600, rue Fullum
8e étage
Montréal (Québec)
H2K 4L1
(514) 873-4670

Centres anti-poison

Hôpital Sainte-Justine
3175, chemin Côte Sainte-Catherine
Montréal (Québec)
H3T 1C5
(514) 731-4931

Hôpital de Montréal pour enfants
2300, rue Tupper
Montréal (Québec)
H3H 1P3
(514) 937-8511

Centre hospitalier de l'université Laval
2705, boul. Laurier
Sainte-Foy (Québec)
G1V 4G2
(418) 656-8090

Service consultatif sur le cadre de vie de l'enfant
Bureau national
Rue Albert
Ottawa (Ontario)
K1A 0P7

Cartoons by Addison
Additional Artwork by Kathleen Bullock

Print Edition ISBN 978-1-62950-018-8
E-book Edition ISBN 978-1-62950-019-5 (PDF)

World Book, Inc.
233 North Michigan Avenue
Suite 2000
Chicago, Illinois 60601 U.S.A.

For information about World Book and Incentive Publications products, call **1-800-967-5325,** or visit our websites at **www.worldbook.com** and **www.incentivepublications.com.**

Printed in the United States of America by Sheridan Books, Inc.
Chelsea, Michigan
1st Printing August 2014

Contents

The *School DayZ* plan is a way to address behavioral issues through vignettes that, though fictional, represent real situations in school.

- Through the metaphor of a story, teachers gain more skill at mediating events, and students are drawn into meaningful encounters with the issues of their everyday school lives.

- Kids grapple with problems, stretching their minds to offer solutions. They examine the emotions, social issues, and values that form the backdrop of the stories.

- As they do this, they practice a host of literacy skills—many of them in cooperation with classmates.

- And at the same time, they begin to understand the roots of their behavior and make positive changes based on this understanding.

- Other things change for the better as a part of this cooperative venture: self-esteem, pride, understanding, compassion, voice, power, and a sense of belonging to a community.

A Different Approach to Discipline

In today's middle school and high school environments, a maelstrom of problems, including bullying, cheating, stealing, harassment, truancy, vandalism, drug use, and chronic rudeness, result in countless detentions, suspensions, and expulsions. The nonstop disruptions steal hours of instructional time. Teachers are often at a loss as to how to address these behavior issues beyond the typical admonition or ejection from the class.

With *School DayZ,* the response to the problem shifts away from a punitive after-the-fact action. Instead, students are actively engaged—delving into the roots of the "fictional" problem—before a blow-up occurs in real classroom life. The story is a parable through which students . . .

   . . . confront a real issue head-on.

   . . . reflect on their own attitudes and values.

   . . . relate events and characters to their own experiences.

   . . . watch and analyze how characters act.

   . . . seek to understand underlying causes of behavior issues.

   . . . identify consequences of various actions.

   . . . imagine constructive ways to avoid or react to troublesome situations.

The Three-Part Lesson

1. Each *School DayZ* lesson begins with an "anticipation guide." This pre-reading activity asks students to consider whether they agree or disagree with statements related to the issue. The statements are not about the content but the understory of the content—the behavior of the class or of individuals. Each lesson brings an issue to the surface and hands it to the students to correct through a cognitive experience. The students respond to each statement, and discussion ensues.

2. Next, a short vignette is read. The collection of stories covers a variety of behavioral, social, academic, group, and personal issues that are familiar to middle and high school students and teachers.

3. The third part of the lesson offers questions that deepen student involvement in the dynamics of the issue. In a setting of cooperative literacy, students write and compare opinions, then discuss and expand ideas. Each lesson also includes an optional activity that offers another way to extend the process. Students script and stage scenes, compose interior monologues for characters, role-play alternative outcomes, create art representations, give advice to characters, or prepare arguments.

Focus on Core Values

In addition to confronting a common school problem or issue, each story also calls on students to examine the need for inner core values. These are values that enable humans in a group to get along together satisfactorily and that contribute to an enjoyable, successful life for all members of the community. Students identify traits that demonstrate core values related to the story—such traits as honesty, tolerance, humility, respect, self-control, and many others. In discussing the story, they define the traits and reflect on how their presence (or absence) affects the story and the characters in the story.

Literacy and Self-Management—A Winning Combination!

As they engage in the *School DayZ* process, students sharpen an amazing array of literacy skills, including reading, writing, reasoning, and speaking abilities. At the same time, they make great strides in understanding and managing their own behavior.

Make the Stories Your Own

Students and teachers inspired these stories when they asked for help with specific issues. Write your own stories about the very issues that trouble you most. Encourage students to do the same. (Pages 158-168 give clear guidelines to help you do this.)

6

SCHOOL DayZ

Classroom-Tested Success with SCHOOL DAYZ

The *School DayZ* plan has been tested in many classrooms and in many different schools. Teachers and students responded with great enthusiasm and begged the author for more stories. Here are just a few of the email messages sent to Ron Klemp:

"These stories are fun to work with."
6th-grade student

"I like talking about things that really happen to students in schools."
7th-grade student

"Some kids are pressuring me. Could you please write a *School DayZ* lesson about that?"
8th-grade student

It has been a positive experience working with the *School DayZ* plan. Issues such as bullying, peer pressure, and harmful gossip are not usually the subject of our lesson plans, but can have a devastating effect on our students' academic performance. Using the *School Dayz* lessons with my students gave me the perfect opportunity to discuss these issues with the class and together come up with strategies to deal with these situations. The students look forward to our discussions and tell me about issues they are dealing with so I can find a lesson to connect with their current need. I noticed much growth and maturity in my students during the course of the semester in how they approached dealing with these situations, and subsequently they were able to focus more on academics during instructional time. It is imperative that educators address all issues that impact our students' academic performance. *School DayZ* is an outstanding tool for addressing some of these concerns.
Thank you, Angela
middle school teacher and counselor

We did the *School DayZ* activity today, and it went really well. Some of the kids had a lot to say. It was really great to hear them talking about this stuff and sharing their opinions. We learned that one student feels picked on by the teachers. He says if three people are talking, he's the one who gets in trouble. Other students had great insights on why students find stealing to be easy.
Thanks so much, it really helped.
Anna, *middle school teacher*

I did a few more *School DayZ* lessons. The lessons generated rich discussion about controlling anger and how one can be angry without hurting others. It allowed the students to share positive ways to deal with one's anger. I am using the lessons in my homeroom also. Thank you for the great lessons.
Arum, *middle school teacher*

"Norm the Storm" is a HUGE hit. We started off with this story, and it was great. I have a student named Kaylee who is always goofing off, talking, and disrupting the class. Before the lesson, I had to give her several warnings. After a few minutes of discussing the statements concerning behavior, Kaylee quieted down. Then she picked up her binder to cover her face as we were reading the story. As we were answering the final questions, she actually contributed to the discussion. She did some self-reflection, and the lesson was immediately effective. It was awesome! I'm hoping this self-discipline will carry on!
Thanks! Don, *middle school teacher*

Using the SCHOOL DaYZ Stories to Teach and Strengthen CCSS

The School DayZ lessons offer fantastic opportunities to teach Common Core State Standards. Each lesson uses numerous English Language Arts anchor standards and grade-level content standards in grades six through eight. Many other reading, writing, speaking, listening, and language standards are easily woven into the School DayZ approach.

As a part of each lesson, students are asked to
- do close reading
- look for explicit ideas in the text
- make logical inferences from the text
- draw conclusions from the text
- cite evidence from the text to support inferences and conclusions
- find central ideas and themes in the story
- identify key details in the text
- examine characters--their actions, their words, their motivations
- analyze and compare the ways events and actions develop in the story
- compare the actions and viewpoints of characters in the story
- discuss story-related ideas with other students
- participate in reaching group consensus about story-related ideas
- speak coherently to explain ideas and conclusions
- listen to ideas and conclusions of other students
- write explanations, conclusions, and inferences based on evidence in the story
- make decisions about word and phrase meanings within the context of the story
- read a range of texts with real-life scenarios, issues, and values
- understand and interact with texts of challenging complexity

The next page (page 9) shows Common Core English Language Arts Standards strengthened by lessons in this book. Teachers can extend the connection with these standards and many others at the middle grades level by adding vocabulary exercises, broadening discussion and listening opportunities, expanding writing activities, or matching specific language skills to stories. See pages 13-14 for more ideas to extend learning in ways that will deepen CCSS understandings, skills, and processes.

Common Core State Standards Supported by the SCHOOL DAYZ Lessons
English Language Arts Standards, Grades 6-8

Number	Anchor Standard	Corresponding Grade-Level Standards
CCRA.R.1-3	**Reading: Key Ideas and Details** Read closely to determine what the text says explicitly and to make logical inferences from it; cite specific textual evidence when writing or speaking to support conclusions drawn from the text. Determine central ideas or themes of a text and analyze their development; summarize the key supporting details and ideas. Analyze how and why individuals, events, or ideas develop and interact over the course of a text.	RL.6.1-3; RL.7.1-3; RL.8.1-3
CCRA.R.4, 6	**Reading: Craft and Structure** Interpret words and phrases as they are used in a text, including technical, connotative, and figurative meanings, and analyze how specific words shape meaning or tone. Assess how a point of view or purpose shape the content and style of a text.	RL.6.4, 6; RL.7.4, 6; RL.8.4, 6
CCRA.R.8	**Reading: Integration of Knowledge and Ideas** Delineate and evaluate the argument and specific claims in a text, including the validity of the reasoning as well as the relevance and sufficiency of the evidence.	RL.6.8; RL.7.8; RL.8.8
CCRA.R.10	**Reading: Text Complexity** Read and comprehend complex literary and informational texts independently and proficiently.	RL.6.10; RL.7.10; RL.8.10
CCRA.W.3	**Writing: Test Types and Purposes** Write narratives to develop real or imagined experiences or events using effective technique, well-chosen details, and well-structured event sequences.	W.6.3; W.7.3; W.8.3
CCRA.W.4	**Writing: Production and Distribution of Writing** Produce clear and coherent writing in which the development, organization, and style are appropriate to task, purpose, and audience.	W.6.4, W.7.4, W.8.4
CCRA.SL.1	**Speaking and Listening: Comprehension and Collaboration** Prepare for and participate effectively in a range of conversations and collaborations with diverse partners, building on others' ideas and expressing their own clearly and persuasively.	SL.6.1a-d; SL.7.1a-d; SL.8.1a-d
CCRA.SL.4	**Speaking and Listening: Presentation of Knowledge and Ideas** Present information, findings, and supporting evidence such that listeners can follow the line of reasoning and the organization, development, and style are appropriate to task, purpose, and audience.	SL.6.4; SL.7.4; SL.8.4
CCRA.L.1-2	**Language: Conventions of Standard English** Demonstrate command of the conventions of standard English grammar and usage when writing or speaking. Demonstrate command of the conventions of standard English capitalization, punctuation, and spelling when writing.	L.6.1-2; L.7.1-2; L.8.1-2
CCRA.L.3	**Language: Knowledge of Language** Apply knowledge of language to understand how language functions in different contexts, to make effective choices for meaning or style, and to comprehend more fully when reading or listening.	L.6.3; L.7.3; L.8.3
CCRA.L.4-5	**Language: Vocabulary Acquisition and Use** Determine or clarify the meaning of unknown and multiple-meaning words and phrases by using context clues, analyzing meaningful word parts, and consulting general and specialized reference materials, as appropriate. Demonstrate understanding of figurative language, word relationships, and nuances in word meanings.	L.6.4-5; L.7.4-5; L.8.4-5

How to Use the SCHOOL DAYZ Lessons

Follow these steps to guide the process that involves students in meaningful reading, consideration of issues, discussion, critical thinking, writing, and problem solving. These lessons will ultimately lead students toward engagement with their own behavior.

I. Before you read …

- Make copies of the "Response Sheet" for the *School DayZ* experiences. (This is found on page 12.) Give one of these to each student when beginning a new lesson.

- Make copies of the two pages for each story. (Copy these back to back.) Distribute the pages to students, with the "Before & After" side facing up. Note that these pages are NOT intended to be consumable but should be collected for repeated use.

- Students consider the anticipatory statements and respond individually. These statements are found in the "Before You Read" section. They write their responses on the Response Sheet. Note that the directions ask students to check statements with which they agree and write a note explaining their response to each statement.

- Students gather in groups or pods. Together, they decide if they can agree on a response to each statement. Gently push groups to reach a closed-end consensus—where they all try to agree or disagree with the statement. They may not come to an agreement, but trying to do so leads to a lively discussion of the issue.

- The teacher then facilitates a discussion about each statement to determine the collective "wisdom" of the class.

II. Read the story …

This can be done orally, silently, or both. The teacher may read to the class; a student may read to the class; students may read to each other; or students may read silently.

III. After you read . . .

- Students respond individually in writing to the study guide questions (found in the "After You Read" section). The Response Sheet forms should be used for answers.
- Next, students meet in their *pods* (groups) to determine if they can agree on answers to the questions.
- The teacher facilitates a whole-group discussion. During the discussion, approach these kinds of things:

  A. Have students identify the problem or issue in the story.

  B. Have students identify the problem from the perspective of each character in the story.

  C. Ask students to discuss whether or not the problem is realistic.

  D. Ask students to connect the story to their own lives, thinking about whether they can identify instances or similarities to incidents they have witnessed or experienced. Allow time for storytelling.

  E. Ask students to identify core values or traits that story characters have or need as related to the issue.

  F. Discuss the answers to the questions that came from the pods' responses.

  G. Discuss the message, metaphor, irony, or other insight offered by the cartoons accompanying the story.

  H. Request that students offer some concluding remarks regarding how situations could be avoided, changed, or resolved. Include specific actions recommended by students that could be taken in such a situation. Also include ways students think behaviors or attitudes in their own lives might be changed by the experience of reading and discussing the story.

IV. Think more about the story . . . (optional)

If time permits, pursue the optional "Think About It" section. This pushes students to expand their reasoning skills and deepen their responses to the story.

Flexible Lessons

The plan above is a suggestion. Adjust the steps, the focus of the discussion, or the process as best fits your students and your class needs.

SCHOOL DAYZ

Response Sheet for

_____
story title

Before You Read

Carefully read each statement on the School DayZ sheet. If you agree with a statement, put an X on the short line to the left of its number. Otherwise, leave it blank. Then, on the longer lines, write notes to yourself explaining why you made your choices.

_____ 1. _____

_____ 2. _____

_____ 3. _____

_____ 4. _____

_____ 5. _____

After You Read

Read the questions that follow the School DayZ story. In the space below, write your answer to each question. Use complete sentences.

1. _____

_____

2. _____

_____

3. _____

_____

4. _____

_____

5. _____

_____

Name _____

EXTEND THE LEARNING

The School DayZ stories form the heart of this book's mission. Each lesson brings student focus to an issue. With the anticipatory exercise ("Before You Read"), students gather in small groups to start exploring their background knowledge, experience, biases, and beliefs on the issue. The story itself draws students into a familiar scenario that involves a problem for some of the characters. The "After You Read" questions and "Think About It" suggestions ask students to engage even further with the real-life issue and dig deeply to offer solutions.

Beyond the lesson, there are many other questions, discussions, and activities that can extend engagement with the issues and with literacy skills. Look for opportunities to do this. **However** (and this is a strong however!), take care not to overextend. If every lesson is accompanied by more activities, assignments, or projects, students will lose their enthusiasm for the stories or lose the emphasis on the problem solving that affects management of their own behavior. But when an issue naturally grabs deep interest, you might find ways to strengthen more skills and move toward deeper understandings. Here are some ideas:

Good Questions to Accompany Reading or Listening

• Model and teach the asking of questions such as these. Students can apply these to their discussions of the story, as well as to their interactions with one another's ideas:

What is the author's purpose? Does the writer accomplish his/her purpose? How can you tell?

What can you infer from this sentence? What parts of the story are behind your inferences?

What conclusion have you reached? What led you to this conclusion?

What is the theme of the story? What portions of text establish the theme?

How is the meaning of this phrase different from the meaning of that one?

What is _____'s (character name) view of the situation? How do you know?

How do the events in the first paragraph affect the events in the rest of the story?

How does the writer use humor (or dialogue) to further the message of the story?

What is the effect of using this word (or phrase or idea)?

How does this idea affect one that came after it?

How are these words:_____ used in this passage?

What attitudes lie behind _____'s (character name) behavior? How can you tell?

What portions of the story are most helpful to you as you consider a solution for the problem?

What mood builds throughout the text? What passages in the story create this mood and help it build?

How does the illustration compare to the written text? How does it add to or change the message?

The character _____ claims to be neutral on the issue. What portions of the text confirm or contradict this claim?

What does _____ (character name) say that changed the situation? How does the text show this change?

Debates and Arguments

- Give students a chance to share their "After You Read" responses and ask questions about (though not debate) one another's ideas.

- Students might be drawn to debate or prepare written arguments on hot topics. This will offer great opportunities for extending reading, research, writing, speaking, and listening skills. The issues and core traits tackled by the stories (see pages 15 and 16) provide rich substance for spoken or written arguments!

Reflections, Journals, Interviews

- As an individual student (or a class) grapples with one of the problems, issues, or traits, he (or she, or they) can record and reflect on a personal process of examining and changing behavior. This can take a variety of forms, such as journal entries, essays, poems, blogs, or video journals.

- Students can create, administer, and summarize interviews or surveys related to the topics, issues, or core traits. These processes can help them find out about about others' experiences or beliefs or about how the story-reading experience affected behavior.

More School DayZ Stories

- Students love to write their own stories. (Many stories in this book were inspired or co-written by students.) Creating a School DayZ-style lesson strengthens a long list of literacy skills and standards. Pages 158-168 give detailed instructions for writing their own School DayZ lessons. Students can use one of the story templates or create their own formats. Once original stories/lessons are created, use them as lessons for the class!

Vocabulary

- Help students get into the habit of quickly noting any words or phrases that are unfamiliar. Encourage them to make decisions during their reading about what the word or phrase means.

- Give a brief time right after story-reading and before the "After You Read" exercise for students to ask about a word or look it up IF he or she feels that the "After You Read" exercise cannot be done without understanding the word. Caution: take care not to interrupt the flow of the post-reading response by stopping to conduct a vocabulary lesson.

- After the post-reading activities, ask students to point out words or phrases that were unfamiliar or confusing and share their ideas about the meanings. They can consult references to further explore meanings.

- Keep a list of words, phrases, or expressions from the School DayZ stories. Find ways to use these in other classroom activities. Challenge students to use the words often.

ISSUES, OVERVIEW

Here is an at-a-glance view of the issues, topics, themes, and problems that are found in the *School DayZ* stories. Page numbers direct you to stories that focus on these topics.

Issue	Story Numbers
Accusations — 14, 22, 61, 65, 69	
Advocacy — 28, 34, 50, 54, 57	
Anger — 4, 19, 20, 21, 22, 28, 29, 34, 39, 41, 45, 46, 56, 57, 51	
Arguing — 22, 28, 41, 57	
Assemblies — 2, 21, 40	
Attitude — 2, 19, 20, 21, 23, 26, 27, 34, 39, 41, 42, 45, 46, 49, 65	
Breaking rules — 7, 8, 12, 13, 17, 19, 21, 25, 26, 31, 32, 37, 38, 40, 58, 66	
Bullying — 2, 3, 15, 23, 34, 39, 45, 48, 50, 67, 69	
Bus behavior — 67	
Cell phone use — 1, 17, 35	
Cheating — 14, 38	
Cliques — 34, 36, 48, 65, 67	
Destructive behavior — 9, 13, 21, 25, 32, 52, 55, 56, 66	
Detention, suspension — 13, 40, 58	
Discomfort or fears about school abilities — 11, 27, 30, 37, 46, 51, 53, 63, 68	
Discrimination — 11, 15, 23, 28, 56	
Disrespect to other students — 1, 2, 6, 10, 11, 15, 16, 23, 34, 37, 40, 42, 48, 55, 67	
Disrespect to teachers or other adults — 16, 18, 19, 20, 27, 46, 62	
Disruptive behavior — 2, 10, 13, 17, 20, 27, 53, 57, 59, 60, 62	
Dress code — 7, 19, 44	
Drugs — 32, 47	
Embarrassment, shame — 1, 2, 6, 11, 15, 19, 24, 29, 30, 37, 46, 51	
Exclusion, inclusion — 15, 23, 34, 48, 50, 56, 63, 65	
Fairness — 7, 19, 22, 30, 61	
Feelings/fears about school — 3, 30, 37, 46, 51, 64, 67, 68, 69, 70	
Fighting — 13, 22, 28, 34, 39, 41, 54, 57	
Friendships, relationships — 5, 6, 8, 14, 21, 23, 24, 29, 32, 33, 35, 36, 37, 38, 41, 43, 47, 48, 56, 57, 65, 69, 70	
Gangs — 21, 43	
Gossip, rumors — 6, 18, 48, 65, 69	
Grading issues — 38, 46, 54	

Issue	Story Numbers
Group work — 42	
Homework — 5, 38, 42	
Hypocrisy — 65	
Impatience — 20, 60	
Inattention — 10, 19, 29, 59	
Individual differences — 10, 11, 15, 34, 45, 50, 51, 56, 59, 64	
Internet and video game activity — 9, 52, 69, 70	
Jealousy — 29, 36, 41, 56, 65	
Lying — 22, 45	
New student — 5, 37, 51	
Over-commitment — 33	
Parents — 35, 54	
Peer pressure — 1, 2, 5, 6, 9, 21, 31, 32, 35, 37, 38, 43, 47, 57, 63, 67, 69, 70	
Personal problems affecting schoolwork — 19, 29, 37, 53, 67	
Popularity (or lack of it) — 11, 15, 20, 23, 24, 36, 63	
Pranks — 1, 13, 17, 21, 40, 55, 66	
Profanity — 4	
Romance — 8, 41, 43, 55	
Rudeness, meanness — 2, 6, 11, 15, 20, 23, 28, 32, 34, 37, 39, 45, 47, 48, 50, 56, 57, 62, 65, 67	
Self-image (including body image) — 11, 24, 36, 63, 68	
Selling stuff at school — 12	
Sexual harassment — 49, 67	
Skateboard behavior — 56	
Skipping school — 31, 37	
Stealing (or "borrowing") — 22, 35, 57, 61	
Stress — 29, 33, 67, 68	
Success (or lack of it) with schoolwork — 2, 5, 30, 33, 37, 38, 42, 43, 46, 51, 53, 54, 59, 63, 64, 68	
Teachers — 3, 4, 16, 18, 22, 30	
Teasing, name-calling — 2, 3, 6, 10, 11, 15, 19, 28, 34, 37, 48, 50, 65, 67	
Trust — 16, 29, 36, 41, 42, 47, 61	
Vandalism — 13, 21, 66	
Vanity, conceit — 20, 23, 34, 36, 48, 49, 65, 67	
Violence — 21, 29, 34, 41, 45	

CORE TRAITS, OVERVIEW

These are traits that demonstrate specific inner core values—positive traits that educators and parents hope kids will integrate into their way of thinking and their actions. Page numbers direct readers to stories that link to specific traits.

Trait	Stories
Acceptance	11, 15, 18, 23, 24, **28**, 32, 34, 36, 37, 42, 47, 48, 51, 61, 63, 65, 68, 69
Achievement	2, **5**, 24, 33, 38, 42, 43, 46, 51, 53, 54, 63, 64, 68
Advocacy	15, 18, 28, 34, **50**, 57
Appropriate behavior	1, 2, 4, 8, 9, 10, 13, 17, 19, 21, 25, 26, 27, 30, 31, 32, 34, 40, 41, 47, 48, 49, 53, **55**, 60, 62, 66, 67
Appropriate dress	**7**, 9, 19, 44
Caring, empathy, understanding	1, 2, 6, 10, 11, 14, 15, 18, 23, 24, 27, 28, 29, 30, 34, 38, 48, 50, **53**, 59, 62, 65
Confidence, self-confidence	3, 11, 24, 30, **51**, 67, 68
Cooperation	16, 20, 26, **42**, 57
Courage	2, 24, 28, 32, 34, **39**, 47, 67, 68
Courtesy, kindness, encouragement to others	1, **2**, 10, 11, 15, 16, 18, 21, 23, 24, 26, 27, 28, 34, 40, 48, 50, 60, 61, 62, 65, 67, 68
Fairness	**22**, 33, 38, 42, 61
Friendship	6, 14, 21, 23, 24, 29, 32, 33, **36**, 38, 43, 47, 56, 69, 70
Good judgment	4, 5, 6, 8, 9, 12, 13, 14, 17, 18, 20, 25, 31, 32, 33, 35, 36, 38, 40, 41, 43, 44, 47, 53, 55, 56, 60, 61
Honesty, truthfulness	14, 22, 24, 35, **38**, 45, 47, 61, 65
Humility	**20**, 23, 34, 36, 48, 49, 65
Inclusive behavior	15, 23, 28, 34, **48**, 49, 65
Patience	20, 60
Problem-solving ability	All stories
Respect	1, 2, 4, 6, 11, 15, 16, **17**, 18, 19, 21, 23, 24, 25, 26, 27, 28, 29, 34, 37, 39, 40, 41, 45, 48, 50, 53, 55, 56, 61, 62, 65, 67, 69
Responsibility	1, 5, 10, 14, 16, 17, 20, 21, **25**, 26, 27, 31, 32, 33, 35, 38, 40, 42, 45, 46, 47, 52, 59, 60, 61, 66
Safe behavior	9, 13, 21, 29, 32, 41, 47, 52, 56, 66
Self-advocacy, self-care	7, 9, 29, 30, 32, 43, 47, 51, 52, **54**, 64
Self-control, self-discipline	2, **10**, 13, 16, 19, 20, 21, 22, 27, 28, 29, 34, 40, 41, 45, 53, 55, 56, 59, **60**, 62
Self-esteem, self-respect, positive self-image	3, 9, **11**, **24**, 27, 29, 30, 32, 36, 39, 41, 43, 47, **49**, 51, 53, 63, 64, 68
Tolerance	10, 11, **15**, 18, 23, 28, 34, 37, 48, 50, 57, 59, 65, 69
Trust, trustworthiness	16, **29**, 34, 36, 41, 47, 61, 65

Bolded numbers indicate stories where students are asked to write and discuss definitions for the trait.

THE
SCHOOL DAYZ
STORIES

Seventy Stories

Along with

Pre-Reading and Post-Reading Literacy
Experiences

CAUGHT ON CAMERA

Bo did so well on his most recent math test that his parents gave him $50. He had been saving for a long time for a cell phone with all the latest features. And now he finally had the picture phone he had been wanting. He couldn't wait to show everyone, especially his best friend Luke.

Hanging around outside school before the bell one morning, Bo pulled the prized phone out of his backpack.

"Wicked awesome!" Luke whispered. "Take a picture, already! Kate's not looking and she has a zit! Take her picture."

Bo snapped Kate's picture secretly. It really cracked him up when he saw it. Later that day, he put it on the Web for the whole school to see, and he told people to "check it out!"

The next day, Bo's teacher pulled him aside and sent him to the principal's office. Kate, her parents, and his own parents were waiting for him.

Principal Adams started the discussion: "Bo, Kate complained that you took a picture of her and posted it on the Web. Is that true?"

"Yeah, but so what? I didn't do anything wrong! It's a free country!" Bo said.

"Did you ask Kate if you could take her picture?" the principal asked.

Bo looked at the floor, and then at his parents. "No, but why should I? I mean, she's out there in public. Everyone could see her anyway."

Kate's father shook his head. "When you put the picture on the Web, you added a caption that told people to check out Kate's 'monster' zit! Do you think that's appropriate?"

Kate loves social networking— but not tonight.

"I don't know," Bo admitted. "What difference does it make? She didn't try to hide her zit. Besides, Luke told me to take her picture!"

18

Before You Read

Consider each statement below. Decide whether or not you agree with it. Use your Response Sheet to record your decisions and reasons.

_____ 1. It is okay to take someone's picture without his or her permission.

_____ 2. Using cell phones to take pictures doesn't violate anyone's privacy.

_____ 3. People should not be allowed to use cell phones for taking pictures.

_____ 4. New technology should be used in any way that is possible.

_____ 5. Anyone who takes a picture without permission should be charged with a crime!

Sweeet!

After You Read

On your own, answer the questions below. Write your answers on the Response Sheet.

1. Why do you think Bo wanted to take Kate's picture?

2. How do you think Kate feels about this whole issue?

3. If you were the principal, what action would you take?

4. How do you think Luke is involved in this incident?

5. Should there be any rules about the use of picture cell phones at school?

Think About It

Imagine that you are one of Kate's parents. Write a letter to Bo that might convince him to think differently about the way he uses his phone.

AUDITORIUM MADNESS

Word spread around the school that the teachers were planning a Friday awards assembly for end-of-the-semester projects. Excitement grew, and many students really looked forward to it. After the presentations, students would get a chance to view the film *Demons in the Hood* created by Mrs. Hanratty's English 10 class. Finally, Mr. Moon would show his annual slide show—a collection of candid pictures of students—set to rap and rock music.

Jesse worked even harder on his project when he heard about the upcoming assembly. He had never won anything before, and once he decided to go for it, he was all business.

On the day of the event, students crowded into the auditorium at the start of the period. Confident of winning an award, Jesse hurried to find a seat. During the week, his teachers had made positive comments about his project. Even the principal had given him a compliment on his work.

As usual, the assembly is a showcase for respectful behavior.

The program got underway. Students had to be reminded several times to calm down and maintain self-control. Shelly and her friends were being loud and boisterous, as usual. Shawn and his gang sat in the back making rude comments to everyone within earshot. While teachers were busy getting awards organized, more kids joined in the rowdiness—making crude remarks and shoving anyone trying to get to a seat.

When the presentation of awards started, the ruckus just got worse. Some kids in the audience seemed to think it was cool to badger the winning students who stepped forward to accept awards. Mean, nasty comments were made about their personal appearance, intelligence, or friends.

Names were being called in alphabetical order, and Jesse knew his was coming up soon. He was embarrassed and nervous. He wasn't sure if all his hard work was going to be worth the razzing.

Before You Read

Consider each statement below. Decide whether or not you agree with it. Use your Response Sheet to record your decisions and reasons.

_____ 1. It is acceptable to make loud and rude comments from the audience as long as everyone laughs.

_____ 2. There is no such thing as "self-control" for teenagers. They need outside control.

_____ 3. People don't really care about earning awards at assemblies anyway.

_____ 4. Students get awards because they play by the rules.

_____ 5. If assemblies get out of control, it is because the program is not interesting or relevant to the students.

CERTIFICATE OF ACHIEVEMENT

This award is presented to

Jesse

For being the biggest oser!

This is the award Jesse fears getting.

After You Read

On your own, answer the questions below. Write your answers on the Response Sheet.

1. Why would some students in the story be looking forward to an awards assembly?

2. Why do you think some of the people in the story would be so rude to their classmates?

3. How do you think this teasing could have been prevented?

4. What do you think the teachers should have done after the behavior erupted?

5. How would you define the term "courtesy"? (Use your own words.)

Think About It

Write a diary entry about the assembly experience as Jesse might write it. Tell what happened and how he is feeling now.

BEING IN MIDDLE SCHOOL

Mrs. McLean pulled an essay from her pile. "Good grief!" she exclaimed. "The assignment was to write about what it's like to be in middle school. Some of the kids make it sound as if they're in reform school. How can we get these guys to understand that they're here to learn exciting things?"

Mr. Jones chuckled. "When you think about it, we went through the same issues when we were in middle school, or junior high as we called it then. It's no different."

"I agree, but from a teacher's point of view, some of these essays are discouraging!"

She read two that she had just received:

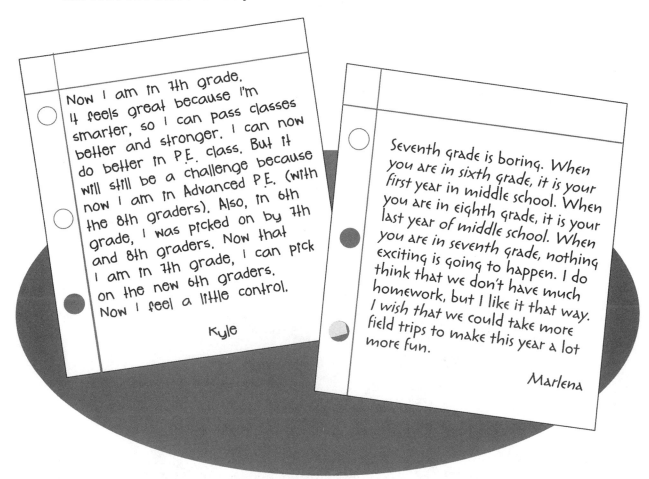

Now I am in 7th grade. It feels great because I'm smarter, so I can pass classes better and stronger. I can now do better in P.E. class. But it will still be a challenge because now I am in Advanced P.E. (with the 8th graders). Also, in 6th grade, I was picked on by 7th and 8th graders. Now that I am in 7th grade, I can pick on the new 6th graders. Now I feel a little control.

Kyle

Seventh grade is boring. When you are in sixth grade, it is your first year in middle school. When you are in eighth grade, it is your last year of middle school. When you are in seventh grade, nothing exciting is going to happen. I do think that we don't have much homework, but I like it that way. I wish that we could take more field trips to make this year a lot more fun.

Marlena

Mr. Jones shook his head. "I see your point."

"One thing is sure," replied Mrs. McLean. "I am going to think about how I can make my classes more interesting. If I have students that are bored, then I'll continue to have problems."

SIXTH GRADE   SEVENTH GRADE   EIGHTH GRADE

One student's view of
being in middle school

Before You Read

Consider each statement below. Decide whether or not you agree with it. Use your Response Sheet to record your decisions and reasons.

_____ 1. The second year of middle school is not as fun or important as the first year.

_____ 2. Middle school gets harder with each grade in all ways—not just academically.

_____ 3. The only difference between middle and elementary school is that you have more teachers each day.

_____ 4. Any student who is new to a middle school is going to be teased or harassed.

_____ 5. The hardest part about middle school is worrying about what other students might think of you.

After You Read

On your own, answer the questions below. Write your answers on the Response Sheet.

1. Why do you think some kids find middle school to be boring?

2. In your opinion, how is a student's experience different in the different grades of middle school or junior high?

3. One essay describes the tradition of older students picking on younger students. What are your thoughts on this issue?

4. What do you think the teachers learned or should learn from reading these two essays?

5. What part of either essay seems most familiar to your experience?

Think About It

Create your own short essay describing what it is like to be in your grade or in middle or high school, in general.

SHE SAID WHAT?!?!?

Yesterday in my social studies class, two students got into a huge argument and started cursing at each other. The teacher totally freaked out. She grabbed each kid by an arm and started yelling. Then she said **it**. She used a word that we never hear our teachers use! I was so shocked that my mouth dropped open.

The teacher goes ballistic.

Later, I tried to explain to my friend Matt what had happened. I told him it didn't seem right for Mrs. Applegate to swear at students even if they were acting like jerks.

"So what?" said Matt. "I mean—we hear that word every day. Kids say that **and** more all the time. Big deal!"

Matt's attitude got on my nerves. "I suppose you think it's okay for anyone to use that word whenever they feel like it—even a teacher?"

"Sure, why not? Look, Alison, you'll probably hear it again when you walk to your next class." Matt got a half smile on his face. "Lighten up; people swear all the time. These days, swearing on TV shows and in movies—even in real life—is normal."

"It might not bother you, Matt, but bad language upsets a lot of other people." I thought for a second. "If your mother heard you swearing, what would she do?"

Matt laughed. "Shoot, she swears a lot more than I do!"

I doubted that. "Well, if my mother ever caught me swearing, I'd be in big trouble." I picked up my backpack. "So, let me get this straight. If your teachers talked the way some kids talk in the halls, you don't think it would matter? What if you were working at your dream job, would you use that language?"

Matt screwed up his face. "Well, if you're talking about my dream job, that would be different."

"Why?" I could tell our conversation had caused him to think.

He shrugged. "I don't know. It's just **different** . . . a different situation."

I have #@%*& had it with you two!!

Before You Read

Consider each statement below. Decide whether or not you agree with it. Use your Response Sheet to record your decisions and reasons.

_____ 1. People are too uptight about profanity.

_____ 2. If we really do have "freedom of speech," people can say what they want.

_____ 3. It's impolite to swear in public—no matter what the situation.

_____ 4. Cursing is just a way of expressing yourself.

_____ 5. Calling people names and swearing is usually just done in fun.

After You Read

On your own, answer the questions below. Write your answers on the Response Sheet.

1. Why do you think people use profanity so often these days?

2. Is it ever appropriate for a teacher to swear in a classroom?

3. What makes it okay for kids to swear, but not adults?

4. Why do you think some people get embarrassed when others use profanity?

5. What are some situations in which it might be okay to use profanity?

Think About It

What do you imagine the teacher is thinking now? Write a list of statements or questions she might be saying to herself or a close friend.

HOMEWORK (OR NOT)

Julie left school and headed straight to the library. On her way, she ran into Brad and Ashley, two of her new friends. Julie had recently moved to the school and was just getting to know some of the students in her classes.

"Hi, Julie," said Brad. "What's up?"

"Hi, Brad. Hi, Ashley," she answered, waving and trying not to drop her books.

Brad gave her a hand. "Hey, we're going over to the skateboard park where the really cool kids hang out. Wanna come along?"

Julie hesitated. She'd been one of the top students in her old school and she was used to spending most of her after-school time studying and doing homework. "Thanks for the invite, but maybe next time. I have to get a book from the library. Then I have to write that paper Mr. Ruiz assigned in Science today. Wow, did you guys finish it already?"

Unlike Brad and Ashley, the dog takes homework seriously.

Brad laughed. "Finish? Heck no, we haven't even started. It's just a waste of time. Ruiz never even grades those papers!"

"Yeah," Ashley echoed. "We don't do homework if we can get away with it. We have more interesting, fun things to do! Teachers just give it to please the parents, anyway."

"If you don't do your homework, how can you get a good grade?" Julie felt bewildered.

"They always let us make it up," Brad explained with a shrug. "So why bother, if there's something better to do like skateboarding? Even when I have to do **something** to keep my folks off my back, 10 minutes later it's a done deal! Half the time I don't even bother turning it in."

"Interesting. Well, thanks again for the invite," Julie said, "but I'm meeting a study partner at the library. Maybe I'll see you guys tomorrow?"

Julie walked on, still wondering about their conversation.

Before You Read

Consider each statement below. Decide whether or not you agree with it. Use your Response Sheet to record your decisions and reasons.

_____ 1. Most students think homework is a waste of time.

_____ 2. Students who do their homework usually get good grades.

_____ 3. Teachers mostly assign homework because parents want it.

_____ 4. A student who doesn't do the homework but gets A's on the test should get an A in the class.

After You Read

On your own, answer the questions below. Write your answers on the Response Sheet.

1. Why do you think teachers assign homework?

2. How would you respond to Brad's comments about homework?

3. What do you think that Julie will do after this discussion?

4. What suggestions would you give teachers regarding homework?

5. How would you define the term "achievement"? (Use your own words.)

Think About It

What might Julie be thinking about this situation? Draw a thought balloon. In it, write something to show what is on her mind.

SATURDAY NIGHT RUMORS

When Shaunna heard the buzz around school about Melissa, she got mad. She knew from personal experience that unsubstantiated rumors (like this one) hurt people. When she was in elementary school, she'd been the subject of a nasty rumor that had caused her family a lot of pain. Now the same thing was happening to her best friend.

The rumored "incident" had occurred at Mark's party the Saturday before. Everyone knew his party would be a blast because his parents were expected to be out of town for the weekend. Shaunna hadn't gone. She'd been on a trip with her family and missed out on all the "fun."

On Saturday night, her friend Melissa had gone to the party without her. Now, the word around school was that something happened—something that involved her friend. Melissa wouldn't talk about it, and Shaunna felt weird asking. She could see how much her friend was hurting, though.

Jenna and Brianna, friends of both Melissa and Shaunna, supposedly knew what happened Saturday night. Shaunna was reluctant to ask them because that might just feed the rumor. She knew firsthand the embarrassment and humiliation that Melissa must be feeling, but she didn't know how to help.

If only a certain jerk in Melissa's class hadn't opened his big mouth, maybe the rumor wouldn't have started! This guy, R.J., came to school on Monday morning and taunted Melissa in front of the whole class: "Hey, Melissa, what's this I hear about you at Mark's party?"

Even though Melissa ignored him and walked away, everyone had heard the rumor. It quickly spun out in a dozen directions. Now the whole school was gossiping about Melissa and what they thought had happened Saturday night.

Before You Read

Consider each statement below. Decide whether or not you agree with it. Use your Response Sheet to record your decisions and reasons.

_____ 1. It's okay to pass on a rumor if it's just to my friends.

_____ 2. Rumors almost always get passed on.

_____ 3. Talking about others is fine as long as they don't find out.

_____ 4. Sometimes a person passes on a rumor just so they can be seen as the only person who knows what's happening.

_____ 5. It doesn't matter if I tell a rumor or if someone else tells, since people are going to find out anyway.

After You Read

On your own, answer the questions below. Write your answers on the Response Sheet.

1. How would you analyze Shaunna's problem?

2. What do you think Melissa could do to stop people from talking about her?

3. Why would Shaunna describe the rumor as "unsubstantiated"?

4. What is a good ending for this story?

5. What would you say to someone (like R.J.) who likes to get into other people's business?

Think About It

Create a caption for the cartoon on the story page.

DO YOUR PANTS HANG LOW?

Isaiah sauntered into Washington Middle School with his best buddy, Al. "Looks like another boring day."

"You got that right," Al agreed. Then he pointed at the assistant principal and a boy down the hall. "Hey, isn't that Derek getting yelled at by Mr. Henry?"

"I'm not letting you into school looking like a gangster," Mr. Henry insisted. His voice rose when he said the word **gangster**.

Derek thinks Mr. Henry could use a little sagging himself.

Derek pleaded, "I am not saggin'! This is the way we like to wear our pants. It's the style. I'm not a gang-banger! Look around, everyone dresses this way." He pointed at Isaiah and Al. "Even wimps like those two wear their pants down—like I do!"

"Hey!" Isaiah bristled. "Who are you callin' a wimp?"

"Hold it!" Mr. Henry put up a hand. He turned and scrutinized Isaiah and Al. "Come here, boys. Raise your shirts!"

"Oh, man," Isaiah thought, lifting his shirt. A minute earlier and he would have made it to class. Al looked at him and groaned. Sure enough, both boys had boxers showing for all to see.

Mr. Henry pointed toward his office. "Come with me, all three of you. I'm calling your parents to take you home. And don't come back until you are properly dressed!"

"Wait!" Isaiah remembered a court case in Florida that he had read about. "Mr. Henry," Isaiah said politely. "I don't mean any disrespect, but you can't tell us how to wear our pants. A court of law said you have no right—that sagging pants are just a style choice."

Mr. Henry's brows came together as he looked at Isaiah. "As long as I'm in charge of this school's dress code, you **have** no rights. If I say 'no' to baggy pants, then that's the rule."

"Man, this is just not fair!" Isaiah grumbled. Al and Derek nodded their heads and slouched in seats in Mr. Henry's office.

Mr. Henry held out the phone. "Okay, Derek, call home."

Isaiah turned to Derek. "By the way, who were you callin' a wimp?"

30

Before You Read

Consider each statement below. Decide whether or not you agree with it. Use your Response Sheet to record your decisions and reasons.

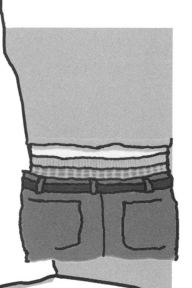

_____ 1. Kids should have the right to wear what they want to school.

_____ 2. The idea of a school dress code is out of date.

_____ 3. You can't assume someone is a troublemaker just because he wears baggy pants.

_____ 4. If underwear is showing, the pants are too low.

_____ 5. It is a waste of teachers' time to have to enforce dress codes.

After You Read

On your own, answer the questions below. Write your answers on the Response Sheet.

1. Why do you think Mr. Henry is so opposed to the boys' style?

2. What do you think about the way Isaiah handled the situation?

3. Is it a good idea for schools to control students' attire?

4. What should the boys have done?

5. How would you define the term "appropriate" as related to clothing at school? (Use your own words.)

Think About It

With a partner, create the dialogue that might take place between Mr. Henry and Derek's parents.

THE PDA BAN

Alicia and Frankie were in love. True love. They knew they would be soul mates forever. They spent every free moment together, meeting between class periods, sitting together at lunch, and walking home together after school.

One spring day between second and third periods, Frankie felt he just had to show Alicia how much he loved her. He grabbed her in his arms and gave her a big kiss. Just then, the principal, Ms. Delkins, rounded the corner. Her eyes narrowed, and she scowled. She took each student by an arm and separated the two.

"Stop that!" she said sternly.

Frankie and Alicia looked at her in surprise. "Why? We weren't doing anything wrong."

"We don't allow PDA's here. You should know that." Ms. Delkins sounded angry.

"PDA's?" Alicia asked.

"Public displays of affection!" Ms. Delkins snapped. "It's against the rules at this school. Come with me."

A crowd of students had gathered. "Whoooooeeeeee!" Gonzalo hooted. "You're in trouble now. She's gonna tell your parents!"

Before disappearing into the principal's office, Alicia turned to the other kids. "Mind your own business and . . . and . . . just shut up!"

Ms. Delkins directed Frankie and Alicia to chairs while she searched for their folders in the file cabinet.

As the minutes ticked away, Frankie grew impatient and angry. "Man, this is stupid. Our day is ruined, and for what? They're making a big deal out of nothing."

Alicia shook her head. "They don't understand how much we mean to each other. But when my mother finds out I've been kissing a boyfriend, she'll ban me from seeing you."

Frankie grabbed her hand. "You're right, they don't understand us. But just remember, I love you!"

Alicia smiled.

32

Before You Read

Consider each statement below. Decide whether or not you agree with it. Use your Response Sheet to record your decisions and reasons.

_____ 1. Students should not be allowed to kiss at school.

_____ 2. Some people think hugging another person in public is not appropriate.

_____ 3. Schools should not control displays of affection when two students love each other.

_____ 4. Watching two students "make out" with each other at school is nasty!

After You Read

On your own, answer the questions below. Write your answers on the Response Sheet.

1. Is it appropriate to have a rule against students hugging or kissing in school?

2. Why do you think that Ms. Delkins is so adamant about this issue?

3. What are your thoughts about students who publicly display affection?

4. In your opinion, when does a PDA cross the line and become improper?

Think About It

Prepare an argument for the School Board that will persuade them to change this policy (the PDA ban).

THE JIG IS UP

Emma invited Molly to her house after school. "Come on, Molly. We'll have the whole place to ourselves. This is our chance to go online and check out Stephanie's social networking page."

After running through the house to make sure they were really alone, Emma hurried Molly into the family room and turned on the computer. Both girls were anxious to see their friend Stephanie's page online. They'd heard talk about it at school; someone even said she got messages from older boys! Emma and Molly wanted to see for themselves.

Stephanie's page did look pretty cool. She had posted tons of pictures of herself (including some in a skimpy bikini). She also wrote lots of nonsense about parties she went to, and how she had just gotten her driver's license. The girls read through all of Stephanie's messages. It was true—many were from boys who wanted her phone number or asked to chat with her online.

The lure of the Internet is hard to escape.

"I want to meet older boys, too," Emma said. "Let's set up our pages just like hers. And definitely, let's lie about our age just like she did."

Molly wasn't so sure. Her mother had talked to her about Internet safety. Some of those "boys" who contacted Stephanie could be predators. Molly knew she should tell Emma not to do it, but she didn't want to seem like a loser. Emma went ahead and set up the page. Then she jumped up and ran from the room.

She returned dressed in a bathing suit, wearing a lot of makeup and holding a digital camera. "Take my picture, Molly. Then I'll take yours."

Molly shook her head. "No way! I'm not going to pose in a bikini or lie about my age. And you shouldn't either. It could be dangerous!"

Come on," Emma pleaded, "what's the danger? No one can actually find out where we live. It will be so much fun, and it's just a joke anyway. Besides, no one will really think that a 12-year-old is 16."

34

Before You Read

Consider each statement below. Decide whether or not you agree with it. Use your Response Sheet to record your decisions and reasons.

_____ 1. Kids have a right to put anything they want on the Internet.

_____ 2. Even if you put something risky on the Internet, you can always keep your real identity a secret.

_____ 3. The Internet is a great way to meet new people.

_____ 4. The Internet has serious drawbacks.

_____ 5. Social networking sites are safe these days.

After You Read

On your own, answer the questions below. Write your answers on the Response Sheet.

1. Why might Emma's actions be unsafe?

2. If you were Molly, how would you react to what Emma wants to do?

3. What do you think Molly and Emma should say to Stephanie?

4. Why do you think kids like to share private information on the Internet?

5. What would you do if you were Molly's parents?

Think About It

Write a list of sensible guidelines for using social networking sites.

NORM THE STORM

Norm enrolled in school several days late. After lunch each day, he buzzed up and down the halls, stopping to talk to everyone he met, arriving at his history class late, of course. Unprepared to study, he would ask to go to the restroom, or sharpen his pencil, or borrow paper from another student. Some days he came to class without his book—which seemed to excuse him from doing any work at all. He just squirmed and twisted in his chair and talked at the other students who were trying to do their assignments. Or he roamed around the room, bumping into all the desks.

One of his favorite pastimes was pestering Greg and Justin during class. He loved to play one against the other, just to start as many sparks as possible. Norm also enjoyed picking on Rachel and Lauren, teasing them about everything from their clothes to their hair.

Somehow, Norm managed to create a disturbance wherever he went. No wonder his other teachers constantly nagged him about his behavior. When the history teacher realized she had to solve this problem or there would never be peace in her classroom, she "invited" Norm to come in after school for a conference.

Actually, Norm never realized he was doing anything wrong, so he was surprised. "Why me?" he asked.

"Because we have to talk."
Ms. McLellan walked away.
"Please be here right after school."

Amazingly, Norm did show up.
Ms. McLellan was ready with a list of things Norm did that bothered the other students and disrupted the classroom. Instead of reciting the list, she simply asked, "Norm, how do you feel about your role in my classroom?"

We interrupt your regular classroom activities with this special alert. A Normado has been sighted in Ms. McLellan's history class. If you are in his path, take cover immediately!

Although she had not accused Norm of anything, he was defensive. "I just can't help bothering everybody. That's the way I am!"

The teacher lowered her already-soft voice and said, "Will you help me figure out how to help you have a better experience in this class?"

Before You Read

Consider each statement below. Decide whether or not you agree with it. Use your Response Sheet to record your decisions and reasons.

_____ 1. Some people like attention all of the time.

_____ 2. It is acceptable in some cases to disturb the class.

_____ 3. People need to know that you are angry with them.

_____ 4. If someone is a bother in class, it is best just to ignore him or her.

_____ 5. People ridicule others because it makes them feel good about themselves.

After You Read

On your own, answer the questions below. Write your answers on the Response Sheet.

1. Why do you think people thrive on getting attention?

2. What did you expect the teacher would say to Norm at the conference?

3. How can a teacher show that he or she cares for all the students?

4. What does Norm need to learn to resolve his problem?

5. How would you define "self-control" as it relates to this story?

Think About It

Write down some some friendly advice or encouragement you can give to Norm that may help him improve his behavior.

A COMPLEX SITUATION

Candelario hangs with the "Crazees" clique at school. When surrounded by his "homies," he doesn't talk much. He is a big guy, and sometimes this cool attitude gives him the appearance of being threatening or even menacing. Students have nicknamed him "The Silent One."

Actually, beneath the swagger, Candelario is a bright young man capable of captivating anyone when he talks. When he's alone, he writes interesting stories and even illustrates them. He rarely shows his artistic or intelligent side. Only his closest family members know how smart and creative he can be. At school he goes out of his way to protect his "silent" image.

The cosine of the corresponding angle is the square root of three over two.

Candelario, The Silent One

One Monday morning during math class, Ms. Cleary asked Candelario to name the cosine of a corresponding angle. He knew the answer cold but kept quiet and shook his head. He did not want to let on that he knew it.

The teacher rapped a pen against the board and asked him again. "Think hard, Candelario . . ." When she saw that he was not going to give her an answer, she moved on to another student.

Later that day in civics class, Mr. Casilli began a discussion about the correlation between law and morality. Candelario was especially interested in and knowledgeable about this subject.

Uncharacteristically, he cracked his silence and offered a comment: "Morals are contextual. Laws are based on morals. So breaking a law out of the context of that moral might not, in every case, be immoral."

Silence fell over the room as the teacher and the other students digested Candelario's unusual contribution. Mr. Casilli nodded. "Well stated, Candelario."

A student in the back snickered, "What a nerd!"

The rest of the class collapsed in a group cackle. Candelario felt his cheeks burning. He turned around with a scowl and glared at his accuser. He wondered if he would ever bother to answer a question again.

Before You Read

Consider each statement below. Decide whether or not you agree with it. Use your Response Sheet to record your decisions and reasons.

_____ 1. Some people base their opinion of themselves on what other people think of them.

_____ 2. If you are smart in school, you should be proud of your ability.

_____ 3. Some people who are smart are afraid to stand out among their peers.

_____ 4. The most important thing to students is their "image."

_____ 5. Most students come to school to be with friends and not to learn.

After You Read

On your own, answer the questions below. Write your answers on the Response Sheet.

1. Why do you think Candelario is hiding his talents?

2. What do you think of the way the math teacher asked the question?

3. What inferences would you make about Candelario's clique, the "Crazees," and why he hangs out with them?

4. How would you define the term "self-image"? (Use your own words.)

Think About It

Write a short interior monologue that describes what Candelario is thinking, including his decision about what he will do next in school.

THE ENTREPRENEUR

David turned to the kid behind him in pre-algebra class and asked, "Hey, Jim, you want any Atomic Fire Balls? Jolly Ranchers? Milk Duds?" The kid behind pulled out a couple of quarters and purchased a bag of Fire Balls.

"I also have that one in a low-cal strawberry flavor."

Another sale for David! He attended a good school in a good neighborhood, but he wasn't one of the rich kids. Most of the other students got generous allowances and bought hot lunches and other treats every day. David had to bring his lunch from home. His allowance was zero.

A few months ago, David bought bulk candy from a discount store on a whim and started selling pieces in small bags at school. To his delight, the other kids were ready customers. He made a $20 profit in the first week. He was so excited that he went right out and bought even more candy. He imagined the piles of money he'd make. Selling candy to rich kids—now that was a great idea, he decided.

David made good profits. He could buy lunches whenever he wanted. Business boomed—until some other students decided to get in on the action. Soon, selling candy became as popular as eating it. The competition brought David's profits down. He found himself spending more and more time searching for bigger and better candies to sell.

One day, the school's principal announced that students were prohibited from selling anything to their classmates. David ground his teeth and clenched his fists. This ruined everything. He was angry that other kids had horned in on his enterprise. They had made it into such a big deal that teachers had noticed the selling and reported it.

The other kids, who never needed the money in the first place, dutifully stopped selling candy. They feared punishment. David did not. He continued to sell candy secretly. Everyone knew he'd eventually get caught.

David's luck ran out a week later. He was suspended for one day and warned against selling anything on school grounds in the future. Yet David sees this as only a minor setback. In fact, he's learned a great business lesson. He has new plans underway—this time, for an enterprise that will not be so easy to imitate.

Before You Read

Consider each statement below. Decide whether or not you agree with it. Use your Response Sheet to record your decisions and reasons.

_____ 1. Selling candy during class is a good way to make money.

_____ 2. Students should not be allowed to sell anything to other students.

_____ 3. Selling anything to other students can create problems.

_____ 4. School is a place to learn, not a place to make money.

_____ 5. Entrepreneurship should be encouraged at school.

After You Read

On your own, answer the questions below. Write your answers on the Response Sheet.

1. Why would some people say that David was wrong to sell candy at his school?

2. How did David justify his plans to continue selling?

3. What could David's friends have done to prevent his suspension?

4. Why should students be allowed (or not allowed) to sell things at school?

5. What are some other ways David could have earned money?

Think About It

With a partner, write a school policy that would allow students to run money-making enterprises that are safe and nondisruptive.

FOOD-FIGHT FRENZY

The Bull Horn

McCuffy Middle School

March 4, this year   *Volume 8, Number 11*

Flying Soda Can Sends One Student to the Hospital

Story by Jake Pampas and Rich Timbers

27 Students Face Detention

Students who were identified as being actively involved in Wednesday's food fight will spend the next five Saturdays cleaning and repainting the school cafeteria.

Damages, including broken glass and furniture, will be paid for from the seventh and eighth grade end-of-year party fund.

The students involved will also write apologies to their fellow students, the faculty, and the cafeteria workers. Each apology must be signed by the student's parent or guardian.

Last Wednesday during lunch, the school cafeteria erupted in a food-fight frenzy. Seventh-grader Tess Nellson allegedly started the fracas when she grabbed a piece of lemon crème pie and smacked eighth-grader Roger Boyle in the face. The place went nuts! Soon, dozens got into the act, and the food really started flying!

Rollicking students, drenched in Italian dressing, French fries, Spanish rice, Canadian bacon, and American cheese, cheerfully bombarded each other with any edible thing they could find.

Orin Peeples slid halfway across the room on a banana peel. Missiles of mush peppered the walls. The scene really turned ugly, however, when someone started throwing full cans of soda. By the time teachers and administrators arrived with school security, at least one student had been injured.

Tess Nellson was beaned with a soda can and was taken to the emergency room for five stitches.

McCuffy Middle School Cafeteria: Combat Zone

When we interviewed Principal Whimple about the incident, he told us, "Steps are being taken."

He plans to address the student body on Friday about the incident.

Before You Read

Consider each statement below. Decide whether or not you agree with it. Use your Response Sheet to record your decisions and reasons.

_____ 1. Throwing food at lunchtime is just what kids do. A food fight is really not that big a deal.

_____ 2. Most people would agree that a food fight in the cafeteria is poor judgment on the part of everybody involved.

_____ 3. Kids who start food fights should be punished. But after the fight starts, kids who throw food are just defending themselves.

_____ 4. It is unacceptable under any circumstance to throw food at someone.

After You Read

On your own, answer the questions below. Write your answers on the Response Sheet.

1. Why might some students think it is funny to start a food fight?

2. How would you have reacted to this situation if you had been in the cafeteria when it happened?

3. Was the punishment (as described in the newspaper) appropriate for this situation?

4. What do you think Principal Whimple will say to the students on Friday?

Think About It

You overhear a plan for a food fight at school. List four things that you could do about it. Start with the one you're most likely to do.

YOUR CHEATIN' HEART

When Jenny happened to walk past the table where Serena and Anne sat in the cafeteria, she thought she heard sobbing. Jenny didn't mean to eavesdrop, but she couldn't help overhearing.

"What am I supposed to do?" Anne whispered to her friend, choking back tears. "I can't fail this exam. I just don't understand the material! There's no way I'm going to learn this science before next period. My parents are going to be so disappointed, and I'll lose my driving privileges!"

Jenny knew that Serena and Anne were inseparable best friends. Both were honor students—two of the most accomplished girls in school. They worked together in student government, ran together on the track team, and took all the same classes. What a bad break for Anne if she couldn't grasp some of the concepts in their science class!

Serena, good friend that she was, hugged Anne and assured her that everything would be okay. "We'll find a way. You'll pass the test. I won't let you fail."

Jenny wondered how the girls could pull off such a task. Surely they wouldn't cheat! Serena's dad was an administrator at their school. If Serena got caught cheating, she would be in trouble—big time.

Jenny's worst fears were realized when the teacher passed out the science tests. Serena had cleverly positioned herself to make sure Anne, sitting directly behind her, could see her answers. It seemed certain now that their plan was to keep Anne from failing by letting her copy Serena's answers. Jenny decided to keep a silent watch on them during the exam.

*Jenny watching Anne watching Serena—
Is anyone taking the test?*

Before You Read

Consider each statement below. Decide whether or not you agree with it. Use your Response Sheet to record your decisions and reasons.

——— 1. Cheating on a test is sometimes justified.

——— 2. You should be able to help your friends out during a test if they need it.

——— 3. Students should always report cheating whenever they see it happening.

——— 4. If you think you see someone cheating on a test, you should mind your own business.

——— 5. If a student feels he or she has to cheat on a test, there is something wrong with the teaching in that class.

After You Read

On your own, answer the questions below. Write your answers on the Response Sheet.

1. If Serena did help Anne during the test, why would she do that?

2. What could Anne have done to be more prepared for this test?

3. Why do you think Jenny is so concerned about this possible cheating situation?

4. How would you handle a situation where a friend asked you to give her or him help during a test?

5. What should Jenny do in this situation?

Think About It

Assume the girls did cheat. Write two arguments Jenny might have with herself: one about why she should tell, and one about why she should not.

THE BRUSHOFF

On the first day of school, most students are excited to be back among their friends. It's a time to show off new clothes and cell phones and to brag about their summer activities.

Tom was one of the few students who returned without new clothes or supplies. He wore the same dirty old shoes, shirts, and pants, and sometimes he didn't smell particularly fresh. Predictably, he had few friends. Most of the kids didn't want to be seen with him. Nevertheless, he came to school every day, even when he was sick.

Some people thought that because he was poor, Tom came to school regularly for the free breakfasts and lunches. But the real reason he came every day was his favorite class—Art. He loved drawing, even as a young child. He was especially good at sketching animals, people, and places. His art teacher gave him a lot of praise.

Lucy and Marcie were in Tom's art class. They went out of their way to make fun of him because he was poor. Lucy would whisper loudly in Marcie's ear, "Do you smell something nasty?"

Marcie always answered, "I do!"

Then they would look at Tom and say, "Nasty. Nasty."

Nasty Lucy makes nasty comments to her nasty friend.

It wasn't Tom's fault that he was poor. He couldn't buy new shoes or new clothes to wear to school, and he didn't have a mother to remind him to keep clean. When he did have a few dollars to spend, he only thought about art supplies. He'd draw his pictures during class and lunch, and after school. Unfortunately, that wasn't enough to make him friends.

His art teacher heard about an art contest and encouraged Tom to enter. Pleased at the challenge, Tom spent a lot of time on a pencil drawing of stampeding mustangs and submitted it.

When they heard that Tom had entered the art contest, Lucy and Marcie scoffed. They walked around the school and made sure everybody heard: "What a joke! Nasty can't draw! He'll never win!"

46

Before You Read

Consider each statement below. Decide whether or not you agree with it. Use your Response Sheet to record your decisions and reasons.

_____ 1. Most people feel that it's important to have friends.

_____ 2. People usually have a good reason when they tease someone.

_____ 3. It's okay to make up nicknames for others, even if they don't like it.

_____ 4. It is natural for people to look down on others who are less fortunate.

_____ 5. It is better to ignore negative remarks, but sometimes you have to take action!

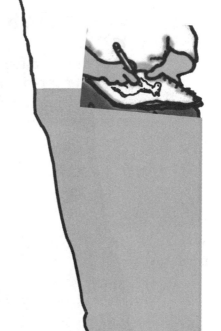

After You Read

On your own, answer the questions below. Write your answers on the Response Sheet.

1. Why do you think people find negative names for others?

2. How would you talk to someone about their poor hygiene?

3. Why do you think the other students neglect to stand up for Tom?

4. If you were someone watching this happen, what would you do?

5. How would you define the term "tolerance"? (Use your own words.)

Think About It

Write a note to Tom that describes how you feel about his situation and how you can help him solve his problem with the other students.

THE WONDER YEARS

After working as a teacher in a small town for many years, Mrs. Gee moved to the city and got a job at Olno Middle School. She loved her job and her students, but she was very disturbed by the lack of respect students showed one another and teachers. It mystified her that the faculty, and even the principal, tolerated this behavior.

Mrs. Gee felt hopeless. A month had gone by and she thought of quitting. But because that wasn't what she wanted to do, she tried some different approaches. She set aside 15 minutes daily for open discussions about the students' concerns—as well as hers. Students were given a chance to role-play different situations and to get and give feedback to Mrs. Gee.

One day, a few months into the term, Mrs. Gee got some bad news about an old friend. This news preoccupied her thoughts all morning. After third period, she went to her car in the parking lot where she could sit and think in solitude. She lost track of the time.

Suddenly, Mrs. Gee realized that she had missed almost half of her fourth period class—a catastrophe! Fourth period was her absolute worst class of the day, and they were all alone! She raced back into the school and down the empty hall, imagining the dreadful scenario: students fighting, coming and going at will, and leaving her classroom in shambles.

Silence. This can't be the right classroom.

However, the hall outside her classroom was very quiet. "Oh, no," she thought, "the principal has taken my class, and I'm really in trouble now!"

When she opened the door, all the students were at their desks, quietly waiting. Mrs. Gee looked around for a grownup, but there was no adult in sight. She calmly put down her purse and began class. At the end of the period, she asked the class if anyone had monitored them while she was out.

Antonio, one of her rowdiest students, said, "We knew something was wrong when you didn't meet us at the door. No sweat! We can handle ourselves now, and we knew you would be proud of us."

4th Period
Worst
class in
the school!

Before You Read

Consider each statement below. Decide whether or not you agree with it. Use your Response Sheet to record your decisions and reasons.

———— 1. Middle schools are supposed to be a little wild and crazy.

———— 2. It's okay to let students express themselves, even if it seems disrespectful.

———— 3. Many students look forward to seeing the teacher get upset.

———— 4. Students act up because the teacher does not respect them.

———— 5. When the teacher is strict, students never act up.

After You Read

On your own, answer the questions below. Write your answers on the Response Sheet.

1. Why do you think Mrs. Gee's "worst" class came through for her?

2. What are some things that Mrs. Gee might not understand about her students?

3. Why do you think this story is titled "The Wonder Years"?

4. How does Olno Middle School compare to your school on the issue of student respect for one another and the teachers?

Think About It

Create a poster that students in this class might have made with some drawings and thoughts about what happened.

TEXTING CONCERTO

Evan and Lisa organized an innocent prank on their favorite teacher, Mr. Williams, who usually had a good sense of humor. They planned to have all the students in his second-period social studies class receive text messages at exactly the same time. Each student would arrange to have a kid from another class text a message at the right moment. If it worked, the ring tones would create a unique concert.

Mr. Williams was just beginning to show some video clips on current events when the clock ticked 9:45. Right on schedule, the room erupted in a cacophony of sounds. The plot went off like . . . well, like clockwork. Evan and Lisa gave themselves a high-five. The class laughed and applauded. Everyone waited for Mr. Williams' reaction.

As expected, he looked up with a smile of surprise and rolled his eyes. "Great precision," he said. "You really got me this time. Now, before we continue with the next clip, would each of you bring your cell phones up and place them on my desk? You can pick them up from me at the end of the day."

The class grumbled, but obeyed.

Fifteen minutes later, the assistant principal appeared at the door and asked Mr. Williams to step outside. The students watched and waited nervously. Were they in trouble?

Mr. Williams returned. "I'm sorry, Evan and Lisa. Mrs. Bennett is waiting for you in her office, and she isn't too happy. It's a hard lesson to learn for such a harmless prank, but it's always important to consider the consequences of your actions—especially when texting is expressly prohibited during class time."

A current event interrupts the lesson on current events.

"Oh, I never thought about that," Lisa whispered to Evan.

He just shrugged and picked up his books. "It was fun while it lasted."

All eyes were on them as they walked out of the room.

Before You Read

Consider each statement below. Decide whether or not you agree with it. Use your Response Sheet to record your decisions and reasons.

_____ 1. Text messaging is the best way to stay in touch with your friends.

_____ 2. If you try to text during a test, you should automatically fail.

_____ 3. It's okay to text during class if you are texting about a lesson.

_____ 4. If kids are allowed to text during class they will be less disruptive.

_____ 5. It's okay to break rules to play a harmless prank.

After You Read

On your own, answer the questions below. Write your answers on the Response Sheet.

1. Why do you think that students do so much text messaging?

2. What could have happened to cause the assistant principal to come to Mr. Williams's classroom?

3. What are some good reasons to prohibit text messaging during class?

4. Why do you think Mr. Williams was fairly casual about the "concert"?

5. How would you define the term "respect"? (Use your own words.)

Think About It

What would Evan and Lisa say to each other as they walk to meet the assistant principal? Create a dialogue for them.

DID YOU HEAR ABOUT MR. SMITH?

Mr. Smith is one of those teachers who is easy to mock. He's rather timid and shy and a terrible bore. That makes him an easy mark, I guess. I think he is a good science teacher. I feel bad about some of the things the other students say about him, or the jokes they play on him.

One day when students had taken the screws out of his lectern, he plopped his books down and the thing fell apart. Everyone got a good laugh. Mr. Smith didn't get mad or anything. He just picked up his books, put them on a table, and then went on with his teaching.

Once I heard a student say, "Have you noticed how Mr. Smith never looks at us? He teaches to the wall in the back of the classroom."

"I hear he still lives with his mom!" This came from someone who wasn't even in his class.

"And the symbiosis is related to the mitosis which is directly in opposition to the meiosis which causes halitosis . . ."

I laugh with the other students, because I know I would look stupid if I said anything to defend Mr. Smith. I keep quiet about what I really think.

Rumors about Mr. Smith continue to spread. "I heard he was in a mental hospital before he became a teacher. Maybe he still belongs there."

"They say he is schizo, or something. He thinks everyone around him is spreading germs and making him sick. He's germ-a-phobic, or a hypochondriac, or something."

I figure they say those things because of the heavy workload Mr. Smith gives, or because of his strictness about completing assignments. It is so easy to poke fun at his mannerisms and at his insistence on an organized classroom. Yeah, I laugh at him with all the rest.

Mr. Smith seems unaware of the mockery and rumors. He just keeps teaching. The sad thing is, he seems to get smaller as the other kids laugh at him, and I feel sorry for him.

Make it stop!

Before You Read

Consider each statement below. Decide whether or not you agree with it. Use your Response Sheet to record your decisions and reasons.

_____ 1. Students have the right to be critical of their teachers.

_____ 2. Rumors usually start with something true.

_____ 3. It's harmless to make up stories about other people as long as they aren't aware of it.

_____ 4. Students should know something about teachers' private lives.

_____ 5. Someone in authority should always be shown respect.

After You Read

On your own, answer the questions below. Write your answers on the Response Sheet.

1. Why do you think the students treat Mr. Smith in this manner?

2. How do you think the students will treat other teachers similar to Mr. Smith from now on?

3. Why do you think that Mr. Smith seems to get smaller for the student who is telling this story?

4. What do you think the narrator in this story should do?

5. "What he doesn't know won't hurt him." Do you agree or disagree with this statement as it relates to the story?

Think About It

Create a scene in which two students are spreading rumors and one student is attempting to get the others to stop spreading them.

HATS OFF!

Mrs. Paculabo leaned over her desk and shouted, "Take off that filthy hat, Danny. Take it off, I said!" It was the fifth time she had asked him to remove his hat.

Danny pulled the knit cap tighter around his ears and slumped in his chair, looking as if he'd rather be any place but trapped in Mrs. Paculabo's math class.

"I'm trying to tell you," he said. "I can't take it off because of the stupid haircut I got last night."

His stepfather had the bright idea to let a neighbor cut Danny's hair rather than take him to a barber. Unfortunately, she didn't do a very good job. Danny's hair looked like Bart Simpson's.

"I don't care if they shaved you bald! Hats are not allowed in this room and I want you to take it off now. Or else."

"Or else, what?" Danny replied, almost in a whisper.

The teacher threw up her hands. "Or else? Or . . . else? March yourself down to the office and let the principal deal with this!" Mrs. Paculabo turned red with fury.

Take it off **NOW** or else...

Which is scarier—the teacher's threats or the bad haircut?

Danny couldn't see any way out of his predicament. He rose quickly from his seat, brushed past the teacher, and stormed out the door. As he left, he screamed over his shoulder, "I hate this place!"

Mrs. Paculabo turned to the class, her face still a shade of crimson. "Listen to me, kids. There are no hats allowed in this school. And there are no exceptions to the rule. And anyone who won't follow the rules has to face some consequences. Now, open your books and get down to work."

The students did as they were told.

Before You Read

Consider each statement below. Decide whether or not you agree with it. Use your Response Sheet to record your decisions and reasons.

_____ 1. Not all school rules are fair.

_____ 2. Someone who breaks a school rule usually has a good reason.

_____ 3. People who break the rules need to be punished.

_____ 4. There should be no exceptions to rules.

_____ 5. If people don't feel a rule is fair, they have a right to refuse to follow it.

After You Read

On your own, answer the questions below. Write your answers on the Response Sheet.

1. What could the teacher have done differently?

2. Why might some people think that Danny has a right to wear the hat in this case?

3. What advice would you give the principal (or other person at the office who will talk to Danny) about what to say to Danny?

4. Which caption is best for the cartoon on the story page?
   a. The caption that is already there.
   b. "This would be a good day to skip school."
   c. "This is more interesting than math."

Think About It

Prepare a speech about how to explain, disguise, or otherwise deal with a bad haircut or a bad hairdo.

RYAN: BMOC

Ryan was clearly the Big Man on Campus. His athletic abilities in basketball were well known. Some of his coaches talked about him as if he were the next Michael Jordan or Kobe Bryant. With all this talent, he grew used to special attention and treatment from coaches. So he was upset to learn that his favorite coach had left to take a different job. He was in no hurry to meet the replacement—a young woman from out of state.

The new coach whittles BMOC down to size.

When he finally made it to gym class, the new coach was methodically going over the rules for the gym and explaining how her class was going to be run. The new rules were strict and the coach seemed like a "no-nonsense" kind of person. Ryan guessed that in this class he was going to be "just another student." After listening to the coach ramble on and on about the rules, he finally lost his patience!

"Lady, when are you going to cut through the bunk and let us shoot hoops? We know all this stuff already. Just let us play!"

The coach looked at him. "Do I detect a little attitude? And it's Coach Parsons to you." She looked at her clipboard. "We'll listen to your comments when I finish explaining the rules. Sit down, please."

Ryan felt his cheeks burning. "Don't tell me what to do!"

Coach Parsons put her clipboard down at her side. "Young man, you are free to go. Please remove yourself from my class. Now!"

Shocked, he looked around at his classmates, expecting them to back him up. Not a voice rose to support him. Angry and humiliated, he walked out the door, letting it slam shut behind him.

Once outside the gym, Ryan dropped his head. As he cooled off, he began to panic. "What did I do that for?" he asked himself. "I've just ruined my basketball chances for the whole year."

Slowly, he realized that he was going to have to swallow his pride and figure out a way to get back into the good graces of that coach if he was ever going to play there again.

RYAN
EXIT

Before You Read

Consider each statement below. Decide whether or not you agree with it. Use your Response Sheet to record your decisions and reasons.

_____ 1. School athletes deserve special treatment.

_____ 2. Teachers play favorites with some students.

_____ 3. Every school needs a BMOC.

_____ 4. Students who act up now will always regret it later.

_____ 5. Once you get an "attitude," it's hard to lose it.

After You Read

On your own, answer the questions below. Write your answers on the Response Sheet.

1. How would you explain the coach's reaction to Ryan?

2. Why do you think the other students did not support Ryan during his outburst?

3. How would you compare Ryan's behavior to how you behave when you lose your temper?

4. What do you think caused Ryan to regret what he had done?

5. How would you define the term "humility"? (Use your own words.)

Think About It

Draw a talk balloon for Ryan and one for the coach. In them, write the opening sentence that each will say when they meet again.

THE WRITING'S ON THE WALL

"Jeez, another boring 'Be a good citizen' lecture," Martin grumbled from the back of the auditorium. He hunkered down and tried to zone out the speaker from the local police department.

"Graffiti. It costs millions of dollars each year to remove graffiti," the young sergeant began. "In many cases, new tags appear the next day. This is not a question of artistic freedom. This is about defacement of public and private property, usually by gang members."

Martin sat up straight. It felt as if the officer was speaking directly to him. "This is bunk," he thought. "Why do I have to sit here with all these kids and listen to someone lecture us about tagging? Most people don't understand anything about it. They don't get it."

Martin already had a reputation as a tagger. Earlier that week, he and three other boys from his crew had been caught stealing spray paint cans out of an art supply room at the school. Before that, he had earned a demerit and a weekend painting job for leaving his tag BFT (for "Blunt Force Trauma") on the back of the football scoreboard.

Even worse, he'd been caught tagging in town. The police had "tagged" his parents for a bill of two thousand dollars for the damages. Martin cringed. His dad had really blown a gasket at the news, and Martin had a court appearance the following week.

Down on the stage, the police officer was still talking, blah, blah, blah. "If you want to get your name on a wall," he said, "cure cancer, throw an 80-yard touchdown pass, save a life, or join the army and become a hero. Graffiti is just vandalism by another name. Worse, it can lead to violence and gang wars. And, by the way, it IS prosecutable."

Martin was disgusted. He still had a couple of spray cans left along with plans for new places to put his BFT. After the assembly, he found his crew. "We've got work to do tonight," he told them.

The other boys were nervous. "Look, man," said Leonard, "you need to chill. You just got busted!"

"Are you kidding?" Martin scoffed. "We've only just begun!"

Before You Read

Consider each statement below. Decide whether or not you agree with it. Use your Response Sheet to record your decisions and reasons.

_____ 1. Kids use graffiti as a means of expression.

_____ 2. Most people think that graffiti is the same as vandalism.

_____ 3. Tagging walls should be tolerated because it's just "kids being kids."

_____ 4. Kids who use graffiti are not violent.

_____ 5. Cities should just give up on trying to get rid of graffiti.

After You Read

On your own, answer the questions below. Write your answers on the Response Sheet.

1. Why do you think Martin is so dedicated to tagging?

2. What might change Martin's mind about graffiti?

3. Is there any value to graffiti?

4. If you were one of Martin's friends, what would you tell him?

5. What is the best way for cities to respond to the problem of graffiti?

Think About It

Write a humorous caption for the cartoon on the story page.

TO TELL THE TRUTH

Luis and Hunter hardly knew each other. They walked past each other in the school halls without a second glance. They had no mutual friends. That's why everyone was surprised to see the two arguing in Ms. Romero's fifth-period class.

The disagreement concerned Luis's MP3 player—the one that had gone missing that morning. Suddenly, Hunter was showing off a new digital player. It looked so much like the one Luis had lost that Luis was sure it was his and that Hunter had stolen it. He said so—loudly.

Students started taking sides. Voices rose in support of Luis and in defense of Hunter. Emotions grew hot on both sides, and Ms. Romero feared a potential fight. She closed the door to the classroom and told everyone to sit down. The students took their seats, grumbling.

"Put the player on my desk, Hunter," she instructed.

Twinkle twinkle little star...

He did so, reluctantly. She explained that he would get it back when he produced a receipt and a serial number. "You must bring proof as well, Luis," she added. "That's the only way to get to the bottom of this situation." Both boys protested that her actions were unfair.

After school, Ms. Romero got a phone call from Hunter's mother telling her that she had overstepped her authority.

"I had no choice," the teacher said.

As she checked her mailbox after school, Ms. Romero found a note from the principal requesting a meeting at 7:00 a.m. the next day with Luis's father.

Maybe neither boy will want to claim this music.

"Fine!" she thought. "Let's get to the truth of this disagreement. I don't care who owns the player."

Ms. Romero discussed the episode with her fellow teachers. Some agreed with her actions, but several said they would have become involved in the disagreement.

Before You Read

Consider each statement below. Decide whether or not you agree with it. Use your Response Sheet to record your decisions and reasons.

_____ 1. It is usually easy to tell who is telling the truth and who isn't.

_____ 2. Teachers may not always do the right thing.

_____ 3. Kids should be thought of as telling the truth before they are suspected of lying.

_____ 4. Disagreements can always be worked out by talking about them.

_____ 5. Some problems should not be resolved right away.

After You Read

On your own, answer the questions below. Write your answers on the Response Sheet.

1. What could the teacher have done differently?

2. Are there any indications that Ms. Romero had a particular view about who was the true owner of the digital player?

3. Do you think the teacher had the right to interfere in this situation?

4. What could Luis have done once he realized that his player was missing?

5. How would you define the term "fairness" as related to this situation?

Think About It

Create a response that Ms. Romero could give to her fellow teachers who thought she should have stayed out of the argument.

A TALE OF TWO DIARIES

Brooke's Diary

Dear Diary,

That annoying Luella something-or-other, the girl from the trailer park who sits next to me in third period English, is always hanging around now. I can't shake her. I made the mistake of offering her one of my needlepoint gel pens when she couldn't find anything to write with last Thursday. Never do a good deed. It always backfires. Now she thinks I actually like her. As if!

She follows me around like a stray puppy. I know Luella is poor, but jeez, does she always have to dress in secondhand clothes? It's embarrassing. My BFFs are beginning to notice. "Get rid of her," Tiffany told me. "She makes us all look bad."

I've tried; but the girl is so dense. She doesn't know when she's being dissed. I have to do something drastic. Here's the plan — I'll be really nice to her for a day, and then invite her to a sleepover at my house next Friday night. What she won't know is that the sleepover is actually at Tiffany's house and my parents will be away for the weekend. When she shows up, the place will be dark and deserted.

If that doesn't give her an idea of how I really feel, then nothing will. Hope this works....

Brooke

Luella's Diary

Dear Diary,

Brooke Briars, the one I wrote about before, is so-oo nice. She loaned me a pen at school, and even smiled and said, "Keep it." Brooke is just about the most popular girl in school. I didn't think she had even noticed me before. I know she has a lot of friends, and when she tells me she's busy doing stuff with them, I understand. I'm just happy she talks to me at all.

I told my mother about Brooke. She said, "Brooke is lucky to have you as a friend." Of course, mothers always say things like that. I'm the lucky one.

Guess what? Brooke invited me to a sleepover at her house on Friday. Her other friends will be there too. I'm so excited, and nervous. My mother is going to buy me new pajamas and then take time off work at the diner to drive me over! I hope my cousin will lend me her sleeping bag. It's better than mine.

Well, Diary, I'll write more about the party when it's over.

Luella

Before You Read

Consider each statement below. Decide whether or not you agree with it. Use your Response Sheet to record your decisions and reasons.

_____ 1. Do whatever you have to do to get rid of someone annoying.

_____ 2. You can be kind to someone without being her (or his) friend.

_____ 3. It is okay to only be friends with people of your own social class.

_____ 4. You should not be friends with people who are mean on purpose.

_____ 5. Sometimes people do mean things without intending to be mean.

Brooke can't seem to shake Luella.

After You Read

On your own, answer the questions below. Write your answers on the Response Sheet.

1. How do you feel about this situation?

2. What do you hope will happen?

3. Why do you think Brooke wants to get rid of Luella?

4. What would you do in Brooke's situation?

5. What do you believe causes people to be mean?

Think About It

Write a note to either girl, telling her anything you would like to say to her. Assume that the sleepover has not taken place yet.

CHEERS FOR GINA

Mrs. Day, the cheerleading sponsor, asked Gina to try out for the squad. On her own, Gina would never have considered such a notion. She was somewhat overweight and quite self-conscious about her looks.

"I'm not very athletic, Mrs. Day. Besides, I'd never fit into any of those uniforms. I don't think I'm cheerleader material."

Mrs. Day put a reassuring arm around Gina's shoulders. "You're wrong, dear. I think you have real talent. We need someone with the kind of spirit you've shown, and your great voice would rally our spectators to cheer the team on."

Gina looked dubious.

"Why don't you think about it?" Mrs. Day urged.

At lunch, Gina sat with her long-time friends, Tanya and Cassie, and thought. Timidly, she brought up the subject of trying out to be a cheerleader. Her friends laughed at the idea.

Team spirit comes in all shapes and sizes.

"Come on, girl," Tanya said. "Mrs. Day couldn't have been **serious**. Maybe she meant to say she wants you as a mascot." Tanya regretted her statement and quickly added, "Well, you **are** a great team fan, the best yeller in the school."

Cassie worried. "Gina, please don't go out for cheerleading. People will laugh at you. You'll embarrass yourself and make us look bad."

Gina couldn't hide her disappointment. "Call me crazy, but I expected my best friends to support me," she said.

After a long silence, Tanya finally said, "You're right, Gina. Why shouldn't you be a cheerleader? I say, go for it. I'll be there for you."

Gina's resistance vanished. She practiced hard and even lost a few pounds. She went out for the squad and made it. The other girls were cool to her at first. But Gina's spirit, good humor, and enthusiasm forced the squad to work harder. They soon became a close team. Gina had cleared her first hurdle. Now, how would the rest of the school react when she appeared with the squad?

Before You Read

Consider each statement below. Decide whether or not you agree with it. Use your Response Sheet to record your decisions and reasons.

_____ 1. In terms of being successful or popular, looks always matter the most.

_____ 2. You shouldn't be a cheerleader unless you look a certain way.

_____ 3. Friends must always be truthful even if it hurts someone's feelings.

_____ 4. You can be successful at anything as long as you believe in yourself.

After You Read

On your own, answer the questions below. Write your answers on the Response Sheet.

1. How would you analyze the first responses from Tanya and Cassie?

2. Why do you think the cheerleaders accepted Gina as part of the squad?

3. How does it make you feel to see other people ridiculed or teased about their physical appearance?

4. How would you define the term "body image" as it relates to this story? (Use your own words.)

Think About It

Write some advice to middle school students to help them be accepting of all kinds of physical appearances.

FOOD FOR THOUGHT

Mrs. Jacobs is extremely proud of her computer lab. She spends a lot of time and some of her own money keeping it in tiptop shape. She is just as proud of her students this semester. Working as a team, they have done an excellent job on the video project they plan to enter in the annual statewide competition. This year her class has a good chance of winning a top spot.

Even so, Mrs. Jacobs gets frustrated. Almost every day someone brings food, candy, or drinks into the computer lab. The rules of the class specifically prohibit food and drinks, and she has to remind the students all the time about this fact— explaining and re-explaining why the rule is so important. But someone always forgets. Although she conducts a daily inspection, Mrs. Jacobs can't catch everything that comes through the doorway.

On the day the class gathered to finalize the video project for the competition, the room buzzed with excitement. All that was left were a few minor changes and saving it to DVD for the final version. Everyone was sure they had created a winning entry.

The day was hot, and the computer lab was especially stifling with all the students rushing around attending to last-minute details. The bag of chips Marlena had eaten at lunch made her mouth dry. She remembered the can of cola in her backpack. Without thinking, she pulled it out and took a drink. Her fingers slipped, and the soda spilled and drenched the entire laptop. Immediately, smoke billowed out and the computer screen went blank.

A loud groan rose from the students as they ran to see what had happened. Marlena felt miserable to think that she'd been the one to cause this disaster.

Mrs. Jacobs tried repeatedly to reboot the computer, but it was no use. The computer would not turn on. Later, when she took it to the technician, they discovered that the hard drive was damaged and no files could be retrieved.

The next day, the class learned that their video was lost and nothing could be done to recover it. There was no time to create a new video for the contest. Needless to say, everyone was devastated.

Cola and computers—
a winning combination.

Before You Read

Consider each statement below. Decide whether or not you agree with it. Use your Response Sheet to record your decisions and reasons.

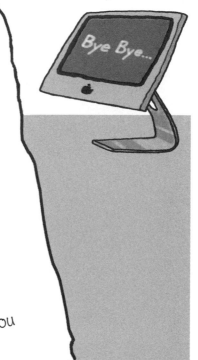

_____ 1. Some school rules are just too silly.

_____ 2. As long as you're careful, food is acceptable in the computer lab (even though it's against the rules).

_____ 3. A student who gets hungry should be able to eat whenever he or she feels like it.

_____ 4. Teachers have the right to make up any rules they want.

_____ 5. You should follow rules at school even if you are not sure they make sense.

After You Read

On your own, answer the questions below. Write your answers on the Response Sheet.

1. Why do you think some students just can't seem to follow the rules?

2. If you were going to give Mrs. Jacobs some advice on preventing this situation, what would that be?

3. What consequences should Marlena face for her actions?

4. What would be your best ending for this story?

5. How would you define the term "responsibility"? (Use your own words.)

Think About It

Plan to write a song about food in the computer lab. Create a title and a chorus for the song.

ZING TALKS TRASH

Zing's nickname was well-earned. He did everything fast. On the track, he seemed to move at the speed of sound. The rest of the time he walked, talked, and ate in a kind of blur. At lunch, he reminded his classmates of someone competing to see how many pancakes he could eat in a minute. One second, Zing had a sandwich, a piece of chicken, or a burrito in his hand. The next second, it would be gone! And he always left the cafeteria in a whirlwind of litter.

The announcement of a new clean-up campaign meant the students would have to pick up their own trash after lunch.

"No way!" Zing sputtered. "I have to get out on the field for track practice. I don't have time to do the custodian's job!"

"What do you think will happen if one of the teachers catches you leaving your usual mess?" Brody asked.

"They'll never catch me. I'm too fast for them!" was Zing's quick answer.

The next day, Zing ate and ran as usual. He left behind a bag of chips, sandwich wrappers, a crushed soda can, and a wad of bubble gum.

At the door, a hand reached out and caught him. "Rudolph, slow down!" Mr. Wagner yelled. (A bunch of nearby kids began to titter. No one knew Zing's real name was Rudolph.) "Didn't you hear about our clean-up campaign?"

Zing got red and spun around. "Yeah, but I'm in a really big hurry, Mr. Wagner. Let the janitor clean that mess."

Mr. Wagner shook his head. "The school has cut back on custodial services due to budget cuts. Now the students need to help keep the lunchroom clean. What makes you think you're different?"

If you blink, you might miss him.

"Well, I have better things to do!" Zing said.

"Yes, you do. You have trash to pick up for the rest of the lunch period— unless you'd prefer to spend your afternoon in detention?"

Zing saw he couldn't win. He raced around the room picking up papers— and fast!

68

Before You Read

Consider each statement below. Decide whether or not you agree with it. Use your Response Sheet to record your decisions and reasons.

——— 1. Keeping a school clean is not the responsibility of the students.

——— 2. People throw trash on the ground because they don't care.

——— 3. Kids should not have to clean up after themselves, because they are just kids.

——— 4. Everyone should take responsibility for his or her trash.

——— 5. Most people litter without even thinking about it.

After You Read

On your own, answer the questions below. Write your answers on the Response Sheet.

1. Why do you think Zing believed it was okay to leave his trash behind?

2. What was right or wrong about the way Mr. Wagner handled the situation?

3. If you were Zing, how would you have responded to Mr. Wagner?

4. What would you recommend to solve the lunchtime trash problem at your own school?

Think About It

Create a comic strip about Zing. Base it on characteristics you have learned about him in this story.

THE CONSTANT QUESTIONER

Abrianna is one of the most annoying kids in my class. She sits behind me in science and drives me nuts asking stupid questions. Not only does she risk getting both of us in trouble, but most of her questions aren't even relevant.

Sometimes in the middle of a lesson, she'll wave her arm in the air and ask the teacher something dumb, like, "Does the cafeteria serve pizza on Thursdays?"

Does she know how lame she sounds? Or does she just like hearing herself talk? Whatever the reason, we're all fed up with Abrianna.

We took a science quiz today. Ms. Lu made the mistake of asking if anyone had any last-minute questions. I did, in fact, have a question, but Abrianna was quick to out-wave me.

OH, OH...
Mizz Lu?
Mizz Lu!!

Curiosity killed the cat, but it doesn't even faze Abrianna.

I could tell Ms. Lu wanted to avoid her. She called on another student. Before the girl could open her mouth, Abrianna shouted out, "Mizz Lu? Mizz Lu? Do mosquitoes have lips?"

All the kids in the class rolled their eyes. Ms. Lu tried to be nice, and asked Abrianna to stay on topic.

"Hmmm. In that case," Abrianna said, "what kinds of rocks are in the Great Wall of China? And what about . . . ?"

Ms. Lu cut her off and started passing out the quizzes. I never got a chance to ask my question. Luckily for me, it didn't come up on the quiz. But I was still pretty angry with Abrianna.

After class I caught up with her. "What's with you and your jerky questions? How about letting the rest of us have a chance?"

Surprised, Abrianna tried to laugh it off. "What do you care? When are we ever going to need to know about rocks, anyway?"

"Who knows?" I said. "Besides, some of us actually want to get good grades."

"You're just trying to kiss up to the teacher!" she groused. "Well, I couldn't care less!" She stormed off.

Before You Read

Consider each statement below. Decide whether or not you agree with it. Use your Response Sheet to record your decisions and reasons.

_____ 1. It is always okay to ask a question.

_____ 2. Some people's questions are more important than others.

_____ 3. It is okay to tell someone to "shut up" if they are bothering you.

_____ 4. People who talk all the time and interrupt are in need of attention.

After You Read

On your own, answer the questions below.
Write your answers on the Response Sheet.

1. Why do you think Abrianna asked so many questions?

2. What could the narrator do to get his questions answered?

3. What could the teacher do to change the situation?

4. How should the other students react to Abrianna's questions?

5. What do you do when you need attention in class?

Think About It

Make a list of guidelines that could help Abrianna become a more effective questioner?

DON'T CALL ME THAT!

Lydia, the new student body president, heard shouting at the end of the hall. She hurried down to see what was going on.

"Don't call me that!" shouted the shorter boy, a new student.

"What's your problem? They told me that was your nickname!" Miguel crossed his arms and frowned.

"It's not! And it's insulting to call me that. How would you like it if I called you 'Jose' or 'Mex' instead of your real name?"

Lydia knew that lots of kids called the new boy "Woo." She didn't know if it was an ethnic slur or not, but clearly the kid himself didn't like it. By the look of it, he'd had enough!

She hurried forward and stood between the boys, a brave thing to do because Miguel was inches taller, and the other kid seemed ready to throw a punch. "Hey, cool it, guys!" she shouted. "What's going on?"

Miguel glared at the other boy. "I don't know! I called out his name, and man, he just came at me."

"What is his name?" Lydia asked.

"Woo. That's what everyone calls him."

Lydia steps into a hornet's nest.

"That's not my name! It's insulting!" The boy's hand clenched again. "My name is Michael."

"Man, you're touchy! Everyone calls you Woo!" Miguel shouted back. "And how am I supposed to know your real name when that's what everyone calls you?"

Continuing to hold the boys apart, Lydia said, "Well, Miguel, people do get tired of being called stereotypical racial names just because it sounds funny." Lydia said. "How would you like it?"

"Hey!" said Miguel "They call me names, too. That's just what we do! And Woo had better get used to it."

72

That's not my name!

Consider each statement below. Decide whether or not you agree with it. Use your Response Sheet to record your decisions and reasons.

—— 1. It's normal for people to tease each other about their ethnicity.

—— 2. When you mention someone's race, you are asking for a fight.

—— 3. There's nothing wrong with teasing other kids as long as you don't mention race or religion.

—— 4. When people call each other racial names, it usually indicates hate.

After You Read

On your own, answer the questions below. Write your answers on the Response Sheet.

1. Why do you think "Woo" is so angry?

2. Why do you think Lydia decided to get involved in this fight?

3. Why do you think Lydia asked Miguel if he knew "Woo's" real name?

4. What do you think "Woo" should do from this point forward?

5. How would you define the term "acceptance"? (Use your own words.)

Think About It

Compose an interior monologue in which Miguel analyzes the situation for a few minutes and decides what he should do next.

SAMANTHA'S SOLUTION

Samantha slumped in her desk and kept her face down. She didn't want anyone to see the red mark on her cheek. It still stung!

She couldn't concentrate on the lesson. She kept going over the ugly incident that had happened before class. Mariah, once a friend, had hit her in the face! Sam was hurt and shocked, especially when Mariah warned her, "Stay away from my boyfriend, or I'll hit you again."

"She thinks I'm trying to steal him," Sam thought. "What a joke. We're just good friends. I've known Jason since first grade."

Sam looked up to see the teacher staring at her. "Samantha, you're usually one of the first students to make a comment on our reading. I always look forward to your contribution. Is anything wrong today?"

Samantha slumps to a new low.

"No, I'm just tired," Sam said, holding a hand to her cheek.

Mrs. Morrow gave her a curious look, but let it go. She called on another student.

After class, instead of hurrying away, Sam lingered in the back, dragging her feet. She was trying to gather the courage to confide in her teacher. Mrs. Morrow sat at her desk patiently, as if waiting for Samantha to make up her mind. She smiled kindly.

Sam realized she really needed her teacher's advice. "Mrs. Morrow, I feel like I can tell you anything." She flushed. "I have a problem and I don't know what to do." She blurted out the whole story. "I'm worried now that Mariah doesn't believe me and will try to hit me again."

Mrs. Morrow shook her head and asked, "Did you report this?"

"No, I'm afraid she'll get even madder." Sam's answer made her sound like a wimp, and she began to regret talking at all.

"That's understandable. Tell me, what would you like to see happen?" Mrs. Morrow's response reassured Sam. She knew then that she had made the right decision.

Samantha and Mrs. Morrow began to work on resolving the problem.

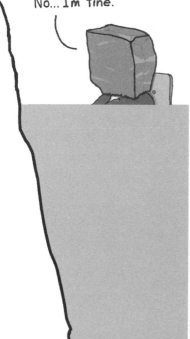

No... I'm fine.

Before You Read

Consider each statement below. Decide whether or not you agree with it. Use your Response Sheet to record your decisions and reasons.

_____ 1. If someone hits you at school, you should report it.

_____ 2. Very few teachers can be trusted.

_____ 3. People who are eager to fight are usually having personal problems.

_____ 4. It is not possible for girls and guys to be "just good friends."

_____ 5. Personal problems don't have to affect your schoolwork.

After You Read

On your own, answer the questions below. Write your answers on the Response Sheet.

1. Why might Mariah have a problem with Sam being friends with her boyfriend?

2. How can a person's personal problems affect his or her performance in class?

3. What might Samantha's solution be?

4. How would you define the term "trust"? (Use your own words.)

Think About It

Write a list of characteristics that you would look for in a person to help decide if you could trust him or her.

CORNERED AGAIN!

Mr. Barton, my language teacher, hates me and won't give me a chance. He moved me into a corner because he thinks I'm too "disruptive." I don't know why. I act like all the other kids. That one time he caught me, I was just asking my neighbor a question about the assignment. Mr. Barton blew up and moved my seat into a corner. It makes a person self-conscious to be sitting away from everyone.

For the first few minutes of every class, we do "bell work." When we come in, the question is always on the screen. Sometimes I don't understand the question, but I don't dare ask for help. Mr. Barton says that we have to do our bell work independently.

I just sit there looking stupid, while he says in an irritated tone, "Carlos, read the question and answer it in your log. You should know this! It's a review of what we learned yesterday."

Mr. Barton calls only on his favorite students, the ones who always have the right answers. Sometimes I'd like to have a turn if I think I know the answer, but the teacher won't give me a chance. He only calls on me when he's sure I don't know the answer. And then I get to look stupid in front of the class again.

There's another reason I'm sure Mr. Barton hates me. He yells at me more than the other kids. I do something to set him off almost every day. Today it was the Renaissance. I guess I'm stupid, but I've never heard of that. He seems to think I'm supposed to know stuff before we learn it. He yelled at me again. I don't know why.

I don't bother asking for help anymore. Barton will just give me the same old reply: "Not now, Carlos!"

I wish I could at least sit in my old seat. I know that would boost my confidence. Instead, I do what I can to survive for 55 minutes, and try not to think of the big fat 'F' I'll be getting on my report card. When the bell rings for lunch—I fly.

class 6

English

"The Renaissance"

The Renaissance was a kind of popular salad dressing used back in the olden days by peasants who couldn't like the real good stuff. About the thousand island, that all the rich folks ate. It was invented by a chef named Da Vinci, and he got real famous for it!

Before You Read

Consider each statement below. Decide whether or not you agree with it. Use your Response Sheet to record your decisions and reasons.

_____ 1. Sometimes teachers think kids are acting "bad" when they are not.

_____ 2. Teachers usually don't believe students' stories.

_____ 3. Not all students deserve help during every class period.

_____ 4. It's appropriate for teachers to give less attention to the smarter students in the class.

_____ 5. If you think a teacher doesn't like you, it is hard to know what to do.

After You Read

On your own, answer the questions below. Write your answers on the Response Sheet.

1. Why do you think this teacher moved Carlos to a different seat?

2. What behaviors did Carlos show that could be mistaken for seeking attention?

3. If you were one of Carlos's classmates, what would you do to help the situation?

4. What do you think Mr. Barton should do differently?

5. If nothing changes for Carlos, what do you think needs to happen?

Think About It

Create three different humorous captions for the cartoon on the story page. Get your classmates to vote for their favorite.

SKIPPING OUT

These notes were found, crumpled, on the lawn outside the middle school cafeteria. The finder read them and pondered what to do.

Hey Jimbo—
Mr. Cravelle, the P.E. teacher, is out today, and we have gym last period! Let's cut out and go to the Comic Shop at the mall. The substitute teacher will never know the difference.

Ben

COOOL IDEA, BENNY! I HEAR THE COMIC SHOP HAS THE LATEST "DARK AVENGER." I'M IN! WHERE SHALL WE MEET? IT WON'T BE EASY GETTING PAST OLD EAGLE-EYE, PRINCIPAL RUNSAK. HE'S ALWAYS ON THE PROWL AFTER LUNCH.

JIM
P.S. SHOULD WE INVITE WILL? YOU KNOW HE'LL BE TICKED OFF IF WE DON'T.

Duh, Jim!
We'll meet out back at the bike racks, of course. Where else? Go out through the cafeteria door, and be careful!!! Yeah, invite Will. He's cool, but that's it. Nobody else must know, especially my snooty sister, Jenna.

Ben

Jim and Ben,
I NEED the new "Dark Avenger"! Don't have a bike, though. I'll take my skateboard and meet you at the mall. Good plan, Ben.

Will

Ben!
DON'T YOU DARE PLAY HOOKY. I'LL TELL, I PROMISE. I OWE YOU ONE FOR SNITCHING TO MOM WHEN I WAS GOING TO GET MY EARS PIERCED WITH CARA.

JENNA

JENNA THE DARK AVENGER
I'm telling.

Crime never pays (especially if you leave evidence lying around).

Before You Read

Consider each statement below. Decide whether or not you agree with it. Use your Response Sheet to record your decisions and reasons.

_____ 1. There is no harm in skipping a class now and then.

_____ 2. People who drop notes on the ground want them to be read.

_____ 3. A student should adhere to all school rules.

_____ 4. A kid who skips class should be given a detention or suspension.

_____ 5. It is better to break a rule than to lose a friend.

After You Read

On your own, answer the questions below. Write your answers on the Response Sheet.

1. Do you think Ben went ahead with his plan?

2. Who is responsible if all three of these boys skip class?

3. Should any of these note-writers have said anything different than they did?

4. What would you do if you found these notes?

Think About It

Think of two (or more) different people who might have found the notes. Tell what you think each of them might have done.

NOT MY ROLE MODEL

Who knew middle school would be so much better than elementary school? All my friends are here, plus all kinds of new kids. It's great, most of the time. We see old friends, but we're all making new friends, and we want to hang with them, too.

Once in a while I catch up with Mike, my friend from grade school. Sometimes we'll kick a soccer ball around like we used to, but he has cool new friends and he wants me to hang with them, too.

Mike says things like, "My homie Dylan scored some really good weed. You should try it. I swear it's the coolest thing, sort of like floating in your head or flying around the room."

I don't think it's a good idea for Mike to smoke pot. But that's his choice. I'm just not interested. Besides, it's against the law and my dad would ground me for life if he found out. So, I avoid Mike and his friends most of the time. I miss his friendship.

One day, Mike invited me to his house after school to watch a movie. Better than doing homework, I figured, and I hadn't seen Mike in a while. "Why not?" I responded.

When I got there, his mom wasn't home. I found Mike in his room—with Dylan.

"Hey, Rob, buddy! You made it," Mike said, holding a joint.

"Yeah," I answered, realizing what I had walked into.

Rob declines a chance to fly.

"Grab a seat then," Mike said. "You got to try some of this weed!"

"Naw, man, I'm cool," I said.

Dylan sneered. "What's the matter, dude? Are you so straight you won't even try it?"

"You heard me. I don't want to."

That's when I knew it was time to leave. I heard Dylan mutter, "What a doofus!" as I left.

I don't see Mike much anymore. I wish things were different.

A friendship
goes up in smoke.

Before You Read

Consider each statement below. Decide whether or not you agree with it. Use your Response Sheet to record your decisions and reasons.

_____ 1. Most people feel that keeping friends happy is more important than doing what's right.

_____ 2. It is okay to do something you believe is wrong as long as you believe it won't hurt you and you think you can get away with it.

_____ 3. It's not cool for friends to try to make you do something you don't want to do.

_____ 4. If someone you know is smoking pot, the best thing to do is to tell their parents.

After You Read

On your own, answer the questions below. Write your answers on the Response Sheet.

1. How would you define the term "peer pressure"? (Use your own words.)

2. Why do you think kids try to pressure their friends into doing what they don't want to?

3. How do you tell your friends that you don't want to do something they are pushing you to do?

4. What do you think about the way Rob handled the situation?

5. Do you think Rob should try to maintain any kind of friendship with Mike?

Think About It

Assume that Rob wants to make another try at keeping his friendship with Mike. Role-play him making a phone call to Mike.

81   SCHOOL DAYZ

THE JOINER

Bill is addicted to joining clubs. When he enrolled in his new middle school, he joined Mathcounts, the yearbook staff, a service club, the debate team, band, and track. If an activity comes along that he can add to his schedule, Bill will always try to squeeze it in somehow.

He gets up early every morning for track practice before school. He attends lunchtime meetings for various clubs. He stays after school on Tuesdays and Thursdays for yearbook staff meetings. On Mondays, Wednesdays, and Fridays, he has additional track practice. Two evenings a week he rehearses with the band, and by the time Bill gets home, he is exhausted. He still has homework to do.

Mr. Hansen assigns a lot of reading in English class, and Bill finds it easy to let these assignments slide, as they usually aren't due until the end of the month. Last week, out of the blue, Mr. Hansen reassigned the month's reading as a group project. Each student was to find a partner and compare three assigned books.

Will the joiner join again?

Bill chose a friend from the track team. Chris was eager to start, and he had a lot of good ideas. As for Bill, he was already in over his head. He had been too busy to do more than skim the books, and his schedule now was so packed that finding time to connect with Chris was almost impossible. They agreed to meet on the weekend before the project was due. Then Bill remembered that the band was going out of town for a competition that weekend.

When Chris discovered that he had to finish the project by himself, he blew up. He wouldn't even talk to Bill at track practice. Bill had lost a friend. Worse, Mr. Hansen called Bill's mother and informed her that Bill seldom participated in class, didn't contribute much to his team project, and slept through most of the period. If he didn't come to class alert and better prepared, there would be serious consequences.

Bill knows he has to let go of some activities, but how, and which ones? All of his clubs mean a lot to him. Yet if he doesn't keep his grades up, he won't be able to stay in track or band.

82

Before You Read

Consider each statement below. Decide whether or not you agree with it. Use your Response Sheet to record your decisions and reasons.

_____ 1. All students should be involved in as many activities as they can.

_____ 2. If a friend lets you down, you need to "write him or her off."

_____ 3. True friends will always cover for each other.

_____ 4. It's normal for good friends to have a disagreement now and then.

THE CLUB CLUB!
The perfect club for students who can't join enough school clubs
Room 301, M-F   5-7:30 am

After You Read

On your own, answer the questions below. Write your answers on the Response Sheet.

1. Why do some students like to get involved in multiple school activities?

2. What do you think Bill should have done in this situation?

3. If you were one of Chris's friends, what advice would you give him?

4. Is it ever okay to take advantage of a friend?

5. How do you handle the pressure of school activities?

Think About It

With a partner, make a list of questions Bill should ask himself to help him decide how to cut down on activities.

FREAKS & JOCKS

Jeff pointed. "Hey, man," he said to his football-player friend, Zach. "You see that dude over there? He never talks. He's a freak."

The "freak" was Keith Flynn, a short kid who dressed weirdly and kept to himself. He had spiked hair with lavender tips, proudly sported multiple piercings, wore baggy clothes and yellow high-tops, and never looked up or talked to other students as he walked slowly down the halls.

"Whaddya mean 'never talks'?" Zach was an offensive lineman on the football team and one of the biggest kids in school. "Everybody talks. I'll bet I can get a rise outta him."

He went over and blocked Keith's way. "Hey, Weirdo. Are you walking your snail to the snail races?" Zach laughed at his own joke. He considered himself a funny guy. His friends laughed, too.

Keith totally ignored him, sidestepped, and continued walking.

"Look, I'm just trying to be friendly." Zach grabbed Keith by the shoulder. Keith shrugged off his hand, walked around the bigger boy again, and slowly shuffled away.

Zach's face burned. "Hey, nobody disses me in front of my crew." He shoved Keith against the wall. Keith put up his fists.

Quite a few students had gathered to watch. Some of them, hoping for a bit of excitement, chanted, "Fight, Freak. Fight."

. . . and in this corner, representing the Jocks . . .

Zach sneered."Fight me? Are you kidding? I'll cream him."

Keith kept his head down, his fists up, and his mouth shut. Zach pushed Keith in the shoulder again. "Let's get it on," he urged.

A student known as "The Bookworm" pushed through the crowd. She shook her finger and glared through her glasses. "What's the matter with you? Are you an idiot?"

Zach turned to stare at her.

Before You Read

Consider each statement below. Decide whether or not you agree with it. Use your Response Sheet to record your decisions and reasons.

_____ 1. It's natural for people to form cliques at school.

_____ 2. You should respect everyone's personal style choices.

_____ 3. If someone picks on you in public, you have to fight him or her.

_____ 4. People who behave or dress differently deserve to get picked on.

_____ 5. It is wrong not to speak to someone if they speak first.

After You Read

On your own, answer the questions below. Write your answers on the Response Sheet.

1. In what ways can Keith's and Zach's actions be interpreted?

2. How might Keith and Zach be similar?

3. Why do you think Keith acts and dresses the way he does?

4. Do you think Keith should have responded differently to Zach?

5. What impact do you think "The Bookworm" will have on the events?

Think About It

To which of the four characters can you relate best? Choose one and tell why.

RUNAWAY PHONE

Walking to school one morning, Jodi's best friend, Rachel, said, "Hey, I have a cool idea."

"I can only imagine," Jodi laughed. "What is it this time?"

"Let's do some slam texting. You know, like a crank call, only texting people instead? It's fun!"

Jodi thought for a minute. "I don't know. I don't have a phone in the first place, and what if we text a message to someone and they get mad?"

The thought of texting a cute boy turns this no-no into a yes-yes.

Rachel scrunched her face. "Look, just borrow your mom's phone for one day and we'll have fun. We won't do anything outrageous. In fact, the boys have baseball practice after school tomorrow. We can sit in the bleachers and text silly messages to the cute guys on the bench. Especially Jason . . . ."

That caught Jodi's attention. She had a not-so-secret crush on Jason, the cutest boy she knew. She reluctantly agreed, and the next morning quietly "borrowed" her mother's cell phone.

Things got out of hand almost at once. Leslie, another friend, took the phone and started texting as they walked to school. Jodi nearly had a panic attack when she realized that Leslie had walked off without returning it. She didn't catch up with Leslie until lunchtime, and to Jodi's horror, most of her mother's minutes were gone. Another student snatched the phone right out of her hand and started on another texting spree!

"Come on, don't do that to me. I'm going to get in big-time trouble!"

There were no minutes left when Jodi finally got the cell phone, but she was lucky to get it back at all. At home, her luck held, and she managed to return it to her mom's purse without being noticed.

Then the phone bill came. Her mom started asking questions. Jodi knew she was in big trouble.

86

Before You Read

Consider each statement below. Decide whether or not you agree with it. Use your Response Sheet to record your decisions and reasons.

_____ 1. Most kids use their cell phones in ways that are not appropriate.

_____ 2. If someone lets you use a cell phone, it is yours to use as you see fit.

_____ 3. Cell phones should not be allowed in school.

_____ 4. People who use cell phones all the time are insecure.

_____ 5. Texting is fun and can't hurt anyone.

Jodi learns to slam text.

After You Read

On your own, answer the questions below. Write your answers on the Response Sheet.

1. How would you describe Jodi's reasoning in this situation?

2. Why didn't Jodi do a better job of hanging onto the phone?

3. What would you do if this happened to you?

4. How would you handle the situation if you were Jodi's parents?

5. Should Jodi go back and say anything to her friends Rachel and Leslie?

Think About It

With a partner, create a scene showing how Jodi's mom reacts to the situation and how Jodi responds.

THE PRICE OF POPULARITY

Hannah wondered what it would be like to be one of the Barbies. Claire and Mikayla, her best friends, chattered away at her side, but she zoned them out and stared across the quad to where the popular kids sat. The Barbies all had long, beautiful hair and tanned legs. ("Barbies" was the name everyone gave them, because they looked like Barbie dolls.)

Hannah and her friends often laughed at the way the Barbies dressed alike and talked endlessly about boys, fashion, and makeup. Secretly though, they all wished they could be just like the popular girls.

One afternoon, Hannah saw the perfect Barbie outfit at the mall. She stared at it for a long time before deciding to buy it. The next day, she wore the outfit to school. She even borrowed some of her older sister's makeup. Claire and Mikayla rolled on the grass mocking her and calling her a "Barbie wannabe."

But that very day, Tiffany Rawlings beckoned her. Tiffany was the most beautiful and popular girl in school. "I almost didn't recognize you, Hannah," she said. "Love your makeover."

After that, Hannah began to receive more attention from the popular kids. Sometimes they invited her to join them. Flattered, she left her friends behind. She didn't mean to dump them, but this seemed like the only chance she would ever get to hang with the popular crowd.

Most of the time she sat on the edge of the group listening to them gossip about other students or people she didn't even know. No one ever talked about the things that interested Hannah: sports, art, music, and animals. After a week, Hannah made an important discovery—the Barbies were boring.

Hannah decides to become a Barbie.

At lunch the next Monday, she approached Claire and Mikayla as they sat at their usual table in the quad. They were talking about a movie they had recently seen. They ignored her.

Hannah cleared her throat. "I'm sorry, guys. I thought it would be cool to hang with the popular kids, but I don't fit in. I like my old friends better. I know you're probably mad at me, but I want to be friends again."

She waited for Claire and Mikayla to say something.

Before You Read

Consider each statement below. Decide whether or not you agree with it. Use your Response Sheet to record your decisions and reasons.

_____ 1. It is important not to forget who your real friends are.

_____ 2. Sometimes you can be popular without losing friends.

_____ 3. You don't have to be friends with everyone.

_____ 4. It's a good idea to change friends often and not worry what they think about you.

_____ 5. Popularity is worth just about any price.

After You Read

On your own, answer the questions below. Write your answers on the Response Sheet.

1. What suggestions might you give to a person who wants to be like the popular kids in their school?

2. What price are some people willing to pay for popularity?

3. What price are YOU willing to pay for popularity?

4. What are the consequences of changing friends often and forgetting old friends?

5. How would you define the term "friendship"? (Use your own words.)

Think About It

Compose a response that you think Claire and Mikayla should give to Hannah when she comes back to be their friend.

TOUGH TIMES FOR THOMAS

Each day was a trial for Thomas. It wasn't easy fitting in at a new school in the middle of the year. When he walked into a classroom, he sensed every student judging him. All the other students seemed more confident than he felt.

Between classes he wandered the halls, lost. He hated asking for help; it made him feel like a dork. When he arrived at class late, often the other students giggled. Most of the students had their own friends and cliques. No one seemed ready to befriend him— except Jamal in fifth-period English.

And that cloud looks just like a mom chasing her kid for skipping class.

Thomas lets his laid-back friends lull him into trouble.

"Don't let them get to you," he was fond of saying when Thomas was embarrassed by something that happened in class.

At lunch, Thomas often sought out Jamal and his friend Eddie. They seemed older, but Thomas didn't care. Finally, someone was talking to him! Jamal and Eddie were laid-back and easygoing (when they weren't full of tricks and mischief). Thomas could tell they came to school to have fun and be with their friends. Learning was purely an afterthought.

As time went by, Thomas began to hang regularly with Jamal and Eddie, two guys who were always ready to cut class and shoot the breeze. Soon, Thomas's schoolwork began to suffer. He didn't care much. It was only grades.

"Life is bigger than grades," Jamal said, before he and Eddie quit school entirely. Thomas didn't see them anymore. He was on his own again.

He began to cut class a lot, and he had to visit the principal's office more than once. Now he was always in trouble, both at school and at home. His mom went ballistic when she saw his report card. His parents grounded him from everything.

Life had become a mess, and Thomas was miserable. Something had to change.

90

Before You Read

Consider each statement below. Decide whether or not you agree with it. Use your Response Sheet to record your decisions and reasons.

_____ 1. All new students feel scared and lonely.

_____ 2. Everyone likes the tough guy.

_____ 3. If you are new to a school, other kids will make fun of you.

_____ 4. It's impossible to back down once you've made a decision.

_____ 5. You can make changes in your life if you really want to.

After You Read

On your own, answer the questions below. Write your answers on the Response Sheet.

1. How did Thomas's actions contribute to his loneliness?

2. What is a reputation, and how important is it?

3. What could a school do to help new students avoid this kind of situation?

4. How can you change a good or bad reputation?

5. How do you know that the friends you have now will be your friends ten years from now?

Think About It

What is the one thing you would most like to say to Thomas? Write a short note of advice to him.

ZERO FOR ZOE

When a person has a best friend, she has to help the friend out of a jam, right? Well, that's how it started with Zoe and me.

Zoe has been my friend since her family moved next door to mine in fifth grade. She's really funny, and we laugh at all the same things. Now that we're in middle school, we share most of the same classes.

Reading and studying are hard for Zoe, and her grades are not very good. Sometimes she tries to get her homework done, but other times it seems as if she just isn't interested. Off she'll go to the mall, or she'll spend hours watching television.

It began to look as if she would have to go to summer school if she didn't improve. That would have been terrible for both of us. We practically had the whole summer planned! So I invited Zoe to come to my house to do homework with me. I'm not a genius, but I do get pretty good grades. I thought I could tutor her, at least well enough to help her avoid summer school.

That turned out to be a bad idea. Zoe didn't come to read or study at all; she came to copy my homework.

Zoe's friend tries to help get her out of a jam.

"This isn't right," I told her. "You won't learn anything by copying me. What about tests?"

"Oh, come on," she begged, "you're my best friend. Just help me get through until the end of term, and I promise I'll do better next year." She pouted. "If I have to go to summer school my dad will cancel our trip to the beach."

I gave in, of course, and let her copy my work. We got away with it until a week ago. One of our teachers finally noticed that our papers were identical. When she brought it up, other teachers began to notice the same thing. Our homeroom teacher set up a conference with us and our parents.

This really bugs me. I shouldn't be the one in trouble! I was only helping a friend. On the other hand, maybe it's good for Zoe to get busted. I think she has some sort of problem that forces her to copy in the first place. I've never seen her read a book or anything. Maybe someone will find a way to help her.

Before You Read

Consider each statement below. Decide whether or not you agree with it. Use your Response Sheet to record your decisions and reasons.

_____ 1. Students should always be responsible for their own work.

_____ 2. Letting people copy your work is not going to help them learn.

_____ 3. People who don't do their own work are just lazy.

_____ 4. If you let someone copy your work, you are just as responsible as they are for their actions.

After You Read

On your own, answer the questions below. Write your answers on the Response Sheet.

1. What could be some reasons why Zoe doesn't do any of her own work?

2. If a friend wants to copy your homework, how do you respond?

3. What is the difference between sharing work and copying work?

4. What would you expect the teacher to do at the conference?

5. How would you define the term "honesty"? (Use your own words.)

Think About It

Create a dialogue between Zoe and her friend (the narrator) that takes place after the conference.

THE STAND-UP GUY

"Give me your lunch money **or else . . . .**"

Brett, the bully, always threatened the younger, weaker students. No one was brave enough to stand up to him. Brett had bullied Jon from the first day of school. Maybe it was because Jon was one of the smallest kids in school. Whatever the reason, Brett pushed Jon around in front of other kids and threatened to do worse.

"Hey punk, I want your allowance every week or I'll be on your case every day!" He had obviously found an easy target in Jon. The younger boy was so afraid of the bully that he did as he was told.

Weeks went by, and Jon lost money and lunches every day. He suffered humiliation after humiliation in front of his friends. The other students were scared to stick up for him. No one wanted to be Brett's next victim.

Jon complained to his parents, and his parents complained to the principal. But nothing ever changed. Brett would stop for a while, and then he would start harassing Jon again.

Jon's older brother Jake got sick and tired of seeing his brother abused. He gave Jon some advice. "You need to stand up for yourself or this jerk will never leave you alone. Next time he tries to take something, say 'No!' Call his bluff. Guys like him are all show."

Although Jon was really scared and didn't know if he'd be brave enough, he knew he had to do **something**—even if it meant getting beaten up. He worried about it all weekend but went to school on Monday, determined to follow his brother's advice.

Right on schedule, Brett cornered Jon outside school and demanded his pocket money and lunch. The smaller boy gulped down his fear. "No," he said. Then he carefully removed his glasses and tucked them away. "This bullying ends now."

The other kids began to creep away.

Jon quaked but stood his ground. "I'll never give you anything again, even if I have to fight you every day."

Brett looked puzzled. No one had ever stood up to him before.

Jon knows the bully is full of air.

Before You Read

Consider each statement below. Decide whether or not you agree with it. Use your Response Sheet to record your decisions and reasons.

_____ 1. It's just a fact of life that some people like to bully others.

_____ 2. The only way to deal with a mean person is to be nice back to them.

_____ 3. When someone is mean, it is usually because something bad is going on in his or her life.

_____ 4. Sometimes doing nothing takes a lot more courage than doing something.

After You Read

On your own, answer the questions below. Write your answers on the Response Sheet.

1. Why do you think Brett bullies other kids?

2. Do you think Jake gave Jon the right advice?

3. If you were Jon, what would you do in this situation?

4. How do you or your friends deal with bullying in your school?

5. How would you define the term "courage"? (Use your own words.)

Think About It

Finish the story. Write or tell it from the viewpoint of someone who witnessed the confrontation between Jon and Brett.

THE GREaT TORTILLA TOSS

Bear Tales

Ashville High School Newsletter

Home of the Grizzlies

October 20, 2009

Football Players Suspended After Tortilla Incident

Story by Kelsey Lamoge

Tortillas flew at last Friday's pep rally in a silly prank that brought serious consequences to Ashville High. Students and staff are divided as to whether the joke was harmless, or whether its perpetrators maliciously intended to humiliate the lower classmen.

According to several sources, the seniors on the varsity football team brought packages of soft tortillas to the pep rally and secretly distributed them to all students in the senior section of the gym. The plan was to toss them into the freshman section as the freshmen took their turn at the school cheer.

The plan worked. When the freshmen began to cheer, the tortillas sailed. Many students screamed. Most students laughed. Faculty and staff members were not amused. There were no reports of injuries.

Principal Arnold announced on Monday that all senior football team members would be suspended from school for one week and from the team for two weeks. In addition, she canceled all pep rallies for the remainder of the year.

This will no doubt have grave consequences for Ashville's chances at a championship football season. The question is: Can this team remain undefeated without the seniors?

Parents Demand Answers

According to Principal Arnold, hundreds of parents have expressed opinions about the tortilla incident and punishment.

Other sources indicate that legal action by players' parents may be pending.

An open meeting of school board members and parents will be held Thursday evening at 7:00 in the gym.

The diploma Principal Arnold intends to give this year's graduating seniors

COMMENT CORNER

"This is a major overreaction by the principal."
– *J.R. Skyle, Senior Class President*

"Seniors insulted our class bigtime. They should ALL be suspended."
– *Brittney Losh, Gr. 9*

"It was a harmless joke. Nobody got injured."
– *Terri Glass, Gr. 10*

"Now our winning football season is ruined. I think the principal made a huge mistake. She will never be forgiven."
– *Bradley Frist, Gr. 9*

"This will go down in AHS history as one of the best pranks ever."
– *Jayde Alcolla, Gr. 11*

Before You Read

Consider each statement below. Decide whether or not you agree with it. Use your Response Sheet to record your decisions and reasons.

_____ 1. Pep rallies are all about fierce competition among classes.

_____ 2. It's okay to play pranks that don't physically harm anyone.

_____ 3. Students who are rude to others should face consequences.

_____ 4. Often, the adult staff members in schools have no sense of humor.

After You Read

On your own, answer the questions below. Write your answers on the Response Sheet.

1. Why do you think the principal gave such a harsh punishment?

2. What would you advise the principal to do in this situation?

3. How would you feel about this if you were a member of that freshman class?

4. What sort of rules should be made regarding pep rally behavior?

5. Which of the comments in the "Comment Corner" is closest to what you might say about this incident?

Think About It

Make a brief statement to the principal from a parent of a suspended football player, the varsity football coach, or a 10th-grader.

THE MONSTER GETS TO GUS

Gus and Kirsten were the perfect couple. Gus was a football star, and Kirsten was the pretty head cheerleader. They could have stepped out of the pages of the latest teen magazine. But it all got spoiled when the green-eyed monster got to Gus.

Late in the fall, a new student arrived on campus. This male student had everything going for him; he was tall, strong, and athletic. Rumors soon swirled that this new guy had his eye on Kirsten. Although Gus had yet to meet the new student, he wasn't worried. He and Kirsten had been going together since middle school.

One afternoon as Gus practiced on the football field and Kirsten worked with her squad on the sideline, the stranger appeared in the bleachers. "Great moves, girls," he called.

Kirsten blushed. The new guy was really good-looking. She said, "Thanks. Can I help you?"

"I'm Nate, a new member of the cheer squad."

Kirsten was speechless.

A few days later as Gus walked down the hallway, a fellow football player slapped him on the back. "Don't worry man, there are other fish in the sea."

Gus thought about his friend's remark all afternoon, getting hotter and hotter as he imagined his girlfriend with another guy. He caught up with Kirsten and grabbed her arm. "Are you cheating on me? How dare you go behind my back with someone else!"

"Gus isn't too excited about the other fish in the sea."

"What are you talking about?"

"Don't act so innocent! You know what I mean." Gus was now yelling.

Nate walked up behind Kirsten. "What's going on?"

The moment Gus saw him, his face went purple and his hands came up. "Get away from my girl!" he shouted, thrusting his arm forward just as if he were threading the needle for a touchdown pass.

The punch hit an unintended target as the crowd gasped in horror.

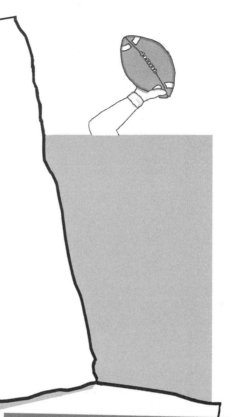

Before You Read

Consider each statement below. Decide whether or not you agree with it. Use your Response Sheet to record your decisions and reasons.

_____ 1. It is never okay to hit someone.

_____ 2. Most people believe everything they hear.

_____ 3. Feeling jealous is normal.

_____ 4. People don't always check out the facts before they take action.

_____ 5. People who love each other usually get into fights. It's all part of the game.

After You Read

On your own, answer the questions below. Write your answers on the Response Sheet.

1. What might be some reasons why Gus believed this rumor?

2. How would you describe Gus's respect for Kirsten?

3. Why do you think the crowd stood by and let this happen?

4. Whom do you think Gus was intending to hit, and why?

5. Who or what is the "green-eyed monster," and how could Gus deal with the monster?

Think About It

Briefly describe four different endings for this story. Ask some classmates to vote for the option they think is best.

99   SCHOOL DAYZ

PAIGE AND THE POD

Gabrielle, Trevor, and Roberto pushed their desks together and began to review their assignment for Mrs. Garcia's government class.

"Aren't you going to help us, Paige?" Gabrielle asked, even though she knew the answer. Paige never did anything. The four of them were supposed to be a pod, a team assigned to research and compare some of the famous civil rights speeches of the 1960's. So far, Paige's participation had been nil.

"Maybe later. If I feel like it." She yawned. "I'm bored."

Gabrielle and the other members of the group just looked at each other. All of them were thinking the same thing: It wasn't fair being stuck with Paige.

Each time the pods worked on their projects, Paige sat with her group and read a comic book or zoned out. The other members of the team chose the speeches, researched the orators, compared the high points of each speech, and explained the effect of the speeches on history.

The week ended and all projects were due. Gabrielle's pod received an A. Mrs. Garcia wrote "Excellent work" across the cover of their report. Each student, including Paige, received an individual grade of A as well.

Paige enjoys the company of the suckers who let her get away without doing any work.

After class, Gabrielle caught up with Paige. "You didn't do anything and still got the same grade we did. That's not fair!" she said.

"Look . . . in this world you make it any way you can. I've got a good system going and it works for me. It's not my fault the rest of you are suckers."

"Oooo!" Gabrielle shook with anger. "You can't cheat forever. You'll never make it in the world that way!" She stormed off.

Before You Read

Consider each statement below. Decide whether or not you agree with it. Use your Response Sheet to record your decisions and reasons.

_____ 1. Everyone should be responsible for his or her own work all of the time.

_____ 2. Most people want to be successful and are willing to work for it.

_____ 3. Some people like to see others fail.

_____ 4. Some students refuse to do work because they are afraid it is too hard.

_____ 5. Group projects usually give some students a free ride.

After You Read

On your own, answer the questions below. Write your answers on the Response Sheet.

1. What could the students have done to make sure that Paige got the grade she deserved?

2. What advice would you give to the teacher in this situation?

3. Why do you think Paige was unwilling to do the work?

4. What experiences have you had with this kind of group work problem?

5. How would you define the term "cooperation"? (Use your own words.)

Think About It

With three other people, role-play a scene in which some students from the pod discuss Paige's behavior with her—early in the project.

SHAY LOOKS DOWN

Shay is very close to his cousin, L. J., who is two years ahead of him at school. L. J. belongs to a gang and keeps urging Shay to join. Shay is not sure, but a girl he likes is also a member of the gang, and she only goes with guys who are "down." Because of Brenna, Shay reluctantly agrees to join the gang.

Much to the dismay of his friends, Shay likes school and tries to keep up because he loves animals and hopes to become a veterinarian some day. He knows he'll need college for that. Studying is hard for him, though. He sometimes has trouble reading and writing.

Shay and Brenna share a class in Career Ed. Brenna agrees to help him fill out a Career Interest Inventory form by reading the career categories aloud to him. She is more interested in talking about his gang membership, however.

"So, you're getting 'jumped in' today. I'm down with that! Now we can go out!"

"Don't talk so loud," Shay whispers. "I don't want anyone to know. I haven't really decided yet."

Will caring for injured animals beat out the gang for Shay's goal?

"What's the problem? Once you're a gang member, the only thing you're going to get is **RESPECT**!"

When Shay doesn't say anything, Brenna adds, "You know, your cousin L. J. can get you some 'work' and you can make bank. Buy me some presents—and you know I'll be happy!"

"I can't think about that right now, Brenna. This career stuff is important. Can you find a category for veterinarian? My mom says there's a vet tech class that I might be able to join. I'll buy you lots of presents some day, I promise."

Brenna slams the table with her fist. "Face it, Shay. You're never going to be a vet; you can hardly read! Get real. Joining the gang is the only chance you'll ever have to make it. And you're blowing it. I don't know if I even want to hang with you anymore."

Before You Read

Consider each statement below. Decide whether or not you agree with it. Use your Response Sheet to record your decisions and reasons.

_____ 1. Friends are the most important things in life.

_____ 2. School is only important for some people.

_____ 3. At a certain point, it's better to face reality than to keep trying when something is hard.

_____ 4. People have to make their own decisions.

_____ 5. There are some decisions in life that seem almost impossible to make.

After You Read

On your own, answer the questions below. Write your answers on the Response Sheet.

1. Why do you think Shay is considering joining a gang?

2. What is your opinion of Brenna's pressure on Shay?

3. Which of these would be your choice for ending this story?

   a. Shay decides to join the gang and run around with Brenna.

   b. Shay decides that the gang life isn't for him, so he dumps both Brenna and L. J. and decides to study hard so he can have a chance to become a veterinarian.

   c. L. J. decides to encourage Shay to go his own way.

   d. Shay gets jumped in, but faces consequences for his hesitation.

Think About It

Make a list of the arguments that could be going on in Shay's head for and against joining the gang.

DRESS-CODE DEBATE

Over the summer, a committee of teachers and administrators at Mt. Stensen Middle School created a proposal for a new student dress code. Parents were asked to review the proposal and respond with notes or emails. Here are a few parent responses:

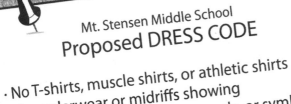

Mt. Stensen Middle School
Proposed DRESS CODE

- No T-shirts, muscle shirts, or athletic shirts
- No underwear or midriffs showing
- No gang-related garments, words, or symbols
- No open-toed shoes or sandals
- No jeans or denim clothing
- No shorts
- No bedroom slippers or pajamas
- No hooded sweatshirts or hats
- No sagging pants
- No spaghetti straps, backless, low-cut, strapless, or halter-style tops or dresses
- Boys: Shirts must have collars, and must be tucked into pants at all times.
- Girls: Skirts or dresses must reach below the length of the fingertips when arms are straight down at sides.

I feel that my daughter's personal style and individual rights are violated by this dress code. It is far too restrictive.
- Dr. Ronald Zimmer

Kids will still find ways to bend these rules. It's time for uniforms. That will assure appropriate dress and eliminate clothing competitions.
- Mrs. Judith McGraw

WE WANT UNIFORMS

Finally!
It's good to see you requiring students to dress decently!
-Susan Jackson

Our family cannot afford to buy one whole set of clothing for school and another for outside school—for three children. Students will not want to wear these "dress code" clothes anywhere but school. This feels like discrimination against less affluent families.
-Anthony Moscheo

Somebody forgot to read the dress code.

Before You Read

Consider each statement below. Decide whether or not you agree with it. Use your Response Sheet to record your decisions and reasons.

_____ 1. Dress codes stifle individual expression.

_____ 2. Without a dress code, students will dress indecently.

_____ 3. Students who dress inappropriately are more likely to behave badly.

_____ 4. The way you dress has nothing to do with your grades or study habits.

_____ 5. Students will dress appropriately without a dress code, if you just ask them to do so.

After You Read

On your own, answer the questions below. Write your answers on the Response Sheet.

1. How would you feel about this dress code for your school?

2. Which of the parent responses would your parent(s) be most likely to support?

3. Who should create a dress code for a middle school or a high school?

4. Who should enforce a dress code?

5. How does the clothing you wear affect your schoolwork?

Think About It

Create your own dress code for your school. Or, come up with another way to get kids to dress appropriately at school.

SOMETHING ABOUT MAX

Max rarely completed his homework or paid attention in class. He used profanity even in front of teachers; he sometimes bullied younger students; and he displayed a lot of "attitude." But these things were not the reasons that teachers and students felt he was different. There was something about him that no one could pinpoint until a certain day in May.

Some younger boys were kicking stones across the schoolyard during lunch break. "Dirt wads," Max mumbled. He slumped against a post and ogled girls at a nearby table.

A stone hurled through the air and smacked Max in the shin. Max exploded. He jumped across the yard shouting obscenities and grabbed the kicker, a young boy named Alex, by the front of his shirt. Max punched him, hard, several times in the face.

Screaming and bleeding from his nose, Alex ran to the nearest teacher. Max acted as if nothing had happened and nonchalantly went back to leering at the girls.

The principal summoned Max to his office and questioned him about the incident. Max's version of the story was different from Alex's. He told the principal that the younger boy had pummeled him with rocks (he showed the mark on his shin) and had fallen on his nose while running away. It all happened so fast that none of the supervising lunch guards had seen the incident, and there were no other witnesses.

Because no one could verify either boy's story, the principal was forced to drop the matter without punishment. But all the teachers believed Alex. They now knew what made Max different from the other students. Max appeared to have no sense of right and wrong, and no empathy for other people's pain.

Max appears to have no sense of right and wrong.

Before You Read

Consider each statement below. Decide whether or not you agree with it. Use your Response Sheet to record your decisions and reasons.

IT'S ALL THE SAME

_____ 1. It is rare that teachers can get the real story about incidents that happen on the school grounds.

_____ 2. Nobody ever gets hit on the school grounds because of an "accident."

_____ 3. Any time a student gets hurt, someone needs to be punished.

_____ 4. Kids can't always control their impulses.

After You Read

On your own, answer the questions below. Write your answers on the Response Sheet.

1. Why might some people feel that Max was justified in hitting Alex?

2. Should the principal have handled this situation differently? (if so, how?)

3. Why do you think Max does not care about this incident or about Alex?

4. Can you think of some ways Max could be helped?

5. What would you do if you were in a class with Max?

Think About It

Give some examples of things you do to control your anger or aggressive behavior.

MAKING THE GRADE

"Class, I have your progress reports ready," Mrs. Lamott said, holding a sheaf of papers. "I'm sure most of you will be pleased." She began calling up individual students by name.

The students scrutinized their reports with varying degrees of groans and grins.

Marcus, sitting in the back of the room, yelled, "Hey, Sarah, how many A's did you get this time? Aced them all, I'll bet. Do you all know why girls and geeks always get the best grades? It's because Mrs. Lamott likes them best."

Robert questions the fairness of his teacher's grading policy.

Robert, a few rows away, crumpled his report. "This isn't right. I didn't make any zeroes this term! I'm not taking this report home! You're hard on me because you don't like me, Mrs. Lamott, and it's just not fair!"

Mrs. Lamott was generally considered a fair teacher by most of her students. Some thought she was a little old-fashioned, but she was always very calm and reasonable.

She walked over to Robert's desk and asked him to carefully read the notes she'd left on his report. "I've written explanations concerning your marks that might help you to understand."

Robert's face grew red. He didn't bother to read her explanations. Angrily, he pushed away from his desk and threw his paper in the garbage. "It's not fair," he shouted again. "I'm telling you, it's just not fair!" Then he kicked the garbage can over and stormed out of the room.

Mrs. Lamott turned to the class. "It's okay. Robert's pretty upset right now. Take a moment and study your own grade reports. If you have any questions, or if your parents want to know how I grade, I'll be happy to meet with them or you."

ROBERT

Before You Read

Consider each statement below. Decide whether or not you agree with it. Use your Response Sheet to record your decisions and reasons.

_____ 1. Teachers favor smart kids and girls.

_____ 2. Grades don't really tell what a student knows.

_____ 3. It is okay to hit or kick something if you get mad.

_____ 4. Most kids can control their behavior if they choose to do so.

_____ 5. Parents should not always expect their kids to get good grades.

After You Read

On your own, answer the questions below. Write your answers on the Response Sheet.

1. Why do you think Robert reacted the way he did?

2. How did Marcus contribute to the situation?

3. What could Robert do to resolve the issue and maintain a good relationship with Mrs. Lamott?

4. What could other students do in response to Robert?

5. Given what the story reveals about Robert and the teacher, how do you think the story will end?

Think About It

With a partner, make suggestions about how the teacher could change grading policies to avoid this situation in the future.

LEFT HOLDING THE BAG

Sydney heard rumors of a party at a friend's house. "What's the deal?" she asked Jennifer. "Why wasn't I invited? It looks like some of my friends are going to be there."

"It's, uh . . . not really your kind of party," Jennifer said, laughing nervously.

"We'll see about that," Sydney decided.

She arrived at the party alone and looked for a familiar face. "Hey, Jennifer, how's it going?"

Jennifer giggled and acted strangely.

"Are you okay?" Sydney asked. "Where are Roger's parents?" Roger was the kid throwing the party. "Aren't there any chaperones?"

Jennifer giggled even harder. "His parents are out of town—hello!!"

"I'm outta here, then," Sydney said. "I'm not allowed to go to parties without chaperones."

"Don't go yet! The fun's just starting!" Jennifer approached with a big candy bowl of candy; only it wasn't filled with candy. "Dig in," she said.

Suddenly, Sydney understood what Jennifer meant when she said Roger's party was not her kind of fun. She ran outside, relieved to get away.

At lunch the next Monday, Jennifer and some of the other kids were cool toward her. "You aren't one of us anymore; you didn't take the pills. You're going to pay for dissing us."

Jennifer pulled out a bag of pills and dropped it onto Sydney's lap. Then she stood back and yelled. "Mr. Maguire! Mr. Maguire! Sydney has something illegal here!"

Sydney was stunned. She sat, paralyzed. Her friend had set her up. The campus supervisor came over and found her holding the bag. He grabbed the pills. "I think I'd better take you to the discipline dean."

Before You Read

Consider each statement below. Decide whether or not you agree with it. Use your Response Sheet to record your decisions and reasons.

_____ 1. It is okay to take other people's prescription medicine, since it came from a doctor.

_____ 2. If a friend ever sets you up to get in trouble, you should never trust that person again.

_____ 3. You should always stay true to your own values—even if it causes you to lose friends.

_____ 4. In order to keep friends, you sometimes must follow the crowd, even if you don't agree with what they are doing.

After You Read

On your own, answer the questions below. Write your answers on the Response Sheet.

1. Why do you think Sydney didn't just tell her friends that she did not want to take the drugs?

2. What should Sydney tell her friends when she sees them next?

3. If you were Sydney, what would you tell the dean?

4. In what situations has peer pressure caused you to do something you really did not want to do?

5. How would you like this story to end?

Think About It

Write a caption for the cartoon on the story page.

THE LIST

Cassandra started a list of girls in her class she considered worthy to be in the "in group" and those she thought should definitely be "out." She shared the list with Mandy, who made comments and passed back her own version.

Cassandra's list:

In

Kayley – her dad gave her a car!

Renatta – new student from Italy, cute accent, cute clothes

Sophie – dates Jeff Parsons, most popular boy in school

Parker – my BFF, dresses so HOT

Reese – her mother owns a ski lodge

Mia – dates high school boys

Out

Ludmilla – potato face

Dora – hangs with nerds

Brittany – stole BFF Parker's boyfriend

Stephanie – looks like a boy

Lorrie – are you kidding? Who can count the ways?

Abby – should hold the world record for being the geekiest student, ever!

Mandy's list:

In

Kayley – her dad gave her a car (?) SHE IS ONLY 13!!!!

Renatta – new student from Italy, cute accent, cute clothes. SHE'S PASSABLE.

~~Sophie~~ – OUT. Jeff Parsons just dumped her!! He's now dating Brittany. So, BRITTANY IS IN.

~~Parker~~ – OUT. dresses HOT, but not enough to keep a boyfriend.

Reese – her mother owns a ski lodge. OK, SHE'S IN, but what's with those zits?

Mia – dates high school boys. DOES SHE DOUBLE DATE?

Out

Ludmilla – potato face   HER NAME ALONE SAYS IT ALL.

Dora – hangs with the nerds   SHE IS A NERD.

Brittany – BRITTANY IS DEFINITELY IN!

Stephanie – looks like a boy. ENOUGH SAID!!

Lorrie – Who can count the ways? I CAN COME UP WITH A DOZEN.

Abby – holds world record for being the geekiest student, ever. AMEN!!!!!!

Chloe – MUST ADD. SHE HAS THE WORLD'S TACKIEST CLOTHES!

Cassandra, Queen of the IN-Crowd

Before You Read

Consider each statement below. Decide whether or not you agree with it. Use your Response Sheet to record your decisions and reasons.

———— 1. All pre-teen and teenage girls are mean and critical.

———— 2. You should never write anything in a note that you wouldn't want seen by the public in general.

———— 3. Words don't hurt people; only actions do.

———— 4. It's okay to have a list of people you like and don't like.

———— 5. Students should be held accountable for any criticisms they put into writing.

After You Read

On your own, answer the questions below. Write your answers on the Response Sheet.

1. What do you think motivated Cassandra to start this list and Mandy to get in on it?

2. If you read these lists and found your name, how would you feel?

3. Suppose one or both of these lists fell into your hands, but that your name was NOT on either list. How would you respond to the writer(s)?

4. In general, how do you feel about this practice of including others in (or excluding them from) the "in group"?

5. How would you define the term "inclusion"? (Use your own words.)

Think About It

Make a list of 10 possible consequences of making such a list (consequences to the writers, the people named, and/or others).

"KING" MARIO

Mario Macarini swaggered down the halls of Midtown Middle School like a preening lion king with five royal escorts. He dressed in black leather and wore a lot of bling, like chains and rings. His hair was slicked back like a hoodlum in a B-movie. His attitude when he walked into a classroom seemed to be: "You lower beings are lucky I deigned to come at all." Then he'd snap his fingers and one of his hangers-on would put his homework on the teacher's desk. Everyone knew that another one of his "peeps" had done the homework in the first place.

If a teacher dared to call him on it, he and his entourage would walk out *en masse.* He only came to school in the first place because his uncle Babaloo "The Boss" Macarini insisted his nephew needed an education if he wanted to get into "the business." On his own, Mario couldn't have cared less.

Mario spent most of his time sizing up the "foxes" who walked past his throne room in the cafeteria (third row, center table—and none dared sit there without an invitation). Mario and his boys would hoot, whistle, and holler "Hot Mama!" at the pretty girls, and bark like dogs at the plain ones.

Lisa Lazarrio finally found the courage to complain to the counselor. "Mario is sexually harassing the girls; it's got to stop!"

When the final bell signaled the end of another school day, the dean of students escorted Mario to her office, informing him that she had called his uncle to come in for a conference.

Mario's face got red. He shouted, "You had no right to do that, you @!*!#@! You have no idea who you're messing with!" Then he called her a name in another language. Even his crew gasped in shock.

She didn't know the word but understood the sentiment. "Let's see what your uncle has to say when we tell him you are this close to being expelled." She held her thumb and forefinger an inch apart.

The "king" of the middle school began to sweat, but he couldn't drop his blustering bravado. "Go ahead and expel me. That's what I want, anyway. But don't blame me when my uncle takes it out on you!"

Is the king's power all an illusion?

Before You Read

Consider each statement below. Decide whether or not you agree with it. Use your Response Sheet to record your decisions and reasons.

_____ 1. Students admire other students who don't follow the rules.

_____ 2. Whistling and "catcalls" to girls are acceptable ways to get their attention.

_____ 3. If you make inappropriate comments in another language to teachers and other school staff members, your friends will think you are "cool."

_____ 4. Every school has someone who acts like the "king" of the school, and most kids are not that impressed.

After You Read

On your own, answer the questions below. Write your answers on the Response Sheet.

1. What might be the reason that Mario is so defiant toward adults at the school?

2. How would you explain the fact that Mario's "peeps" act like slaves for him?

3. Why might some students think of Mario as a leader?

4. What are your thoughts about the line between appropriate comments to the opposite sex and sexual harassment?

5. How would you define the term "self-respect"? (Use your own words.)

Think About It

Review your definition of self-respect. Decide whether or not Mario has it. Prepare a list of reasons to defend your decision.

MEGHAN IN THE "MEDDLE"

My name is Meghan and I'm in high school. I have a class with this guy Geoff. He's kind of geeky but nice. We've been told that he is sick and will be missing a lot of school. I feel sorry for him. When I heard about his problems, I kind of teared up.

Geoff is a bit behind in reading, and he has trouble pronouncing words because of his illness. Some of the other kids are heartless and make fun of his handicaps. I just don't understand that.

First of all, he's not stupid; he's just missed a lot of school. Elijah and his goons like to tease him. Geoff ignores this most of the time, but he has been known to sound off when enough is enough!

Geoff has just started attending classes regularly again. I guess he's a lot better. Elijah and his friends won't stop bugging him, though. Some of the things they pull are downright mean. For instance, they grab his backpack and dump it out on the floor—knowing that it is hard for him to bend and pick things up. Or, they make a human obstacle course that makes it almost impossible for Geoff to get to his desk.

They even taunt me when I stand up for Geoff. "He's a weirdo," they say, "and if you're his friend, you must be one, too."

My real friends tell me to stop meddling in the situation because Elijah has been known to make life miserable for those he dislikes. I don't care. I can take it.

One day, I got so mad and shouted so loudly that Ms. Stone heard me. I let all my frustrations out. I told her that Elijah's gang was mean, even vicious, to Geoff. Boy, I let them have it! Elijah got in trouble, and Ms. Stone is on to them now.

I had to do something, didn't I? Nothing will ever change if someone doesn't take action. But now I walk around school with a big target on my back.

Meghan watches her back.

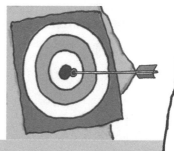

Before You Read

Consider each statement below. Decide whether or not you agree with it. Use your Response Sheet to record your decisions and reasons.

_____ 1. It is okay to make fun of someone as long as everyone is laughing.

_____ 2. Anyone who witnesses cruelty to another person is responsible for stopping it.

_____ 3. There are always risks to sticking up for someone whom others are teasing.

_____ 4. It's fine to meddle in someone's business if your intention is to be helpful.

After You Read

On your own, answer the questions below. Write your answers on the Response Sheet.

1. Why do you suppose that Elijah and his friends are so intent on teasing Geoff?

2. Who do you think is harmed more by the cruelty—Geoff or the kids who are mean to him? (Explain your answer.)

3. In your opinion, what is the responsibility of the other students in this case?

4. Meghan risked having to deal with Elijah's wrath. What possible benefits could result from her actions?

5. How would you describe an "advocate"? (Use your own words.)

Think About It

Make a list of ways you could be an advocate for someone else in your school.

SHEENA'S SLIDE

Sheena's super-sized, vividly colored paintings filled the walls of the tiny apartment. Her sister Bianca cocked her head and squinted at Sheena's latest picture. "I don't get it."

"Great art is never understood. If it were, it wouldn't be great." That's what Sheena told her older sister, but that was just a smoke screen. Deep down she was insecure about her art, her friendships, her schoolwork, and, in fact, everything about her life. She really did feel like an unwanted kid and a misunderstood artist.

Sheena had real talent and a lot going for her, but she had been moved around a lot from foster home to foster home before moving in with her married sister. This new school was just one more place to fail.

Her sister didn't understand her insecurities. She expected Sheena to make something of herself. Sheena didn't like it when Bianca lectured her to work harder. Her grades at the new school were pretty mediocre and quickly sliding downward, and Sheena really didn't care. Her whole attitude, in fact, was on a downward slide. Good grades wouldn't get her anywhere. They wouldn't help her fit in better or to magically get friends. All she cared about was drawing, and there were no decent art classes at Ravenswood Middle School.

Mr. Pitcher, Sheena's counselor, recognized her talent. He called together Sheena's teachers and her sister for a conference. Sheena did not want to be there, but she was resigned to her fate, sure that everyone would dump on her for her grades.

She was right: The meeting **was** about her grades. But it was not all bad. Mr. Pitcher explained that Sheena might be eligible for acceptance into a very prestigious charter high school next year if she could just bring her grades up. This school, on the other side of town, had an excellent art program.

Sheena listened with growing excitement. Then reality set in. What was the use of hoping? She was too stupid to get better grades, she thought. And besides, a poor foster kid like her would never fit in with that fancy high school crowd.

Once you're on this slide, it's a fast ride down.

Before You Read

Consider each statement below. Decide whether or not you agree with it. Use your Response Sheet to record your decisions and reasons.

_____ 1. When you're having trouble at school, it is normal to feel like giving up.

_____ 2. Anybody can rise above his or her circumstances and accomplish anything they want.

_____ 3. It is never easy to fit in at a new school.

_____ 4. If you are really unhappy about something, you should try to find someone to tell about it.

After You Read

On your own, answer the questions below. Write your answers on the Response Sheet.

1. How could Sheena's sister help her feel better and do better?

2. What would you say to Sheena to help her stop her downward slide?

3. How have you felt when you have had to change schools? (Or how would you feel if you had to move to a different school right now?)

4. What do you expect will be the outcome of the conference?

5. How would you define the term "self-confidence"? (Use your own words.)

Think About It

Draw a talk balloon. Write in it what Sheena would like to say to her older sister during the conference.

CELEBRITY WANNABE

Teenage singer-performer and movie star Darcy Dakota was Joelle's heroine. Joelle had been studying tap and ballet and taking singing lessons since the age of three. Now she dreamed of becoming one of Darcy's backup singers! If only she could find someone to film her singing and dancing to one of Darcy's popular songs, she would send a video to her and ask for an audition.

In her quest to be a star, Joelle "borrowed" her parents' video camera, took it to school, and looked for someone to help her. She saw her good friend Connor watching the soccer team practice.

"Hey, Connor," she called. "Will you do me a favor?"

She offered him $10 if he would take 10 minutes and film her doing her best Darcy imitation.

Joelle has big dreams.

"Sounds good," he agreed.

They decided to go behind the climbing wall to block the view of anyone who might be watching. Joelle was too shy to let other students see her performing (before she got the job), and they both knew video cameras weren't allowed on the school grounds. When she was ready, Joelle turned on her digital music player and started to sing and dance while the camera rolled.

At the end of the song, she put her hands around her mouth and shouted, "Hi, Darcy! This song was for you, and if you liked my singing, email me at jjll22@coolmail.com."

She took the video home, copied it onto a DVD, and mailed it to Darcy Dakota the very next day. Connor secretly transferred a copy to his phone, took it home, and uploaded it onto YouTube without telling Joelle.

If Joelle was looking for fame or notoriety, she got it. She received dozens of emails from Internet users, some of them rather questionable! Her parents were not pleased.

She is still waiting to hear from Darcy Dakota.

YouTube

TEXT COMMENTS (43)

funboy15 (1 day ago)
thanx for the laff!! I spit out my coke watching this!

DarceyFan1 (1 day ago)
i am SO sure!!!! U couldn't even be a backup singer for barney the dinosaur!

daFreak23 (1 day ago)
hey joelle...you're a SUPERFREAK! hahahaha!

slimshadey (1 day ago)
the pain!! make it go away!! lol!

Before You Read

Consider each statement below. Decide whether or not you agree with it. Use your Response Sheet to record your decisions and reasons.

_____ 1. Kids who are "wannabe" stars are totally unrealistic.

_____ 2. It is relatively harmless to put yourself on the Internet.

_____ 3. Students should not bring video cameras to school.

_____ 4. If someone on the Internet contacts you, it's easy to figure out if they are a safe person to talk to and if they have harmless intentions.

_____ 5. Most kids think that they have talent.

After You Read

On your own, answer the questions below. Write your answers on the Response Sheet.

1. Why might some people think that it was a mistake for Joelle to make this video?

2. What do you think is Connor's responsibility in this incident?

3. If Joelle had asked you to do the filming, what would you consider before saying "yes"?

4. What could result from the actions Joelle and Connor took (making and posting this video)?

5. Would you define Joelle's "project" as reasonable and responsible behavior?

Think About It

Prepare a text message giving Joelle any advice you think she needs to hear.

THE CLASS CLOWN

I sit next to Gabe in Math and Social Studies. Besides being cute, he is the class cutup and clown. He makes us laugh every chance he gets by imitating the teachers behind their backs, turning every question and answer into a pun or joke, throwing spit wads across the room, or just making silly faces and noises. I've always kind of liked Gabe. Not only is he funny, he's smart, too.

The other day, Mrs. Delgado told him that if he would settle down and do some real work, she would recommend him for honor classes next semester. (She must see the same potential in him that I do.)

He dove into his studies for several days after that, but come Monday, Gabe was back to his old clowning ways. I noticed (not for the first time) that he often showed up on Mondays with bruises and marks on his body. I began to wonder if the bruises were payback for a practical joke, or if he was having trouble at home.

That day he went too far. He went on and on, teasing Mrs. Delgado about her new hairstyle, making the most clever and hilarious wisecracks. The class was hysterical. Mrs. Delgado was a good sport at first, but after several incidents and minutes of chaos, she sent him to the principal's office.

"Maya, why don't you go with him?" she said to me. She handed me a note and told me to give it to the secretary.

"Are you here again, Gabriel?" the secretary asked, looking up from her computer. "Where's your note?"

Gabe sank glumly onto the chair and kept mute. I put the note on the secretary's desk and sat down beside Gabe.

What's really going on behind the smile?

Before You Read

Consider each statement below. Decide whether or not you agree with it. Use your Response Sheet to record your decisions and reasons.

_____ 1. A class clown almost always makes jokes to cover up a lack of self-esteem.

_____ 2. Some people are just naturally funny; they are not necessarily trying to be a problem.

_____ 3. Kids who laugh at the class clown are just as responsible for the disruption as the funny guy.

_____ 4. It is always desirable to have a comedian in a class.

_____ 5. Whether a kid is mean, sassy, hostile, or funny—all disruptive students are equally annoying in a class.

After You Read

On your own, answer the questions below. Write your answers on the Response Sheet.

1. What might really be going on here (in spite of Gabe's constant joking)?

2. It is often said that people who joke just want attention. Do you think this is true of Gabe?

3. How do you think kids would treat Gabe if he stopped clowning around?

4. If you were Gabe's classmate, how would you respond to him?

5. How would you define the term "understanding" as it relates to this situation? (Use your own words.)

Think About It

With a partner, decide what Maya should say to the principal (if anything) and what the principal should do about Gabe.

THE DILEMMA

Jada is struggling with conflicting thoughts. This problem is trickier than most, because it involves her parents, of all things! She's not sure she will ever be able to decide what to do. But she has to—and soon.

I'M SO UPSET ABOUT THE GRADE I GOT ON THAT SCIENCE TEST!
MR. LUCAS DIDN'T GRADE IT FAIRLY. I DO UNDERSTAND PLANT PROCESSES; HE DIDN'T READ MY ANSWERS CAREFULLY. I TRIED TO TALK TO HIM, BUT HE WAS TOO CLOSED-MINDED! HE SAID THE GRADE COULD NOT BE CHANGED.

I NEVER SHOULD HAVE SAID ANYTHING TO MY MOM!

. . . NOW MY PARENTS ARE ALL WORKED UP ABOUT THIS LOW GRADE!
THEY KNOW HOW HARD I STUDIED. THEY ARE GOING TO CALL THE SCHOOL IN THE MORNING AND MAKE AN APPOINTMENT TO SEE MR. LUCAS.

. . . AND THEN WHAT?
MR. LUCAS WILL THINK I'M A BIG BABY GETTING MY PARENTS TO FIX THINGS FOR ME. THIS WILL ONLY MAKE MATTERS WORSE. FROM NOW ON, HE'LL BE EVEN HARDER ON ME. I JUST KNOW HE'LL HOLD A GRUDGE. TEACHERS DON'T LIKE TO BE CHALLENGED BY PARENTS. I SHOULD HAVE PUSHED HARDER FOR HIM TO RECONSIDER MY GRADE.

. . . BUT I CAN'T LIVE WITH THIS GRADE WHEN I KNOW I DON'T DESERVE IT!
MY GRADE POINT AVERAGE WILL BE RUINED, AND IT'S NOT A TRUE PICTURE OF MY WORK IN SCIENCE CLASS. I DON'T WANT A BAD GRADE. BUT I DON'T WANT MY PARENTS SHOWING UP AT SCHOOL TO RESCUE ME EITHER.

124

Before You Read

Consider each statement below. Decide whether or not you agree with it. Use your Response Sheet to record your decisions and reasons.

_____ 1. You should not tell your parents about troubles at school.

_____ 2. Teachers don't like it when parents try to fix things for you.

_____ 3. If you don't agree with a grade, you should discuss it with your teacher.

_____ 4. Most teachers would not be willing to discuss a grade or test score once it is given.

_____ 5. If you get something wrong on a test, it is certainly because you didn't know the material.

After You Read

On your own, answer the questions below. Write your answers on the Response Sheet.

1. How would you summarize Jada's dilemma?

2. When have you had a dilemma similar to Jada's?

3. Is there anything in the story that gives you a clue about what Jada might do?

4. How do you think Jada should solve this problem?

5. How would you define the term "self-advocacy"? (Use your own words.)

Think About It

Write a sentence that students could use to open a conversation with a teacher about a grade they wish to question.

JACKIE HITS THE WALL

My troubles with Jackie started when she decided to become my "wannabe" girlfriend. She practically stalks me. Almost every day, Jackie enters school talking and laughing loudly. She doesn't walk or run; she darts. Lately, instead of going directly to class, she stops at the water fountain and waits to trap me. I usually make a wide circle around the campus to avoid her, but this morning I was way late. I had to take my chances in the corridor.

"Hey, Aaron!"

I cringed when I heard her voice. Before I knew it, she popped up behind me and snatched the chain with my brother's dog tags from my neck. She scampered off, giggling, darting from side to side, and looking over her shoulder as if she expected me to follow. **No way.** Instead, I headed for Principal Simmons's office to snitch. I'd rather let the authorities deal with Jackie.

When Jackie turned to look for me, she ran smack into a wall and knocked her head on the corner. I saw it happen, but couldn't do anything. She fell back on the hallway floor with a bleeding gash over her left eye.

A crowd gathered around Jackie. She was stunned for a moment, and then realized she was bleeding. Hysterical screams filled the corridor, and even a few curses! I rushed to join the crowd. That's when I saw my chain and dog tags curled on the floor. I grabbed them and walked away as casually as I could. My brother gave me his tags when he got out of the army, and I did not want to lose them. They mean something.

Jackie discovers that stalking Aaron is "for the dogs."

The next day, Jackie returned to school with stitches over her eye. I saw her waiting for me by the water fountain.

Before You Read

Consider each statement below. Decide whether or not you agree with it. Use your Response Sheet to record your decisions and reasons.

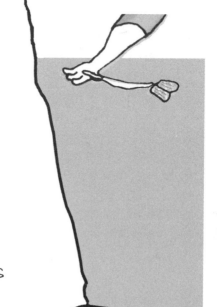

_____ 1. People naturally gather around when something dramatic is happening.

_____ 2. Taking someone else's "stuff" is a good way to let them know you like them.

_____ 3. You should worry about yourself and not care what others are doing.

_____ 4. There is nothing wrong with "stalking" somebody you like in school.

_____ 5. Kids can't always control themselves. It's normal to act crazy now and then!

After You Read

On your own, answer the questions below. Write your answers on the Response Sheet.

1. Why do you think Jackie felt it was okay to snatch the chain from Aaron?

2. What do you think Jackie learned from this incident?

3. If Jackie were your friend, what advice would you give her?

4. What do you predict will happen next?

5. How would you define the term "appropriate"? (Use your own words.)

Think About It

Work with a partner of the opposite sex to make a list of appropriate ways to let someone know that you like him or her.

WHEELS OF MISFORTUNE

After a fall in Elmwood Skateboard Park, Luke sat on his board and caught his breath.

"Hey, Dion, look at that new kid," Luke said, pointing and laughing. "What a geek! No real skateboarder wears a helmet and all those pads. He's a rookie!"

They watched as Gregorio, the new kid, pulled to the lip of the platform, swung down on his board, flew to the other side, did a kick turn, a roll, and came down on the slope of the pit. Then he went to the other side and repeated the move. He was so smooth that everyone stopped to watch.

Jaws dropped. Eyes were glued on the new kid as he went back and forth, flipping and turning. Eventually, he flew up and over the lip, grabbed his board, and landed on both feet. Then he held his board in the air as if acknowledging an applauding audience.

"Luke, I think we were wrong." Dion tucked his skateboard under his arm. "You gotta admit, he *can* skate."

"So what? He's still a nerd. And a showoff. With all that gear he wears, it's no wonder. He's not afraid of getting hurt!"

Dion tried to suppress a snort. "Even if you *had* all that stuff, Luke, you still couldn't skate the way he does!"

"Oh, yeah?" Luke took the challenge. "I can do all of that and more. And without gear. I'll show you right now!" With those words, Luke headed for the pit.

He shoved the board out in front of him, hit the lip of the ramp, and sailed. He swung back up the other side and kicked into his turn. Suddenly, one of his feet came off the board and he dropped.

It did **not** look good for Luke.

Before You Read

Consider each statement below. Decide whether or not you agree with it. Use your Response Sheet to record your decisions and reasons.

_____ 1. People who skateboard are fearless.

_____ 2. Skateboarding without protective gear is self-destructive behavior.

_____ 3. It's not that important to play it safe when skateboarding. Serious accidents are rare.

_____ 4. If you wear protective gear while skateboarding, people will think you are a wimp.

_____ 5. You should intervene when a friend starts to do something stupid or dangerous.

After You Read

On your own, answer the questions below. Write your answers on the Response Sheet.

1. What do you think Luke really thinks about Gregorio's skating?

2. How would you compare Luke and Dion?

3. If you were Dion, would you have done or said anything different in this situation?

4. Does this remind you of any situations you have experienced or observed?

5. How would you end this story?

Think About It

Work with a small group to create two or three different possible humorous captions for the cartoon on the story page.

THE SQUABBLERS

It seemed as if Ben and Michael had been put on Earth to argue over **everything**. They bickered right through elementary school, and now, as luck would have it, they found themselves attending the same middle school. Six weeks into the new school year, their teachers and classmates were already fed up with the rivals.

A foot fuels the feud.

The feuding wasn't limited to shouting matches. Ben had been known to trip Michael with a strategically placed foot; Michael had been caught eavesdropping on Ben's private conversations. Their teachers hoped the two would work out their differences, but as time passed, the problem only got worse.

During a lively class discussion in Science, Ben and Michael started in on each other again.

"Why don't you mind your own business?" Michael snapped at Ben.

"I am. Why don't you shut up?" Ben shouted back.

Michael sneered, "Who's gonna make me?" He waved a fist in Ben's face.

The science teacher sighed. "Here we go again." He separated the two with a warning that fighting would get them both suspended.

Kayla, a classmate of the boys, was tired of the constant disruptions in class. She noticed that Ben and Michael were both loners who seemed to have no friends, and she wondered if the boys could stop hostilities long enough to become friends. She wasn't sure she ought get involved, but something had to be done before the boys got themselves kicked out of school. So she asked some of the other students to help her convince Ben and Michael they'd be better off as friends.

All the kids shook their heads. "It's none of our business, Kayla. Let the teachers handle it. Besides, it's kinda fun watching Michael and Ben 'get into it' with each other."

Kayla thought it over. Maybe her idea wasn't worth the hassle of opposing her friends. They were probably right. The problem was something for the teachers—or Michael and Ben themselves—to resolve.

Before You Read

Consider each statement below. Decide whether or not you agree with it. Use your Response Sheet to record your decisions and reasons.

_____ 1. Some people just can't get along with anybody.

_____ 2. It's easier to go along with what friends say or do than it is to go against them.

_____ 3. When you don't get along with someone, maybe the best thing to do is to stay away from that person.

_____ 4. As long as I see or hear something, then it is my business.

_____ 5. Sometimes a fight is the best way to solve an argument.

After You Read

On your own, answer the questions below. Write your answers on the Response Sheet.

1. What could be the cause of this ongoing argument?

2. Which of the following endings is best for this story?
   a. Kayla finds a way to get the two boys to be friends.
   b. Ben and Michael have a huge fight and no longer speak to each other.
   c. The teacher stops the behavior, but the boys do not become friends.

3. What advice would you give to Kayla?

4. How have you handled the situation when your friends argue?

Think About It

What if Kayla had not dropped her idea?
Tell a partner what Kayla might have done.

DETAINED!

Middle Talk
NEWS from McLaughlin Middle School
JANUARY

Detentions Get Out of Hand

Story by J.R. Zacher

The number of detentions at McLaughlin Middle has soared, while the use of detentions varies widely. This is the conclusion reached by students and staff who reflected on the school's detention system. A recent survey to rate the effectiveness of the policy resulted in opinions ranging from "useless" to "very helpful."

A review of statistics shows that the number of detentions given has increased by 40 percent in the last two years, and that each year the number of students who get detentions rises. Detention rooms are crowded every day after school and on Saturdays. The school is having trouble finding enough staff to supervise the sessions.

Current Policy

Detentions are given for:

- profanity
- vandalism on school grounds
- class disruptions
- excessive tardies to class
- repeated violations of dress code
- verbal or cyber harassment
- repeated failure to do classwork
- other issues as decided by teachers

The detention policy at work

Students report that detention classes are so full and rowdy, they are not able to get any work done. They say they spend their time fooling around or sleeping.

A survey of staff and students showed that almost every teacher applies the detention policy differently. Some of the teachers polled believe there are better ways to help students improve behavior.

According to the school handbook, one goal of the detention policy is to "reduce the number of students getting detention." It is clear that this goal is not being met.

Before You Read

Consider each statement below. Decide whether or not you agree with it. Use your Response Sheet to record your decisions and reasons.

_____ 1. Detention is a waste of time.

_____ 2. Some sort of detention or Saturday school deters people from misbehaving and helps them get serious.

_____ 3. School officials and teachers often disagree on school policies.

_____ 4. If a student is not following the rules or is not getting schoolwork done regularly, there needs to be some kind of punishment.

_____ 5. Schools should make only policies on which all teachers, administrators, parents, and students agree.

After You Read

On your own, answer the questions below. Write your answers on the Response Sheet.

1. What do you think are appropriate reasons to give a detention to a student?

2. What effect do you think this article will have on McLaughlin Middle School?

3. With which of the "Comment Corner" comments do you agree (and why)?

4. What do you think is the best way for a school to reduce problem behaviors, such as those listed in the newspaper under the current detention policy?

Think About It

Write a short letter to the editor in response to the main article on the story page.

ROBIN IN MOTION

"Look, I'm a bird, like my name!" Robin stretched her arms and flew around the art room, bumping into desks and students. "Draw me!"

"Robin, take your seat," Ms. Symmons requested kindly. "Students, take out your art supplies. We'll work on pastel landscapes today."

"Wait! I need a drink first." Robin buzzed out into the hall.

When she came back, a friend's drawing distracted her. "That's so-o good," she said, grabbing the friend's hairbrush out of her backpack and brushing her hair into a ponytail.

"Please, Robin, put the brush away," the teacher said.

Robin wandered around looking at drawings before finally arriving at her desk. She rapidly arranged and rearranged her books and supplies, then looked around to see what was happening. Other students had already started working. "What's the assignment, Ms. Symmons?"

"Use your imagination to create your ideal landscape."

Robin got out her paper and chalk and hummed loudly as she started to draw a cat. A minute later, she turned to the boy behind her. "Devon, do you have an eraser? And some breath mints?"

"Your drawing needs your attention," Ms. Symmons spoke gently. She stood near Robin's desk. "I'll keep you company and watch you draw for a bit. No humming or bothering your neighbors, please."

After a minute, Ms. Symmons suggested. "Your cat is nicely drawn, but it looks very lonely on that blank background. Think about where the cat is, and draw that place."

Robin responded, "I think he's an astronaut cat going into space."

Where will she land next?

Devon snorted. "That's st-u-u-pid."

Immediately, Robin began to scream as she swept her drawing and all her supplies off the desk. She picked up pieces of chalk and flung them at Devon. He covered his head.

Ms. Symmons put a hand on Robin's shoulder and said, "Let's step outside for a moment."

Before You Read

Consider each statement below. Decide whether or not you agree with it. Use your Response Sheet to record your decisions and reasons.

_____ 1. Some kids just cannot sit still, even if they want to.

_____ 2. If a student does not do what a teacher asks, it is obvious that the student is intentionally being rude.

_____ 3. There are no excuses for being inattentive in class.

_____ 4. If a student is not doing the work in class, there is probably something wrong with the way the teacher is running the class.

_____ 5. It is not possible for a teacher to treat all students equally.

After You Read

On your own, answer the questions below. Write your answers on the Response Sheet.

1. How would you describe the teacher's responses to Robin?

2. Is there anything else the teacher might try to help Robin?

3. What could be some reasons for Robin's constant motion in art class?

4. How should other students respond to someone with Robin's behaviors?

5. How would you define the term "empathy"? (Use your own words.)

Think About It

Think of a task or activity the teacher could give Robin that might keep her involved and on track.

THE IMPATIENT ONE

Whitney had a problem being patient. Everything she thought, needed, or wanted seemed more important than anything else. In class, she'd wave her arm frantically until the teacher snapped, "What is it, Whitney?"

She interrupted her friends' conversations, her mother's phone calls, and the family's TV shows to get what she wanted as fast as possible. Ironically, not only were people annoyed by her constant interruptions, but Whitney seldom got the attention she needed.

When Whitney tried to do her math homework, her head swam. The next day, Whitney rushed into class and said, "Mrs. Lewis, I need help with this. Will you show me again how to do these exponents?"

Mrs. Lewis frowned. "I'm beginning a class," she said. "Sit down, please, Whitney. Come and see me after school." She raised one eyebrow, a sure sign that she was annoyed.

Whitney slunk back to her desk. Why was Mrs. Lewis so curt with her? Wasn't it her job to instruct the students?

That night, Whitney desperately needed permission to attend a sleepover at her friend's house. As her parents talked about how hard it was to pay all the bills, she wanted to rush them with her request. Something stopped her. It was the feeling that it wasn't the right time to bother them, mixed with an equally strong feeling that if she made them mad, they wouldn't let her go. She waited until they put the computer and bills away. To her surprise, her mother smiled and said, "Sure, dear, if you want to."

What a surprise! Whitney had been patient and thoughtful for once, and she had gotten what she wanted without demanding it.

The next day in math class, Whitney had more questions. But she remembered how Mrs. Lewis hated being pestered while she was teaching a lesson. Whitney wrote down her questions and waited until the time came for the students to work on their own. Instead of rushing to Mrs. Lewis's desk, she raised her hand.

Mrs. Lewis smiled at her and said, "Yes, Whitney, how can I help you?"

Whitney believes that the world revolves around her.

WHITNEY'S WORLD

Before You Read

Consider each statement below. Decide whether or not you agree with it. Use your Response Sheet to record your decisions and reasons.

_____ 1. Teachers should answer students' questions right away.

_____ 2. Students who always ask for help are annoying.

_____ 3. It's the impatient kids who get the most attention, so patience doesn't pay off.

_____ 4. The following saying is true: "Good things come to those who wait."

_____ 5. Students should be aggressive in demanding what they need.

After You Read

On your own, answer the questions below. Write your answers on the Response Sheet.

1. Do you think Whitney's experiences in this story will change anything about her behavior from now on?

2. What caused Whitney to realize that she shouldn't interrupt her parents?

3. How did Whitney apply her experience at home to her problem at school?

4. Do you think Mrs. Lewis should have done anything differently with Whitney?

5. How would you define the term "self-discipline"? (Use your own words.)

Think About It

Make a list of five things that trigger your own impatience and five things about which you are usually patient. Explain your lists.

THE ACCUSATION

"It's gone," Keiko admitted. He hung his head. He couldn't look at Anson, the editor of the school paper. "I've looked everywhere!"

"What do you mean 'gone'?" shouted the eighth-grade editor. "That's a brand new expensive camera bought just for the newspaper. It can't be gone!"

"I . . . I . . . just put it down some place after taking pictures of the varsity basketball game, and now it's gone. I think Danielle must have stolen it. I saw her going down the hall with a bulging backpack. She had been saying how cool it was. I bet she took it."

"This is your fault, Anson," cried Niki. "Mr. Thomson trusted us with it. You should never have let a sixth-grader use the new camera unsupervised."

Niki went off to track down Danielle. She found her near the lockers, and carefully told her, "Someone suggested that you might have the school newspaper's camera in your backpack."

"You mean someone has accused me of lifting it! Who? On what grounds?" Danielle was angry. "Look anywhere you want. Search my backpack. Search my locker. Search my pockets. I am not a thief! But wait till I get my hands on whoever said this! Who was it?"

The camera was not in Danielle's backpack, locker, or pockets. Niki left a fuming Danielle, and returned to the newspaper office.

Who knows where an accusation can lead?

Meanwhile, Anson organized a search. "We'll search every place Keiko went," he said. "Let's start with the gym."

They followed Keiko to all the places he'd gone after the game: the gym, classroom, halls, vending machines, quad, and back to his locker. They picked up a lot of other lost stuff, but no camera.

"It's been stolen for sure," Anson moaned. "I'm the editor. It's my responsibility. I'll face Mr. Thomson and take the consequences. Let's drop off this other stuff at the Lost and Found first."

The door to the Lost and Found room was locked. Keiko pressed his nose to the glass and peered inside. "Look! There it is!" he shouted.

Before You Read

Consider each statement below. Decide whether or not you agree with it. Use your Response Sheet to record your decisions and reasons.

_____ 1. When something is missing at school, it usually is a case of theft by a student.

_____ 2. Kids accuse each other of stealing things all the time. Nobody should get bent out of shape about it.

_____ 3. People are often too quick to accuse others.

_____ 4. If you lose something that belongs to someone else, you are responsible for it— even if it gets stolen.

_____ 5. It is impossible to undo an accusation.

I bet number three took it.

After You Read

On your own, answer the questions below. Write your answers on the Response Sheet.

1. How many accusations were made in this story, and how did each accused person react?

2. What would you say the long-lasting consequences are of making a quick accusation?

3. What do you think about the way Keiko handled the situation?

4. How would you respond if you were falsely accused of stealing something?

5. What effect will this incident probably have on the way the students feel about Keiko from now on?

Think About It

Draw one or more thought balloons to write Danielle's thoughts about what she should do next.

SURPRISE FOR THE SUBSTITUTE

When our math teacher was out for three weeks to recover from knee surgery, we had the good (or bad) fortune to have Ms. Tanglewood as our substitute.

One day near the end of sixth period, we watched as Ms. Tanglewood picked up a crumpled piece of paper from the floor. She unfolded it, and from the look on her face, we knew what it was. Kelsey is a gifted cartoonist. Most of us had seen the comic strip she had created about the substitute. We all held our breath, wondering what would happen next.

| Ms. Tanglewood (aka Ms. Swine) | Ms. Tanglewood shows her math skills. | The sub calls on Tad, who is not Tad, but is in Tad's seat. | The fourth-period class has plans for the sub. |

Before You Read

Consider each statement below. Decide whether or not you agree with it. Use your Response Sheet to record your decisions and reasons.

_____ 1. It's normal for students to pull pranks on substitutes.

_____ 2. Kids behave badly only for teachers who are weak at classroom control.

_____ 3. Substitutes have it easy. It doesn't matter if kids learn anything that day.

_____ 4. If one kid in a classroom does something mischievous, most of the others will follow along.

_____ 5. It is terrible the way most students treat substitute teachers.

After You Read

On your own, answer the questions below. Write your answers on the Response Sheet.

1. Is it okay for students to make fun of a substitute?

2. Do you feel this cartoon is all in good fun, or is it cruel?

3. What might happen next?

4. What do you hope the substitute teacher will do?

5. How do you think it would feel to be a substitute in your classes?

Think About It

Give some advice to a substitute as to how to survive any class. Write this as a list or paragraph.

JEANNIE THE BRAIN

I was starting to get a reputation—not the one you think—worse. People were calling me "smart." **No one** has ever won any popularity contests by being smart—especially a girl.

I didn't know what to do about it. I had this compulsion to wave my hand in the air like a nerdy smarty-pants and answer the teacher's questions first, and best! Why couldn't I control this impulse?

My teachers were no help at all. "Jeannie," Ms. Crump would say, "tell Alex the difference between protons and neutrons." (Alex, of course, is the coolest guy in school and, of course, he's totally pleased to be shown up by the girl who wears glasses.)

"Jeannie, it's time you stopped thinking about your grade-point average and started making points with the other kids by *acting* average," advised my friend Anna. "Keep your mouth shut. Don't ace every test. And for heaven's sake, quit spending afternoons at the library."

She was right, wasn't she? I needed to cultivate a different attitude.

Now when Ms. Crump calls on me, I act dumb. It wasn't easy at first. But after a while, I began to use the "duh" word so often it became my mantra.

Today in English the teacher asked the class, "What are the consonants that have unusual sounds or are sometimes silent?"

Without raising my hand, I called out, "Oh, I know! The consonants are North America, South America, Australia, and . . . ."

Is it smart for a smart girl to act this dumb?

Too cute? I fretted. (Ironically there's a silent consonant in "dumb.") Then I noticed Alex and some of the other kids looking at me almost with respect. Well, maybe it was not *actual* respect, but at least they looked at me.

At lunch break, I put on a lot of Anna's makeup and rolled up my skirt. Alex caught up with me after school and asked for my phone number. Dumb is better than smart sometimes.

Don't think for a moment that I don't intend to go on getting good grades. I'm not dumb enough to throw my future away! I'm just smart enough to keep it under wraps!

Before You Read

Consider each statement below. Decide whether or not you agree with it. Use your Response Sheet to record your decisions and reasons.

_____ 1. It's not cool to be smart—especially for a girl.

_____ 2. Sometimes you have to pretend to be someone you're not in order to attract attention or be popular.

_____ 3. Girls will go to any lengths to get guys to notice them.

_____ 4. Boys like girls who are smart.

_____ 5. The smart students who speak up in class intimidate most of the other students.

After You Read

On your own, answer the questions below. Write your answers on the Response Sheet.

1. Do you agree with the advice that Anna gave Jeannie?

2. In your experience, do you know girls who play dumb when they are really smart?

3. What do you think will happen to Jeannie's class behavior in the long run?

4. What impression do you have of Alex?

5. How do you feel about Jeannie's final statements (in the last paragraph)?

Think About It

Write a short internal dialogue between the part of Jeannie that is proud to be smart and the part that is acting dumb.

BEING JOE MCCALL

If only I could change my last name! It's not easy being the youngest McCall when all four of your older brothers and sisters have gone to the same middle school.

My problems started on the first day of school. Mrs. Williams singled me out in history class. "Joe McCall? Are you the brother of Rosemary McCall, my star pupil?" I nodded. "Well, then," she continued, grinning. "I'll be expecting big things from you."

Joe can't escape the looming shadows of his siblings.

Great, Rosemary is in high school now, but her reputation lives on.

I took Art because I thought it would be an easy elective. Boy, was I wrong. Mr. Hansen remembers my oldest brother, Mark, and what a hotshot artist he was. "Artistic talent often runs in families," he told me. "I'd really like to recruit you onto my yearbook staff. We're doing cartoon art spots this year!"

Yikes, I can't even draw a stick figure—but I didn't have the guts to tell Mr. Hansen. Now I'm really stuck, at least until he finds out what a doofus I am at art.

My sister Lara, the science nerd, is in the seventh grade. She won first prize at the Lane County Science Fair and got a write-up in the city newspaper. Mr. Sherman has the article pinned to his bulletin board, and it stares me in the face every day during science class. (By the way, I am totally lame at science.)

But the real reason I want to change my name is athletics. My brother Bob excels in all kinds of sports, and it's just not fair. I love sports, especially soccer, and I'm pretty good at it—but not as good as Bob. He'll always be the star, and I'm only second best.

If my name was Joe Smith, I think I'd have an easier time finding my own talent. Maybe people would stop thinking of me as a clone of my older brothers and sisters.

Before You Read

Consider each statement below. Decide whether or not you agree with it. Use your Response Sheet to record your decisions and reasons.

_____ 1. You're better off in school if nobody knows any of your family members.

_____ 2. Teachers should not have expectations about students before getting to know them.

_____ 3. If you have older siblings at a school, people will always compare you to them.

_____ 4. It's your job to find your own talents and let people know what you want.

_____ 5. All kids have expectations to deal with—whether it is from parents or teachers.

After You Read

On your own, answer the questions below. Write your answers on the Response Sheet.

1. What would you like to say to each of Joe's teachers?

2. What do you think Joe should do about these comparisons to his brothers and sisters?

3. How might Joe's brothers and sisters help this situation?

4. What are some expectations that you have to deal with?

5. Are there expectations that should be placed on students? If so, what are they?

Think About It

Write one statement that Joe could make to each teacher as a way of speaking up for his own talents.

THE TWO-FACED GIRLS

"Did you hear about Nora's brother? He got a suspended driver's license for speeding!"

"I guess that means Nora will have to take the bus to school now."

"Maybe she'll stop talking about how 'wonderful' her big brother is all the time."

"Yeah, if she's smart, she'll quit that."

"Yeah, and showing off . . ."

"Or being so stuck-up!"

"You said it—stuck on herself! She's always bragging about how she won that writing contest. Which is weird, because she's really stupid at math **and** science."

"And P.E."

Hypocrisy is alive and well at Nora's middle school.

"She gets away with everything because she has asthma. Last time I stayed overnight at her house, she threw a fit because her dad wouldn't order pizza at midnight. He caved."

"Her teachers cave, too. All she has to do is wheeze a bit . . ."

"Shhhh . . . here she comes . . . "

"Hi, Nora. Whatcha doing?"

"Hi, Beth. Hi, Caitlin. I've been looking for you guys. I'm having a skate party on Friday night. You wanna come?"

"Yeah!"

"That sounds great! I'll be there!"

Before You Read

Consider each statement below. Decide whether or not you agree with it. Use your Response Sheet to record your decisions and reasons.

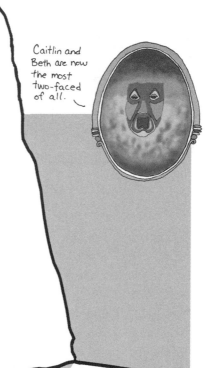

Caitlin and Beth are now the most two-faced of all.

_____ 1. Everybody is hypocritical sometimes.

_____ 2. There's nothing more disgusting than someone who is two-faced.

_____ 3. It's a fact of life in school that people talk about each other behind their backs.

_____ 4. If you criticize someone, you should not turn around and pretend to be their friend.

_____ 5. Gossip is really destructive.

After You Read

On your own, answer the questions below. Write your answers on the Response Sheet.

1. Would you like to have Caitlin and Beth as friends? (Explain your answer.)

2. Why do you think these girls are talking this way about Nora?

3. What have you experienced that is similar to this story?

4. What advice would you give to Nora?

5. Do you think Nora deserves the treatment she is getting from the other girls?

Think About It

Write a letter to Caitlin and Beth that might lead them to reflect on their behavior.

FIRES IN THE BATHROOM

The Grayland Grapevine
Grayland Middle School News
May 13

Fire Mystery Remains Unsolved

Story by Denzel Matthews and Lexie L'Engel

Four fires last fall, few clues, no suspects, no solutions—this is the status of the investigation into the "mystery fires" at Grayland Middle School. On two consecutive days, fires started at the same time in the boys' and the girls' bathrooms. School officials and local police have searched for answers but, as of this time, have found none.

According to news reports, some clues were found at the scenes of the fires. These appear to be: crumpled paper towels on the floor, various footprints, burned matches, cigarette butts, a can of lighter fluid, and a burned card of some sort.

Rumors have run wild about who the culprits might be. There have been stories about timed devices, kids smoking in the stalls, a group of student teachers pulling a prank, a conspiracy to get certain students in trouble, a bad report card being burned,

Not everyone agrees that cameras in the bathrooms would be a good idea.

and a science experiment out of control. There is even one theory that the teachers planned the fires to get some extra days off school.

Dozens of students and staff members have been interviewed. Some parents have complained that their children were being falsely suspected and harassed. Administrators decline to be interviewed. So for now, the investigation is quiet, and the mystery remains.

Fires in Our History

Fire is not new to Grayland Middle School. Bathroom fires were set in 1995, 1999, and 2001. And in 2003, there were simultaneous fires in all the bathrooms on one day. False fire alarms occur several times each year. In each of these cases, the culprits have been promptly caught.

COMMENT CORNER

"No one was hurt, so I don't see that it matters now."
– Angie Barnes, 6th gr.

"All this attention to the matter is probably just what the guilty people want."
– Su Lin, 7th gr.

"Put cameras in all the rooms in the school. That should solve the problem once and for all."
– Shania Turner, Teacher

"There must be some clues. I wonder who the administrators are protecting."
– Lou Grebing, Teacher

"I think we should let the kids form a detecting team!"
– J. R. Kling, 8th gr.

"I love it—a good mystery right here at GMS!"
– Maria Degas, 7th gr.

Before You Read

Consider each statement below. Decide whether or not you agree with it. Use your Response Sheet to record your decisions and reasons.

_____ 1. A little fire in the bathroom wastebasket is harmless.

_____ 2. Smoking or otherwise lighting fire anywhere in school should be treated as a crime.

_____ 3. School wouldn't be as much fun without someone pulling the fire alarm once in a while.

_____ 4. Anyone who sets a fire at school is probably in need of attention and wants to be caught.

_____ 5. When there is a fire in a bathroom, the blame is usually put on students.

After You Read

On your own, answer the questions below. Write your answers on the Response Sheet.

1. Why do you think someone would set a fire in a school bathroom?

2. What should the consequences be for pranks such as pulling the fire alarm?

3. If you heard someone talking about setting a fire in the bathroom, what would you do?

4. At what point does a school prank cross the line and become something that should involve serious consequences or police involvement?

Think About It

Write a few comments that could be added to the "Comment Corner" on the front newspaper page.

BETHANY'S BUS-RIDING BLUES

For the third time in a week, Bethany complained of a stomachache. She dragged herself out of bed so late that she missed the bus. Her mom had to drive her to school. Again.

The week before, she had complained of motion sickness after the bus ride home. On Monday of that same week, cheerleading practice had ended too late to catch the last bus. At least that was what she told her family when she called home.

Her mom began to notice a pattern. "Bethany, is it only my imagination, or are you avoiding the bus?"

After hesitating a moment, Bethany confessed. "The bus ride makes me nauseated. When I go in the morning, I feel terrible by the time I get to school. Then I'm sick half the day. At the end of the day after the ride home, I feel yucky the whole evening."

"Why didn't you tell me sooner?" asked her mom. "We can get you some motion sickness pills, or one of those patches—to keep this from happening again." Her mom sounded relieved that Bethany's problem seemed so minor.

Bethany sighed. She had not told her mother the whole story. It was absolutely true that the bus ride made her sick to her stomach. Every minute on the bus was excruciating. But motion sickness treatments would not cure her ailment.

It was the chaos and roughhousing that went on in the bus that caused her anxiety. Not to mention the raunchy language and teasing. How could she tell her mother about that? How could she tell her about the stuck-up girls in the third row who mocked her every day? And she could never repeat the comments made by Tad's group of guys who controlled the back of the bus! If she talked about the reality of life on the bus, her mom would rush to the school and make a scene. Then her life at school would be as horrendous as those bus rides.

Bethany wondered, "Other kids handle the taunts, the threats, the pressures to do disgusting things. Why can't I?"

Bethany's least favorite place to be

150

Before You Read

Consider each statement below. Decide whether or not you agree with it. Use your Response Sheet to record your decisions and reasons.

_____ 1. If you're going to ride the bus to school, you just have to have thick skin.

_____ 2. Most adults don't really get it: Horrible stuff happens on school buses.

_____ 3. If a school bus is out of control, it is the fault of the driver.

_____ 4. Students who tease, bully, or fight on the bus should be kicked off the bus for good.

_____ 5. There is little that the driver or school officials can really do about bad behavior on the bus.

After You Read

On your own, answer the questions below. Write your answers on the Response Sheet.

1. What do you think about the tactics Bethany used to avoid the bus ride?

2. Should Bethany tell her mom the whole truth? (Why or why not?)

3. How does this story relate to your own experience or to the experience of friends who ride a bus to school?

4. In the last paragraph, Bethany asked herself a question. What are your thoughts about what the answer might be?

Think About It

Write the first verse of a song called "The Bus-Riding Blues."

HIGH SCHOOL TERRORS

Dear Diary,

I have never written in a diary before, but my English teacher gave us this stupid assignment for the end of eighth grade. She promised no one would read this (even her) without our permission. So here goes.

I can't sleep. Middle school is almost over. I've just about made it. Now I'll be going to high school. I don't dare let on to my friends, but I'm scared. I think they are too, but they would never show it.

Devon's dreams about high school are not sweet.

Well, what am I scared of? First, I think freshmen are at the bottom of the heap. I hear horror stories about older kids bullying and threatening freshmen in the bathrooms and outside school. I hear that your lunch money always gets stolen and if you don't carry any money, you get beat up.

Besides that, I am afraid I will look wrong or dress wrong or look too shy or stupid. I don't know how to act. I've just figured out how to be cool in middle school—and now I'm leaving. In high school, I don't want to be called a nerd or a dork. I want to be popular. I don't have to be the most popular guy in school, I just want everything to be okay.

And I'm totally not sure I can do the work in high school. I hear it is way hard. I doubt that high school teachers will help kids as much as the middle school teachers did.

I hope my friends will stay my friends. I hope I can make the wrestling team. I hope I can get in a cool group. I hope I can do the work. Maybe I can survive high school. I hope so. I'm a little excited about it, too.

Well, that's all.
Devon

Before You Read

Consider each statement below. Decide whether or not you agree with it. Use your Response Sheet to record your decisions and reasons.

——— 1. Moving from middle school to high school is intense.

——— 2. Once you get to high school, it's hard to keep your old friends.

——— 3. Being in high school is not as hard as most students think it will be.

——— 4. Students who are new to high school are going to be picked on.

——— 5. Everybody is scared to go to high school.

After You Read

On your own, answer the questions below. Write your answers on the Response Sheet.

1. Which of Devon's fears about high school do you think is greatest? (Tell why.)

2. What do you think would be the best way for Devon to adjust to high school?

3. What fears of Devon's do you share?

4. How do you think the middle school or high school staff can reduce the fears of high school?

5. What do you predict Devon would write in a diary a year from now on the subject of going to high school?

Think About It

Write a diary entry or short memoir containing your thoughts about going to high school or to any other new school.

SCHOOL DAYZ

DEANNA DUMBFOUNDED

Deanna met her best friend, Kirsten, every day at the same time and same place for lunch. If one of them got hung up after class, she would text the other.

Today, after finishing a tough history test, Deannna arrived at the arranged place. Kirsten was not there. She checked her cell phone but there was no text. Just then, another student named Robbie walked by. She usually didn't talk to him much because he had asked her out, and she had turned him down.

Deanna checked her cell phone again—no message from Kirsten. So she headed off to the cafeteria to grab some lunch. When Deanna walked into the cafeteria, heads turned toward her, and people stopped talking. For the rest of the day, people who usually said "hi" to her now ignored her. She sat through her last two classes in a daze.

At the end of the school day, she finally spotted Kirsten, but Kirsten was hurrying away. Deanna caught up and grabbed Kirsten's shoulder. "What's going on? Why weren't you at lunch today? Are you okay? Did something happen?" she asked as if these questions were all one sentence.

"Didn't you see the page?" Kirsten asked.

"What page?" Deanna replied.

"You need to look at your Facebook page. People are saying you told everyone that we are more than just friends. There's even a picture of you and me hugging. Where did that come from? And I just heard that some girls are getting ready to beat up both of us!"

Deanna was incredulous. "I didn't say anything or show anything to anyone!" she shouted.

"Well it's all over the school now. I can't be seen with you. You need to leave me alone." Kirsten shouted, emphasizing the last three words.

Deanna watched as Kirsten quickly walked away. She was dumbfounded. Just then Robbie appeared with a large smirk on his face. Then he abruptly turned in the opposite direction. Deanna just stood alone near the lunch quad-- shaken, wondering how this could have happened.

Conversations on social networks can be hurtful.

Who could be spreading rumors?

Before You Read

Consider each statement below. Decide whether or not you agree with it. Use your Response Sheet to record your decisions and reasons.

_____ 1. It's normal for teenagers to spread rumors about other students.

_____ 2. The use of social networks has increased the chances that someone can be bullied.

_____ 3. People who normally wouldn't pick on another student are more likely to do it through a social network because they think they can remain anonymous.

_____ 4. Someone who is bullied on a social network usually did something that caused it to happen.

_____ 5. People who spread lies about someone are probably jealous of the person they victimize.

After You Read

On your own, answer the questions below. Write your answers on the Response Sheet.

1. Did Kirsten have a good reason to be so upset with Deanna?

2. What part did the other friends play in this situation?

3. From what you read in the story, what do you think Robbie's involvement might be?

4. Is it more likely that boys or girls would spread rumors about girls? Why do you think so?

5. What are some possible actions that Deanna could take in this situation?

Think About It

Deanna, Robbie, and Kirsten are all in the counselor's office. Write a scene from this scenario that contains dialogue between the three characters about the situation.

THE VIDEO GAME TAKE-OVER

Damon and Edwin had been friends since second grade. Even when they got to middle school, they stayed "tight" no matter who else joined their circle of friends.

One day at lunch break, Edwin went to meet Damon for their usual short game of basketball. Damon showed up with another boy, whom he introduced as Oscar. "He just moved here from Arizona," Damon explained. "Cool," Edwin said. "Let's shoot baskets."

Edwin wanted court action,
not couch action!

In the following days, Damon and Oscar shot baskets or played short pick-up games with Edwin. Soon, however, Damon and Oscar stopped coming to the basketball court.

After school one day, Edwin dropped by Damon's house. He walked in to see Oscar in front of the big-screen television. Damon also had some equipment that Edwin had not seen before. "Pretty cool, huh?" Damon asked as Edwin stared at all this new hardware. "Yeah," Edwin answered, more curious than ever.

Oscar jumped up with some kind of control in his hands. "This is my new Xbox 380. It just came out and is really cool on this big screen. I don't have a big screen in my house--not yet anyway. So we set it up here. And," he said as he walked over to a big plastic box and pulled out a cartridge, "I have just about every video game you could imagine."

"Well, I was wondering," asked Edwin, holding out the basketball he had brought along, "do you want to go down to the park and shoot some hoops before it gets dark?"

Damon laughed. "Oh man, I can play with the Lakers, Celtics, Nets, or the Heat right here in my living room!"

Oscar chimed in. "Yo, we can play football, baseball, anything you want, right here without even having to get off the couch."

Edwin thought for a minute. "Yeah, but then you just become couch potatoes!" he said, trying to make a joke.

"I'll catch ya later," Damon said, appearing not to appreciate Edwin's joke in front of his new friend.

Edwin tucked the basketball under his arm. "Okay, catch you guys at school."

Before You Read

Consider each statement below. Decide whether or not you agree with it. Use your Response Sheet to record your decisions and reasons.

———— 1. Video gaming is harmless, even when played for several hours a day.

———— 2. Kids who spend most of their leisure time playing video games sometimes have trouble making friends.

———— 3. Kids who play sports video games a lot become good athletes.

———— 4. Video games, especially violent ones, cause psychological problems for kids and affect their behavior.

———— 5. Sometimes video games can take the place of friends.

After You Read

On your own, answer the questions below. Write your answers on the Response Sheet.

1. How would you describe the way Edwin feels about this situation?

2. How do your own video gaming habits (or those of someone you know) affect you and your friendships?

3. How does the title of the story relate to the situation in the story?

4. What would you expect Edwin to do about this situation?

Think About It

Edwin and Damon run into each other at school. What might Edwin say to Damon? How might Damon respond?

CREaTE YOUR OWN SCHOOL DaYZ STORIES

Once you've used some of the stories in this book, you will see all the parts that are needed for writing your own. Remember that the goal is to share a story that presents a real school-life topic or issue and then ask students to engage with the ideas.

To create your own, follow these steps:

1. Choose a topic, problem, or issue that comes up in your life and your school. (See examples on page 15 of this book.)

2. Choose a positive trait that applies to the characters in the story. This might be a trait that a character does or does not have or struggles to develop. (See examples of these on page 16 in this book.)

3. Choose your characters. Make them like real students that you know or have observed.

4. Use a real-life situation that your readers will know relates to them and their school experience.

5. Choose a format for your story. Pages 160 and 161 of this book offer forms for a standard narrative story like most of the stories in this book. Pages 162 to 168 give you other options for your story format. Select the one that is best for presenting your topic.

Story Form A: Standard Narrative (page 160)
Have a narrator tell the story. Add some dialogue to make the story come alive.

Story Form B: Single Note (page 162)
Tell the story in a letter or note. Add some lines of introduction if you need them.

Story Form C: Two Notes (page 163)
Use notes as a part of the story. Add an introduction to the story to explain the notes.

Story Form D: Diary Entry (page 164)
>   *Tell the story through a diary entry. Add some lines*
>   *of introduction if you need them.*

Story Form E: Two Diaries (page 165)
>   *Tell the story through two different diary entries.*
>   *(These could be written by different people, or by*
>   *the same person at different times.) Add some*
>   *lines of introduction if you need them.*

Story Form F: Comic Strip (page 166)
>   *Tell the story through a comic strip. Add introductory*
>   *or concluding parts to the story if you need them.*

Story Form G: Newspaper Page (page 167)
>   *Create a newspaper page to tell the story.*

Story Form H: Thoughts (page 168)
>   *Tell the story through someone's thoughts.*
>   *Add some lines of introduction if you need them.*

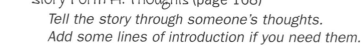

6. Write the story.

7. Get a copy of the Before & After Form (page 161). Write your story title at the top. Next, complete the top section called "Before You Read." Write four or five statements that will set up the story. These will be read and discussed BEFORE people read your story. They should inspire thought and discussion about the ideas or problems in the story.

8. Complete the middle section of the form ("After You Read"). Write four or five questions that will require readers to interact with the story. Ask readers to give opinions, reflect on things that happen, and help solve the problem in the story.

9. Finally, complete the "Think About It" section. Give readers a task that leads them to some deeper thinking about the story and topic.

10. Be sure to add your own cartoon or other illustration to your story. Include a caption, if you wish.

>   *NOTE:* Share your story with others who will read it and do the
>   "before and after" tasks. They can write their responses
>   on the Response Sheet found on page 12.

_____

story title

by _____

caption

_____

story title

Before You Read

Consider each statement below. Decide whether or not you agree with it. Use your Response Sheet to record your decisions and reasons.

After You Read

On your own, answer the questions below. Write your answers on the Response Sheet.

Think About It

story title

Name _____

_____
story title

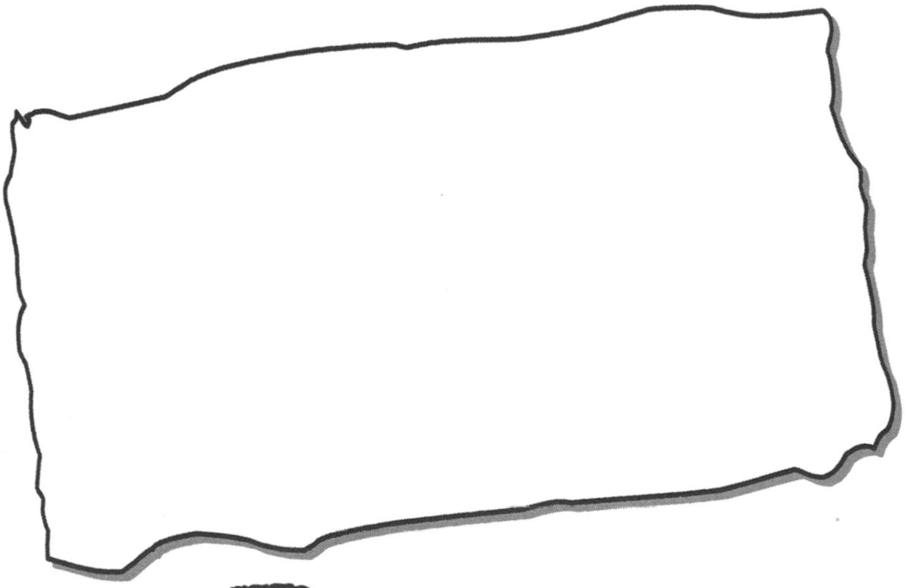

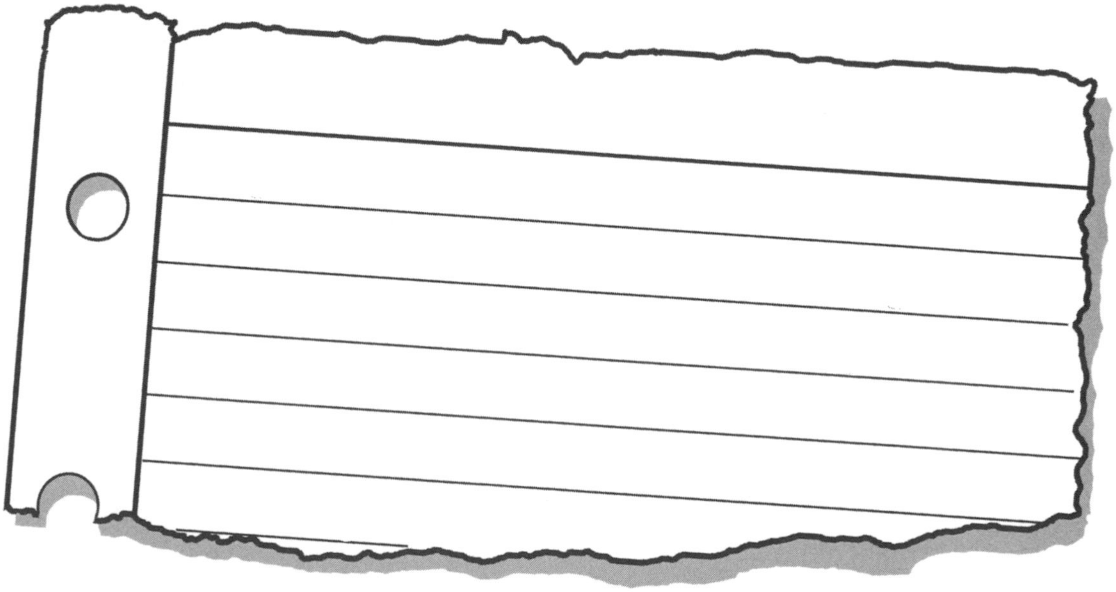

_____
_____
_____
_____
_____
_____

Name _____

_____
story title

Dear Diary,

_____
_____
_____
_____
_____
_____
_____
_____
_____
_____
_____
_____
_____
_____
_____
_____
_____
_____
_____
_____
                                  _____

Name _____

_____

story title

Dear Diary,

Dear Diary,

Name _____

_____

story title

_____

_____

_____

_____

_____

headline (story title)

caption

Name _____

168